Fast Innovation

Achieving Superior Differentiation, Speed to Market, and Increased Profitability

Michael L. George

James Works

Kimberly Watson-Hemphill

McGraw-Hill

New York   Chicago   San Francisco   Lisbon   London
Madrid   Mexico City   Milan   New Delhi   San Juan
Seoul   Singapore   Sydney   Toronto

2 3 4 5 6 7 8 9 0 DOC/DOC 0 9 8 7 6

ISBN 0-07-145789-5

This publication is designed to provide accurate and authoritative information in regard to the subject matter covered. It is sold with the understanding that neither the author nor the publisher is engaged in rendering legal, accounting, or other professional services. If legal advice or other expert assistance is required, the services of a competent professional person should be sought.

—From a Declaration of Principles jointly adopted by a Committee of the American Bar Association and a Committee of Publishers

McGraw-Hill books are available at special quantity discounts to use as premiums and sales promotions, or for use in corporate training programs. For more information, please write to the Director of Special Sales, McGraw-Hill, 2 Penn Plaza, New York, NY 10121. Or contact your local bookstore.

 This book is printed on recycled, acid-free paper containing a minimum of 50% recycled de-inked fiber

CONTENTS

PART II:
BUILDING CORPORATE INNOVATION CAPACITY

About the Authors

Michael George, Chairman and CEO of George Group Consulting, has worked personally with CEOs and executive teams at major corporations worldwide. His primary emphasis is on the creation of shareholder value through the development and execution of critical strategic initiatives. He is the author of Lean Six Sigma (McGraw-Hill 2002), Lean Six Sigma for Service (McGraw-Hill 2003), What Is Lean Six Sigma? (McGraw-Hill 2003), Conquering Complexity in Your Business (McGraw-Hill 2004), and The Lean Six Sigma Pocket Toolbook (McGraw-Hill 2004). Mike began his career at Texas Instruments in 1964 as an engineer. In 1969, he founded the venture startup International Power Machines (IPM), which he took public and sold to a division of Rolls-Royce in 1984. This enabled him to study the Toyota Production System and TQM at first hand in Japan. In 1986, he published America Can Compete and subsequently founded George Group. Mike earned a

BS in Physics from the University of California and a MS in Physics from the University of Illinois.

James Works is President and Chief Operating Officer of George Group. He specializes in working with senior executives in large corporations to build and sustain an innovation and improvement approach that achieves major growth and operating gains. Prior to joining George Group, James held key roles in the areas of Strategy, Product Marketing, Customer Marketing and Business Model Innovation in the personal computer industry with Advanced Micro Devices and Dell. He holds a BA in Economics from Duke University and an MBA from University of Texas.

Kimberly Watson-Hemphill has built a reputation over the last 12 years as a leading expert in the field of Innovation. She currently leads the Design for Lean Six Sigma practice for George Group. Kimberly has assisted companies with innovation and business improvement in such diverse areas as product design, logistics, purchasing, information technology, finance, legal, construction equipment engine design, space flight hardware, chemical processes, discrete manufacturing processes, and business services. Kimberly holds a BS in Aerospace Engineering and BA in French from the University of Michigan, and a Master's degree in Engineering Mechanics from the University of Texas.

Acknowledgements

This book has been strengthened by many who have freely shared their experience and knowledge, including: Clay Christensen of the Harvard Business School, Kyle Rone, a thirty year veteran of IBM Federal Systems; Jim Patell of the Stanford University School of Business; Lou Giuliano, CEO of ITT Industries (retired); Larry Huston of Procter & Gamble; Dr. Alph Bingham of Eli Lilly; Wilfred Pinfold of Intel; Emery Powell of Texas Instruments; Dick Hanschen, former VP of Texas Instruments; Dr. John Evers of Raytheon; and Pete Buca of Parker Hannifin.

Our colleagues who have contributed include Stephen Wilson, Chuck Cox, Richard Spencer, Max Isaac, Tony Curtis, Ken Jacobson, Bill Kastle, Kevin Simonin, and Jeff Howard of George Group North America, and Bill Zeeb, Carmen Beernaert, and Bruno Ternon of George Group Europe.

Thanks also to our editor, ghostwriter, and layout guru, Sue Reynard, to graphic artist Guy Lawson and colleagues at Lawson Communications; and to proofers Brenda Quinn and Ladye Sparks.

Foreword

I first met Mike George at a Fortune Innovation Conference in New York City in December 2004. As he challenged a number of my assertions, it was clear that he possessed an extraordinary understanding of the history of technological change. I subsequently took the opportunity to test my theory of disruptive innovations against his historical examples which appeared to extend the applicability of the theory. I became convinced, as he had been, that the theory of disruptive innovation was more universally applicable than I had understood. My theory was based on the fact that the majority of disruptive innovations had taken root at the low end of industries with lower-performing products whose *price per unit of product* was *lower*. Incumbent producers were consistently paralyzed by a disruptive innovation, the classic example being that of the integrated steel producers who were caught "flat footed" and unwilling to counter the escalating depredations of the mini-mills. Mike George taught me that certain innovations can enter their market with a *higher price point per unit of product* because they offer *lower cost per unit of performance*, and yet still render the existing competitors flat-footed, and unable to respond. He showed me that the disruption of the vacuum tube business by semi-conductors occurred on this basis in computers and military electronics, examples of which are explained in this book. Working with Mike to revise the theory of disruption to account for the anomalies that he had observed has greatly improved its explanatory power.

My understanding of innovation has been enlarged through my interactions with Mike. I am grateful that in the writing of this book Mike has relied upon my research and that I have similarly been able to build upon his understanding. I thank him for providing all of us with the set of practical implementation tools presented in this book.

Clay Christensen
12 April 2005

Clayton Christensen is the Robert and Jane Cizik Professor of Business Administration at Harvard Business School. He is the author of such important texts as *The Innovator's Dilemma*, *The Innovator's Solution*, and *Seeing What's Next*.

Preface

The purpose of our enterprise is the knowledge of causes, and secret motions of things; the enlarging of the bounds of human empire, the effecting of all things possible.

Francis Bacon, The New Atlantis

This book is for CEOs and managers who want to know:

- why it takes so long for innovations to reach the market and why they so often fail

- how to reduce time-to-market and increase the success rate of innovations

- the secrets to creating truly great innovations

- how to balance the need for speed with the need for genuine differentiation

A 2004 survey of 188 global CEOs by *The Economist* indicated that in more than half the companies, at least 25% of their revenue derived from products and services less than three years old, and most companies need to quickly innovate to meet new customer demands.[i] Similarly, a recent Boston Consulting Group survey showed that 90% of CEOs are counting on organic growth through innovation.[ii] But the same report goes on to say:

Despite all the time and money companies have spent on improving innovation over the last ten or even 20 years, hundreds of executives across all industries said their organizations still are:

• Not as fast as they need to be

• Not successful as often as they need to be

• Too fragmented across too many different projects

- *Not well-aligned across the whole organization (functions, geographies, etc.)*

At the same time, when looking at the external environment, executives highlighted recent developments that have made commercialization even more challenging. These developments include:

- *New competition*

- *Intense, and increasing, price and cost pressure*

- *Ever-shrinking product lifecycles*

- *Increasing integration of the world's economies*

- *Major technology shifts*

These insights confirm a preponderance of data that proves few companies have succeeded at the goal of using innovation to drive organic growth. Separate studies by Christensen (of Harvard), Foster (of McKinsey), Zook (of Bain), Slywotzky (of Mercer), and Jim Collins agree that

> *90% of companies cannot maintain adequate growth to sustain above-average shareholder returns for more than a decade* [iii]

Not surprising when you consider that the success rate of innovations is quite low, approximately 25%, according to data by Cooper.[iv]

Why have we seen such poor results from growth through innovation? *The Economist* survey provides some of the answers. According to these executives, the principal obstacles to profitable and sustainable organic growth through innovation include:[v]

1) Time and cost overruns (60% of respondents)

2) Competing development priorities (53%)

3) Poor upfront market research (52%)

4) Failure to gather sufficient or relevant end-user input (44%)

5) Poor interdepartmental communications (39%)

These are staggering numbers. No wonder so few companies are able to use innovation to drive sustained growth, and why there is clearly a huge gap between the goals that CEOs have for growth and the actual performance. This book, for the first time, explains the causes of this gap and what you can do to join the 10% of companies who succeed in sustaining long-term growth.

What's New in Fast Innovation

The stakes couldn't be higher when it comes to innovation—failure to create successful new products, services, and business models means that a company will stagnate or even decline. So you'll find a lot of books and articles already available on the subject. However, many books or innovation models provide an incomplete picture of how to generate sustainable growth through innovation because they do not integrate new knowledge that has emerged only in the past few years:

1) **Why current approaches to innovation fail to maintain growth:** In Clayton Christensen's *The Innovator's Dilemma* and its sequels, he posits the causes of failure of innovation initiatives. In summary, companies fail to react to "disruptive growth opportunities" which may damage a company's viability. Disruptive opportunities arise from new technologies, new processes, and new business models that are often dismissed by good management because they rate poorly on traditional evaluation criteria (such as Net Present Value) compared to "sustaining" innovations (incremental extensions of existing offerings). Incumbent companies are caught flat-footed by disruptions. Fast Innovation provides the strategic and tactical structure to make both forms of innovation into powerful engines to maintain growth.

2) **Real solutions to explain and reduce time-to-market:** Previous product development books[vi] have addressed the tactical issue of making innovation processes faster, and were an important step in the evolutionary process of reducing innovation lead time. But the picture they present is incomplete because they did not provide a definitive solution. The knowledge of the causes of time and cost overruns, as expressed in the two Laws introduced in this book (of Lead Time and of Innovation Variation), is entirely new and presented in book form

for the first time here. A strategic and tactical plan to apply these laws is provided that will allow companies to dramatically shorten time-to-market by 50% to 80%.

3) **Fast differentiation maintains growth:** Differentiation includes knowing how to capture the "heart of the customer"—going beyond what people say they want or like to discover unmet needs. We present methods for translating those needs into differentiated offerings using internal and external sources of knowledge generated by the innovation process. This is in sharp contrast to the current practice of freezing specs early in development and an internal focus, both of which add to schedule delays and often result in undifferentiated offerings that fail in the market.

These three solutions have been applied and proven to varying degrees by firms such as GE, 3M, Eli Lilly, Texas Instruments, Procter & Gamble, Raytheon, Toyota, Intel, Dell, Amazon, and Microsoft. But by consistently applying all three insights, companies can reduce innovation lead times by 50% to 80% and dramatically improve differentiation, which confers greater competitive advantage and hence maintains a higher growth rate of shareholder returns. This is the first book to provide quantitative methods such that a CEO or manager can know that the innovation process will both meet its required delivery date and create a differentiated offering with a high probability of success.

We'll show you the necessary infrastructure and tools to achieve:

- Significantly faster and predictable time-to-market for products or services

- A highly differentiated, exciting product, service, or experience

- Fast innovation lead times (from opportunity to market)

- Greater creativity in the types of innovations you pursue

In short, what you'll get in this book is an answer to the question nearly every CEO asks:

*"How can I drive more innovation faster
to enable sustained profitable growth?"*

Structure of *Fast Innovation*

What is needed is the tough crust of knowledge, not soft mush for fools.[vii]

Erich Maria Remarque
author of All Quiet on the Western Front

Part I of this book looks at Fast Innovation from an executive view, considering its strategic impact and requirements, and outlines new solutions that directly address the CEO's top innovation frustrations. Part I provides in-depth discussions of how innovation can improve shareholder returns—if it's fast, differentiated, and sustainable—and also looks at the strategic importance of exploiting new dimensions of innovation. Mini-chapters called Spotlights delve into key implementation principles and practices (such as what it will take to be fast and differentiated), many of which must be supported by the CEO to succeed.

Part II then looks at the systemic issues and opportunities that must be addressed to make Fast Innovation happen enterprise-wide: specific practices, policies, and cultural changes that build capacity for innovation. The chapters talk about new executive-level innovation positions and their responsibilities, and changes that must be launched at the corporate level in order for departments and work groups to be capable of acting in ways that allow Fast Innovation.

Part III provides detailed and specific solutions for driving Fast Innovation at the project and portfolio level: how to collect "present state" data, screen and select projects, execute innovation techniques, use quantitative methods for judging whether and when to launch a specific project, build highly creative and fast teams, and so on.

What's most important about this book is that it goes beyond good-sounding ideas to explain why innovation is not living up to its potential in most companies, and, more important, provides real solutions you can use to solve the problem in your business.

Why top executives must not delegate innovation

This book discusses many reasons why top executives (CEO, chief strategy officer, P&L general manager, etc.) have to remain actively engaged in leading innovation efforts. Only people at that level have the power, authority, and responsibility to take on issues such as:

- Exploiting the most profitable innovation opportunities which extend beyond product/service offerings to include process, business model, and market definition innovations.

- Achieving innovation speed and effectiveness through mechanisms outside the purview any one department: the number of new initiatives or offerings to be launched (derived from business strategy), valid capture of the Voice of the Customer (involving strategy, marketing, R&D), lead-time-to-market (which touches on everything from initial customer contact to R&D, production/preparation, and delivery), and cross-functional collaboration (which can touch on every area).

- Making sure the company doesn't make what Christensen sees as one of the most common fatal mistakes: ignoring disruptive growth opportunities. The bigger payback of disruptive innovation is often associated with much bigger risks as well, which makes it unlikely that any division would be willing to endorse it on their own.

- Looking outside the company for ideas and solutions (see Chapter 5 on Open Innovation). This is clearly a corporate, not a departmental, challenge, and requires executive-level leadership.

- Building a strong infrastructure to drive innovation from opportunity to reality. Because of the high stakes for making sure this infrastructure works smoothly, most companies will find they want to create a new executive position (such as a Chief Innovation Officer, Chapter 8) to oversee the whole operation.

In summary, effective, fast, and sustainable innovation requires intervention by executives who can champion a corporate-wide view and overcome cultural resistance to the types of change described in this book.

The Moment to Act Is Now!

In 1925, the average duration of a company's membership on the predecessor to the S&P 500 was 65 years. By 1998, it had dropped to 10 years.[viii] Why? Because many companies on the list are not growing fast enough to stay on! And an even larger number drop in the rankings every year without actually falling off the list (at least not yet!). Given how tough it is for most companies to grow, do you have even a year to waste? This book will help you get started on a path of building sustainable organic growth through the use of Fast Innovation.

Endnotes

i "Harnessing Innovation: R&D in a Global Growth Economy," An Economist Intelligence Unit White Paper sponsored by Agilent Technologies, May 2004.

ii "Innovation 2005," The Boston Consulting Group, www.bcg.com.

iii Clayton M. Christensen and Michael E. Raynor, *The Innovator's Solution: Creating and Sustaining Successful Growth* (Boston: Harvard Business School Press, 2003).

Richard Foster and Sarah Kaplan, *Creative Destruction: Why companies that are built to last underperform the market—and how to successfully transform them* (New York: Doubleday, 2001).

Chris Zook, *Beyond the Core: Expand Your Market Without Abandoning Your Roots* (Boston, MA: Harvard Business School Press, 2004)

Adrian Slywotzky and Richard Wise, *How to Grow When Markets Don't* (New York: Warner Business Books, 2004).

Jim Collins, *Good to Great: Why Some Companies Make the Leap... And Others Don't* (New York: HarperBusiness, 2001).

iv Robert G. Cooper, *Winning at New Products: Accelerating the Process from Idea to Launch,* 3rd ed. (Reading, MA:Perseus Books, 2004).

v *See* note i; also in *Creative Destruction*, Foster cited McKinsey interviews with executives at 50 companies. Each said innovation was important, but acknowledged they had difficulty pulling it off. They cited: the inability to grow beyond the core; the lack of ideas compelling enough to change customer behavior; slow product development; the failure to establish an "innovative culture."

vi *See* for example, Robert G. Cooper, *Product Leadership: Creating and Launching Superior New Products* (New York: Perseus Books Group/HarperCollins Publishers, 2000), and Michael E. McGrath, *Setting the PACE in Product Development, A Guide to Product and Cycle-time Excellence* (Burlington, MA: Elsevier Science (Butterworth-Heinemann, 1996).

vii From the novel *The Arch of Triumph* (1946) which has been made into two films.

viii Richard Foster and Sarah Kaplan, *op cit.* (*see* note iii).

Part I

An Executive's Guide to Fast Innovation

With Richard Spencer

Fast Innovation

The process of creating new products, services, business models, processes, and markets with sufficient differentiation and speed such that the company sustains above-average shareholder returns for decades.

Contributor background

Richard Spencer is a consultant and general manager with extensive expertise and a 20-year track record in leading top- and bottom-line performance improvement programs in a variety of businesses. He has profitably grown four businesses, ranging from a small company to one with $750mm P&L. His particular expertise lies in business strategy, sales & marketing, and Lean Six Sigma operational improvement programs for industrial companies. He holds an M.Eng (Mechanical Engineering) from Imperial College, University of London, and an MBA from Harvard Business School.

CHAPTER 1

Using Fast Innovation to Drive Organic Growth

Today, organic growth is absolutely the biggest task. I want imagination breakthroughs... I want game changers... If we don't hit our organic revenue targets, people are not going to get paid!... We are just a moment away from commodity hell!

Jeff Immelt, CEO of General Electric[1]

Across all sectors, the need to create revenue growth amidst new opportunities is joining the pressures to reduce costs and improve processes. Nowhere is this felt more strongly than at GE, whose stock during recent years had dropped as much as 50% from the mid-2000 peak. CEO Jeff Immelt has set an aggressive goal of 7% organic growth per year, compared with a total growth over the past five years of only 4% (which included acquisitions). The market has already taken note of the new emphasis on growth:

> *Morgan Stanley strategist Henry McVey... points to General Electric's success under CEO Jeff Immelt in repositioning the conglomerate to higher-growth areas, in part by selling certain low-return financial units of GE Capital. The stock market has been rewarding General Electric; in the past 12 months, its stock has risen by 18%, to a recent 36.[2]*

Given that GE is a $147 billion company, this organic growth goal is the equivalent of creating an additional $10 billion company in 2005!

Why organic growth? The other major source of growth in the past has been acquisitions, which often proved a valuable way to complement and consolidate existing offerings and expand into new markets. But many companies are finding an acquisitional strategy inadequate to meet growth targets.

Take Parker Hannifin, for example. A $7 billion company in motion and control markets, Parker has historically pursued acquisitions aggressively to grow their business. The strategy worked extraordinarily well for decades, allowing the company to thrive in an increasingly global marketplace. Profitable growth through acquisition, however, is by nature opportunistic—and the opportunities are not as abundant as they once were. Parker is still going to pursue acquisitions, but is now depending on organic internal growth to achieve fully half of the 10% growth target.

The majority of companies have found that most of the attractive acquisitions (from a value perspective) are gone. The stock market has advanced prices in the last two years, and there is over $100 billion of "dry powder" in the hands of private equity firms, the leading competitor to strategic investment by companies.

Strategic investors have typically paid one or two multiples of EBITDA (earnings before interest depreciation taxes and amortization) higher than have private equity firms, depressing ROIC, which is further depressed by changes in GAAP and the tax code. This has had the effect of depressing shareholder returns. Further, Tom Copeland et al., in the book *Valuation*, evaluated a large data set of acquisitions and found that only 23% were ultimately successful.

Interestingly, this is a similarly low percentage to the current success rate of new innovations. There is one substantial difference in acquisition vs. innovation strategies to grow: Acquisitions are an all-or-nothing path since they require the company to commit completely at time of acquisition. Innovation and the subsequent organic growth, *done right*, allows the company to place smaller bets with similar payoff. While targeted acquisitions will always be an important aspect of increasing corporate capabilities, companies will have to rely on organic growth to a far larger extent to sustain above-average shareholder returns.

Innovation's Contribution to Organic Growth and Value Creation

In *Valuation,* Tom Copeland discusses what drives market valuations over the long run and shows decisively the factors that drive stock price appreciation.[3] Copeland studied the stock market performance of hundreds of companies for over a decade, and arrived at empirical values of stock as a function of ROIC (Return on Invested Capital) and growth that are congruent with discounted cash flow.

In Figure 1-01, we plotted Copeland's data into what we call the Value Mountain, which illustrates his points graphically. The vertical axis, "Market Value to Book Value," is the premium the stock market pays for a company's performance beyond its net assets.

Figure 1-01: The Value Mountain

Premier Stock Price Multiples Strongly Driven by ROIC
Data 1994 to 1998, Copeland's *Valuation* (2000 ed), ex. 5.2

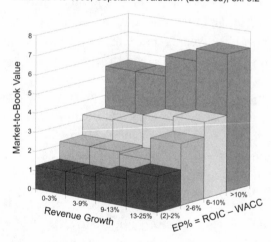

There are two key relationships depicted in the Value Mountain:

1) **The spread between a business's ROIC and its weighted average cost of capital, variously called %economic profit (EP%) or economic value-add% ($EVA™).**[4] The discounted value of economic profit is mathematically identical with discounted cash flow:

> *The value of any stock, bond, or business today is determined by the cash inflows and outflows—discounted at an appropriate interest rate—that can be expected to occur during the remaining life of the asset.*
>
> *Berkshire Hathaway Annual Report*[5]

Companies whose ROIC is about equal to their Weighted Average Cost of Capital (the *front* of the graph) trade at a ratio of about 1 to 2 times book value (while the price does fluctuate during bull and bear markets, over time it will be, in the words of Ben Graham, "gravitationally attracted" to this range). In contrast, a company whose ROIC is greater than WACC (towards the back of the graph) trades at much higher multiples. This pattern has been found by other researchers as well.[6]

2) **The growth rate as reflected in Net Operating Profit Less Adjusted Taxation (NOPLAT).** So long as ROIC is fixed, revenue growth is a proxy for NOPLAT growth. Operating profit can be helped through cost reductions, an important component of organizational effectiveness, but only so far. **Further growth in profit requires revenue growth**, and the stock market knows that.

When a company can combine growth greater than 5% per year with ROIC that's greater than WACC by 5%, it can trade at multiples of 7 to 10+ times book value. As of January 2005, the S&P 500 traded at 2.96 times book value. (Individual companies can do much better or worse, but these figures, calculated from hundreds of companies, are accurate within an industry.)

The mountain reflects a third very important factor that is subjective and hence cannot be shown graphically: that of future expectations. The Discounted Cash Flow models that underlie these valuations are based heavily on the market's expectations for the company's ability to maintain or improve its performance on each axis. This issue underscores the importance of focusing not just on generating a great new innovation or two to pump up the growth, but rather on taking a systemic process focus to creating a Fast Innovation engine that the market will judge to be capable of sustaining your growth and ROIC.

Put simply, if shareholder value is a function of your current and future expected ROIC, WACC, and NOPLAT growth rate (for which revenue growth is a fair surrogate), management must pursue both:

1) Fast Innovation to sustainably increase growth rate and margins

2) Process improvement, such as Lean Six Sigma, Design for Lean Six Sigma and Complexity reduction to increase customer satisfaction, reduce costs, reduce lead times and solve quality problems

The Challenges of Sustained Growth

We have empirical data from the stock market proving that companies the market believes can sustain growth rates above the GDP growth rate receive extraordinary valuations—data supported by many other studies.[7,8] We can all cite stories of sustained growth rates and share prices in companies like IBM, Coca-Cola, Xerox, HP, TI, and Dell—for at least a significant *part* of their histories. But of the companies that constituted the B.C. Forbes list of top 100 companies in 1917, how many remain in the top 100? Only one: General Electric!

> *"If history is a guide, no more than a third of today's major corporations will survive in an economically important way over the next twenty-five years."*[9]

> *"Study after study concludes that about **90 percent** of all publicly traded companies have proved **unable** to sustain for more than a few years a growth trajectory that **creates above-average shareholder returns.**"*[10]

> *"In the 1920s and '30s the turnover rate in the S&P 90 averaged about 1.5% per year. A new member of the S&P 90 at that time could expect to remain on the list, on average, for more than 65 years. In 1998, the turnover rate in the S&P 500 was close to 10%, implying an average lifetime on the list of 10 years!"*[11]

The challenge of maintaining growth is global. We did our own analysis recently of the companies that make up the major indices in Europe. When looked at in combination, the companies that make up the

FTSE100, the CAC40 and the DAX30 have an average lifetime on the index of 10.5 years, a finding substantially the same as the analysis above for the U.S.

The causative factors for failing to maintain growth have been studied by a number of scholars, and their conclusions are consistent and irrefutable.[12] The *reason* firms do not sustain these high rates of growth is because they *do not institutionalize* innovation, and do not change at the pace of the financial markets. The markets engage in what Richard Foster has called Creative Destruction: companies that do not perform are dumped or destroyed in an afternoon; those that do perform are quickly rewarded.

But individual companies per se do not achieve this pace of creative destruction. Bell Labs, a former paragon of innovation, virtually *never killed* a project—which practically guarantees a slow innovation lead time… and growth slower than the market.

> *The perversion you can get into is that you build an incentive system that causes people to keep trying to make something a success and invest behind it when they ought to just quit. Kill it off, take the learning, and recycle.*
>
> Gilbert Cloyd, Chief Technical Officer, P&G

Chris Zook and James Allen found in their 2001 study, *Profit from the Core*, that only 13% of their sample of 1,854 companies were able to grow consistently over a 10-year period.[13] Jim Collins found only 126, or about 9% of his sample, had managed to outperform equity market averages for a decade or more. Clayton Christensen's studies all support the assertion that a 10% probability of succeeding in a quest for sustained growth is, if anything, a generous estimate.[14] Adrian Slywotzky found that from 1990 to 2000, just 7% of publicly traded companies in the U.S. enjoyed eight or more years of double-digit growth in revenues and operating profits.[15]

Throughout this book, we're going to use the statistic cited above—that about **90% of companies cannot sustain above-average shareholder returns for more than a decade**—as a shorthand for all the reasons why innovation efforts have to be raised to a level beyond that currently achieved by most companies. Our message is that a company **cannot be merely** *occasionally* **innovative. It must be** *reliably* **innovative at a rate faster than current (or future) competitors.** This is the rallying cry, the burning platform, that virtually all companies must champion. And it's that challenge that this book will help you conquer.

The Fast Innovation Value Proposition

In the Preface, we promised that this book would show you how to cut the lead time required for innovation by 50% to 80% and dramatically improve the differentiated competitive advantages of your offerings, which are the key innovation issues that most CEOs are frustrated with. Achieving those goals will allow you to use innovation to generate continuous organic growth.

Details on specific innovation tactics will come later in this book. Here, we want to provide the broad perspective. To start, take a look at Figure 1-02, which shows a typical development pattern and provides a picture of the typical relationships between time and cash flow during innovation development with a modest rate of return and a relatively long time to break-even.

Figure 1-02: Typical Pattern of Innovation Development

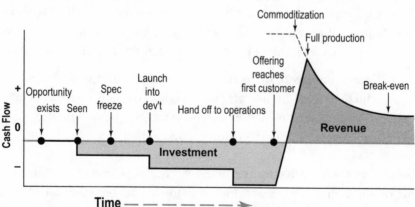

Figure 1-02 also captures the typical cash flow of each phase. The Investment area (in the light shade) covers all investments in monitoring the marketplace and developing and launching the product or service. The Revenue area (darker shading) depicts the positive cash flow that occurs when the offering starts generating revenue.

In most companies, these two areas are shaped by a number of errors and delays at almost every step in development. For example, investments in development are often bigger than necessary because:

- Methods for observing opportunities in the marketplace, understanding the customer's true need, and/or being able to quickly decide to take action are largely ineffective—leading to missed revenue and delays in reaching development.

- Companies have inadequate criteria for predicting the catastrophic impact on lead time, and as a consequence launch too many projects. So *all* projects take longer than necessary (and time = money). We'll talk about this more in Chapter 3.

- Little or no process communication between marketing, development, and operations leads to high costs and poor quality.

- There is a tendency to "over invent," creating all innovations from scratch rather than only inventing what must be new.

Similarly, the Revenue area (which represents the market response to an offering) is smaller than it could be because:

- Companies have astonishingly limited interaction with and observation of customers before and during the development process, which makes it difficult for them to identify true differentiators

- Companies freeze the performance features prior to development, which, as we'll discuss later in this book, virtually guarantees huge schedule overruns and also contributes to undifferentiated offerings… again leading to failure in the market

Because of these problems, the Investment in development (light shading on the chart) is huge, and the company is likely to enter the market late when prices have already fallen due to commoditization (shortening both the height and width of the Revenue area). Given this state of affairs, it's no wonder that many companies fail to maintain above-average growth of shareholder returns. The Fast Innovation techniques presented in this book attack these problems on many fronts:

- Perceiving better opportunities sooner (better means more highly differentiated offerings; sooner means beating your competition)

- Quantitatively determining whether and when to launch a project, giving you control over innovation lead times and time-to-market

- Doing a better job of capturing unmet, unstated customer needs

- Cutting 50% or more of the development time

- Reliably executing the detailed design process and transition from development to operations

The impact of these changes is considerable, as depicted in Figure 1-03.

Figure 1-03: The Impact of Fast Innovation

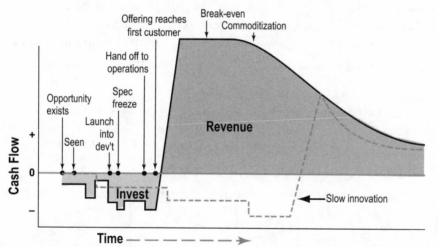

With Fast Innovation, investment in innovation starts earlier (more cash outflow in the detection stages) and there is more investment in quick cycles of learning. (The investment "dips" correspond to specific events during the Fast Innovation development cycle.) The customer knowledge gained upfront, however, pays off in shorter development time and higher margins because of greater differentiation. Being faster also means companies can more rapidly introduce additional offerings or other innovations to the market.

As you can see in Figure 1-03:

- **More effort and dollars are funneled into perceiving and ana-lyzing opportunities:** The result is that you'll pick up on more opportunities and get the best ones into development faster than ever before (which means you can reach the market ahead of your competition). The cash outflow (Investment) starts earlier and initially eats up more dollars than in the traditional (slow) approach—but shrinking the overall perception cycle means that the investment as a whole is not too much larger than that in tradi-tional innovation.

- **Development is shorter and better at delivering on differentia-tion.** Shorter means your investment is smaller and you get to market sooner; better at differentiation means the Revenue area will be taller (more dollars, sooner).

The impact of speed in the investment/profit equation cannot be over-stated. Being able to get attractive offerings to the market quickly means that a company can introduce several offerings in the time it takes a slower competitor to introduce just one. The Fast Innovation value proposition presented in this book is summarized in the resulting changes:

1) **The timeline shrinks dramatically** (Figure 1-04).

Figure 1-04: Timelines of Slow vs. Fast Innovation

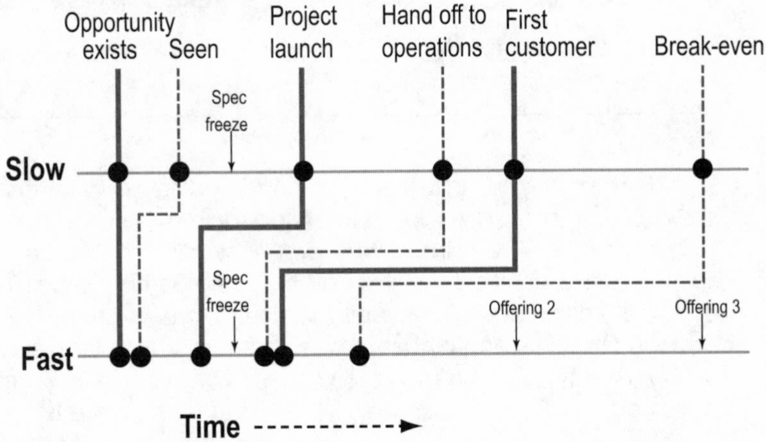

2 The investment in development shrinks dramatically (Figure 1-05).

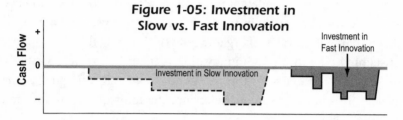

Figure 1-05: Investment in Slow vs. Fast Innovation

3) Revenue generated gets taller and maintains a higher return initially (because you get to the market before commoditization). You'll also reach the break-even point sooner because of the smaller overall investment initially (Figure 1-06).

Figure 1-06: Revenue Generated by Slow vs. Fast Innovation

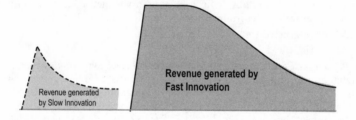

Conclusion

The purpose of this book is to give you the critical approaches that will allow you to change the innovation curve from that in Figure 1-02 to that of Figure 1-03 (as summarized in Figures 1-04 to 1-06). If adopted and built into the fabric of your company, these Fast Innovation approaches will enable you to maintain above-average shareholder returns indefinitely. The next chapter goes into more depth about the three imperatives built into the Fast Innovation curve (differentiation, speed-to-market, and disruption); subsequent Spotlights give an overview of techniques (presented in Part II of this book) for achieving those goals. Later chapters cover other Fast Innovation techniques and review their impact on this development curve.

Currently, 90% of companies cannot sustain above-average shareholder returns for more than a decade. This telling statistic creates the imperative for adopting a new model for innovation. **Most companies will have to significantly change their total innovation process to be able to double or triple their rates of organic growth.** Creating the environment for sustaining growth through innovation is the principal responsibility of the company leadership; the means for achieving this goal is the purpose of this book. Without leadership, the tools of Fast Innovation are of little value.

Endnotes

1 Erick Schonfeld, "GE Sees the Light," *Business 2.0,* July 2004.

2 Cited in "When Giants Awaken," by Andrew Bary, *Barrons,* Jan 3, 2005. (http://www.smartmoney.com/barrons/index.cfm?story=20050103)

3 McKinsey and Company, Inc., Tom Copeland, Tim Koller, Jack Murrin, *Valuation: Measuring and Managing the Value of Companies, 3rd Edition* (New York: John Wiley and Sons, 2000), pp. 76-77. Copeland's book makes valuation accessible to those who do not have an MBA. ROIC is an appropriate metric for the majority of companies, but we use Return In Equity for banks and other financial institutions.

4 EVA is the registered trademark of Stern-Stewart.

5 Berkshire Hathaway Annual Report, 1992.

6 In *Beyond the Core: Expand Your Market Without Abandoning Your Roots*, Chris Zook reinforces the same underlying point by saying that a company that moves from the 0–5 percent growth category in revenues and profits to the 5–10 percent category will triple its shareholder returns from 4.1 percent to 12.4 percent (Boston, MA: Harvard Business School Press, 2004), p. 166.

7 Copeland et al., *op. cit. (see* note 3, above), Ex 5.2.

8 Continuing the Chris Zook citation of footnote 6: According to a Bain study, "A company that moves from the 0-5 percent growth category in revenues and profits to the 5-10 percent range will... over ten years increase shareholder wealth of 320 percent versus only 148 percent for the lower growth rate" (Zook, *op. cit.),* p. 166.

9 Richard Foster and Sarah Kaplan, *Creative Destruction: Why companies that are built to last underperform the market—and how to successfully transform them* (New York: Doubleday, 2001), p. 14.

10 Clayton M. Christensen and Michael E. Raynor, *The Innovator's Solution: Creating and Sustaining Successful Growth* (Boston: Harvard Business School Press, 2003), 7.

11 Foster, *op. cit.,* p. 14.

12 Henry Chesbrough, *Open Innovation: The New Imperative for Creating and Profiting from Technology* (Boston: Harvard Business School Press, 2003); Christensen and Raynor, *op. cit.*; Foster and Kaplan, *op. cit.*

13 Chris Zook and James Allen, *Profit from the Core* (Boston: Harvard Business School Press, 2001).

14 Christensen, *op. cit.,* pp. 19-20.

15 Adrian Slywotzky and Richard Wise, *How to Grow When Markets Don't* (New York: Warner Business Books, 2004), p. 10.

CHAPTER 2

The Three Innovation Imperatives

Differentiated, Fast, Disruptive

The value proposition defined in the previous chapter is captured in our definition of Fast Innovation:

The process of creating new products, services, processes, business models and markets with sufficient differentiation and speed such that the company maintains above-average shareholder returns for decades.

This chapter looks at the three imperatives incorporated into that definition:

1) **Differentiation:** Providing an offering, a process, a business model, or a set of offerings which the customer believes deliver superior performance per unit of cost

   Impact: Drives positive cash flow higher (increasing the profit area in Figure 1-02)

2) **Fast Time-to-Market:** Consistently reaching the market early enough such that differentiated offerings earn high margins, and quickly creating a new innovation to counter the inevitable commoditization of the old

   Impact: Reduces negative cash flow during development AND allows the company to tap into positive cash flow sooner

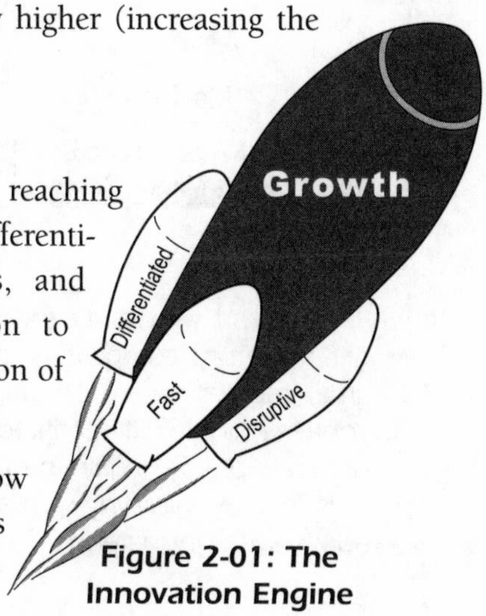

Growth

Differentiated

Fast

Disruptive

Figure 2-01: The Innovation Engine

3) **Disruptive Innovations:** Creating and embracing disruptive offerings that obsolete current offerings, processes and business models will catch the competition flat-footed and may provide great propulsive power to growth

   Impact: Redefines the playing field, making any previous competitive advantages obsolete

Imperative #1: Differentiation

Differentiation in products or services means providing unique or superior customer functionality that commands a premium price, generates a premium profit, or significantly increases market share. As shown in Figure 2-02, highly differentiated products and services have an 82% success rate compared with 18% for me-too offerings.

Figure 2-02: Impact of Differentiated Products

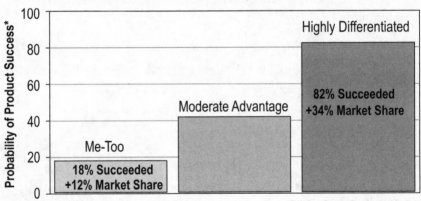

*Data from Product Development Institute

As this chart shows, me-too offerings (those that aren't significantly different from competitors' offerings) succeeded only 18% of the time, generating a 12% gain in market share when they did. In contrast, highly differentiated offerings succeeded 82% of the time, generating a 54% gain in market share. The failure of me-too offerings may explain why so many companies find it hard to maintain above-average shareholder returns.[16]

To generate the kind of shareholder value we're all seeking, the innovation process has to encompass identifying customer needs that are highly valued, and satisfying those needs either *before* a competitor does and/or *better* than a competitor does. Identifying and capturing what will make a product, service, or capability "differentiated" requires a much more sophisticated Voice of the Customer (VOC) process than the traditional combination of focus groups, surveys, questionnaires and competitive analysis. Details are later in this book, but here's a quick look at several key elements:

- **Ethnography:** Closely observing customer interactions with their daily environment so you can identify needs they can't articulate and find opportunities for your capabilities that they can't foresee. This process may also uncover customer frustrations related to the use of your product and service that may help you identify entirely new products and services. Ethnography will uncover these needs early in the process, instead of finding out during development if a customer happens to see a prototype.

- **Rapid cycles of brainstorming, concept development, prototyping, and customer feedback:** Testing everything along the way (your interpretation of customer needs, elements of the product/service design, etc.) speeds up the learning curve and lets designers and developers more quickly come up with offerings that will delight customers. An interesting insight from *The Economist* study we cited earlier is that only 46% of companies involve customers in concept development, and amazingly, 27% of companies wait until testing to get feedback from customers. Imagine the waste and opportunity!

- **Approaching design with multiple performance targets in mind:** Traditional development processes require companies to set performance specs very early in the process, which closes developers off to changes in or a better understanding of customer needs. A flexible approach allows specs to be fixed much later in the process, which allows developers to incorporate lessons learned as the design evolves.

"Differentiation" does not refer solely to unique product or service features. You can achieve differentiation by being faster than competitors at delivering high qualty and lower cost, or by providing a *set* of offerings that helps the customer succeed. Later in this chapter we'll talk about the important concept that low cost doesn't necessarily mean absolute price per unit of product or service, but rather "lower cost per unit of performance" from the customer's perspective.

Imperative #2: Fast Time-to-Market

Speed-to-market maintains profitable growth through at least four mechanisms:

1. Maximizes your share of industry profit pools prior to commoditization

2. Accelerates customer feedback loops and learning cycles

3. Recoups investment sooner and decreases time to break-even

4. Increases our capacity for innovation!

While at Intel, Eamon Malone learned the advantages of fast time-to-market. It's a message he reinforced in his recent position as VP of the Motorola Computer Group, which he helped turn around to become one of the most profitable divisions in the company (details on pp. 166-167). Eamon asserts that at least half the cumulative operating profit for a new product will be generated in the first 18 months after introduction, then commoditization will reduce margins during the remaining 5 to 10 years of life and provide the other half of cumulative operating profit! An analysis of discounted cash flow shows that virtually all the shareholder value is created by the fast innovator. In general, commoditization will reduce prices to a level corresponding to the cost of capital, i.e., to a level that creates little or no shareholder value.

In the pharmaceutical industry, prices are slashed by 80% within a few months of a drug coming off patent.[17] The general pattern is shown in Figure 2-03, next page (the exact shape will vary by business and by product/service).

Figure 2-03: Gross Profit Margin Over Time

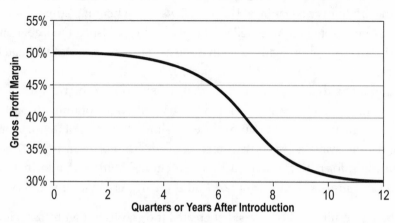

Gross Profit Margin drops over time as commoditization drives prices down.

In addition to a decline in profit margin, the market size and lifetime revenue available to a latecomer is dramatically reduced. The first firms to reach the market and perform adequately will seize and sustain a dominant share of the market. Again, studies in the pharmaceutical industry indicate that the cumulative market share enjoyed by the first three firms to participate in a new opportunity exceeds 80% of the available market, as shown in Figure 2-04.[18]

Figure 2-04: Early Entrant Advantage

The competition to dominate internet auctions is another stark example of the first mover advantage. Despite eBay's overwhelming strength in its auction market, Yahoo beat eBay to Japan and established the leadership position. Even after significant investment, mighty eBay was ultimately forced to withdraw from the Japanese market and leave it to the first entrant. The dynamics of each market depend on the barriers to entry and exit, and each company should estimate the value of time-to-market for its industry or sector. Our experience shows that a lot of the supporting data is available in most companies, but has not been transformed into the information provided by these curves. With this information, you can estimate the value of fast lead time in every market you serve.

When we multiply the curves that created the graphs in Figures 2-03 and 2-04, we obtain the relative gross profit dollars gained from early entry. To make the figures realistic, we use data from the pharmaceutical sector to see how much advantage was gained by the first three entrants (Figure 2-05). In this case, they capture 90% of the gross profit dollars. We strongly suspect this pattern is true for most markets: that when the dollars are adjusted for SG&A expense and the cost of capital, late entrants may generate little if any economic profit and hence no sustaining shareholder value.

Figure 2-05: Cumulative Advantage of Early Entrants

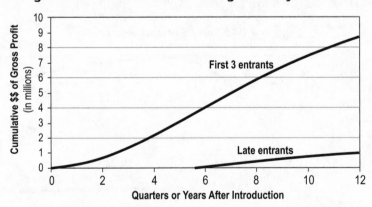

The problem with not being among the first to market with an innovation is clear: late entrants frequently do not earn enough to repay their investment in development, and may be in a significantly weakened condition, unable to fight the next battle.

Late entrants will likely earn a negative economic profit (ROIC < WACC invested). As the Copeland data in Figure 1-01 shows, that negative economic profit will in fact destroy shareholder value. In short, from an innovation standpoint, better *never* than *late!*

Thus far we have dwelt on the internal measures such as operating profit as the cost of being late to market. We have not dwelt on the third factor discussed on page 5, namely future expectations of the market. If the market gets wind that your innovation processes are faltering, and that your previous track record of growth is faltering, then share price and shareholder returns will take a dive. For example, in 2003-04, Intel failed to comprehend that its customers would want a 64-bit Pentium chip separate from Itanium. As a result, Intel delayed launching its 64-bit Pentium, and opened up a window for industry follower Advanced Micro Devices (AMD) to become a technology leader with its Opteron 32/64-bit microprocessors. When the Opteron was benchmarked against Intel, it ran 40% to 400% faster.

Even long-time Intel ally Hewlett-Packard (HP) strayed. Paul Miller, their VP of marketing, commented:

> *We kept asking Intel, what are you going to do for us to be competitive? The plan kept on falling short.*

And not only HP switched. Sun and IBM are using Opteron along with, as unthinkable as it sounds, Dell. The cost of being late to market had major consequences for future customer satisfaction and contributed to a declining share price for Intel (*see* Figure 2-06, top of next page).

Investors learned of these issues in the *Wall Street Journal*.[19] Intel reacted appropriately in 2004:

> *We will develop 90% confidence schedules. We will staff them accordingly. When our engineering managers tell us some-thing is not right, we will fix it. We won't say "we don't believe you." We will make our commitments to our customer such that they can be met, and we will meet them.*

Being late to market has contributed to Intel shareholder returns being strongly negative over the last year despite *record profit performance.*

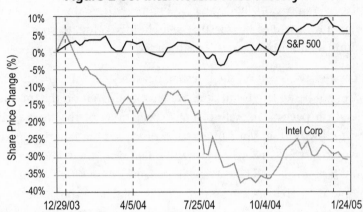

Figure 2-06: Intel Recent Price History

Chapter 6 (p. 126) discusses how Paul Otellini, the new Intel CEO, is turning this situation around using many of the themes discussed in this book. In addition to better market intelligence, he has reorganized the company around product platforms.

Every company should estimate the value of being early to market in their own markets and consider impact on share prices of being late. That's the essential data needed to clearly demonstrate the cost of being late to market in terms of shareholder returns. This is a key input in creating the burning platform—a brief statement of *why* Fast Innovation is necessary to the company—to gain buy-in to launch the Fast Innovation process. One way we have found to effectively make this real for people working in the innovation process is to figure out just what a day or a week or a month of faster time-to-market would be worth. Even more effective is to find out how many hours (days, weeks, months…) of improvement would generate "a million dollars." A statement like "Every week we could get to market faster would add a million dollars to the bottom line" creates the kind of urgency you need.

To the extent that innovation drives growth, you will find that being an early entrant (preferably among the first three) gives you remarkable leverage. And of course the first mover often has the greatest advantage. Sometimes a rapid follower can capture most of the profit, usually because the first mover lacks strong operational execution or a lack of process innovation.

But by and large, failing to be among the first three entrants will minimally result in a loss of operating profit and growth (in a slower market) and can have catastrophic effects when a fast-moving technology or rapidly changing service is involved. For example, American manufacturers were late to market with the 64K memory chip, and the Japanese seized all those profits. The Americans were in a weakened position on the 256K chip, and first Mostek, then Intel, and finally Texas Instruments were driven from the business.

We'll give you an overview of *how* to become fast in Chapter 3 and details on specific practices in Part II.

Imperative #3: Disruption

Imperatives #1 and #2 are about enlarging the positive cash flow area on the value proposition curve defined in Chapter 1. Disruption is about creating entirely new curves altogether—redefining the marketplace in such a way that a new set of factors determine profitability and success. Not surprisingly, innovations that help you redefine the marketplace are called disruptive innovations; those that merely change the dynamics within the existing frameworks are called sustaining innovations.

1) **Sustaining innovations:** Improvements that build on existing technology, products/services, market strategy, etc. (also referred to as

> **Building a burning platform around speed**
>
> The cost of being late to market is a metric all companies should explicitly capture. Historical data can be used to estimate the growth and margin that would have accrued had their innovation lead times been twice as fast. The estimates generally show that a slow and ineffective innovation process costs companies between 20% and 50% of their potential shareholder value. In addition, an estimate should be made of the impact on share price for perceived time-to-market failures. This knowledge helps creates the burning platform for change necessary to gain buy-in at all levels to implement the Fast Innovation process.

"incremental" innovations). Sustaining innovations apply existing core competencies and therefore...

- likely offer only a modest to moderate improvement in cost per unit of product/service or cost per unit of performance

- have a low risk of failure

- can be quickly copied and commoditized

- can be evaluated using Net Present Value analysis

- create growth in revenue and shareholder value without destroying or marginalizing the value-creation potential of incumbent offerings, processes, or market position

- would most likely...
  - be sold to the company's best customers
  - pass through existing channels
  - easily integrate into existing offerings
  - generate predictable volumes and profits

2) **Disruptive innovations**: Offerings, processes, methods, technologies, etc., that represent a major shift from everything that has come before. Disruptive innovations eliminate or marginalize the revenue growth and value-creation potential of an incumbent's offerings. They may offer explosive growth but have a number of challenges and risks:

- may require new technologies or core competencies (so the company will have to develop new knowledge and skills)

- may not interest the company's current best customers (so the company will have to establish a new customer base)

- may require completely different sales channels

- may compete with and cannibalize existing offerings (a problem that can be dealt with only at an executive level)

- will have unpredictable sales volumes and profits (at least at first)

- cannot be evaluated by Net Present Value analysis

Innovations such as automatic transmissions, CDs, and DVDs meet all the criteria for sustaining innovations; they were largely extensions of existing technology. Incumbent producers of those products (GM, Ford, Chrysler, Phillips, Hitachi) immediately reacted to the innovation and captured most of the volume—hence the innovation merely *sustained* incumbent growth. To use Christensen's terminology, these incumbents were *not* caught flat-footed. They were able to immediately react to the innovation. The ability of incumbents to respond to an innovation is a key determinant of whether the innovation is sustaining or disruptive. In the early '60s, car seat belts were sold by independent intruders. When the car companies adopted seat belts as standard, the independents became a dim memory. And what would have happened if an industry outsider had offered a marginally better automatic transmission? Such a product would have appealed to GM's best customers, would have used GM's existing core competencies, etc. In the case of a sustaining innovation, the incumbents will *fight rather than flee.*

Disruptive innovations are, in contrast, very attractive to industry outsiders. Incumbents often cannot, or more commonly *will not,* copy a disruptive innovation—they will *flee rather than fight.* Lack of managerial peripheral vision, dependence on existing core competencies, and the game-changing nature of disruptive innovation can overwhelm a flat-footed incumbent, as shown in Table 2A (next page).

Many of these disruptive innovations began as small, possibly nuisance, markets on the periphery of huge markets in which the incumbents thrived. Because the innovation was on the periphery, the incumbents chose to defend their existing core competency until it finally was a competency that customers no longer cared about:

> *When spring comes, snow melts first at the periphery, because that's where it's most exposed.*
>
> *Andy Grove, Intel*

While all product/service innovations can have strong growth potential, the potential is greater for disruptive innovations (those that incumbents will more likely flee than fight). For example, even products not protected by patents often have a five-year run of high growth and

Table 2A: Disruptive Innovations

Disrupted Company/Industry	Disruptive Product/Service
Vacuum tubes (GE, RCA,Sylvania)	Transistors
Integrated Steel Producers	Mini-Mills
NCR	Electronic cash registers
Keds, Converse	Running shoes
Kendall	Disposable diapers
Friden, SCM, Monroe	Electronic calculators
Kodak, Polaroid film	Digital cameras
Digital Equipment Corp.	Microcomputers
American, Delta, United	Southwest Airlines
Credit Cards at 19.9% APR	Capital One risk-adjusted rate
Swiss watchmakers, Timex	Digital watches
Levi Strauss	Designer jeans
Model T Ford	Used Model T and Chevrolet "K" cars
Compact Discs	Apple iTunes, online MP3 providers
Brick and Mortar Bookstore	Amazon.com
Compaq	Dell's business process model
Local specialty stores	Wal-Mart

Partial Source: "When Entering Growth Markets, are Pioneers Really Poachers?" Steven P. Schnaars, Business Horizons *(March, 1992).*

margins before competition begins commoditizing the offering. As we've noted, the disruptive advantage arises in part because the disruptive innovation is often initially dismissed by incumbents, who may subsequently be too weak to mount a counterattack (they're caught flat-footed).

Disruptions can take the form of a new technology, a new offering, a new process, or even a new business model. Disruptions can also take the form of creating a sequence of sustaining innovations so *quickly* that competitors cannot keep up (using sustaining innovation disruptively). We'll go through examples of all these types of disruptions later in the book.

The Power of Disruptive Innovation

To understand the importance of striving for disruptive innovations, we worked with Clayton Christensen of the Harvard Business School. Clay's favorite way of introducing the power of disruption is through examples:

Integrated producers of steel transform iron ore into a broad range of products, from low-profit commodity re-bars to high-profit sheet steel. The development of the "mini-mill" based on the electric arc furnace made it possible to produce low-quality re-bars from scrap metal at 20% less cost than the integrated producers could achieve. (Note that in this case the product wasn't new—what was new was the process used to produce it.) Rather than invest scarce capital in what, from their perspective, was *perceived* as low-profit re-bars, the integrated producers invested in high-margin, upscale products for their most profitable customers. They were happy to flee rather than fight for the re-bar market.

But from the customers' perspective, the mini-mill re-bar was offered at a *lower cost per unit of product*, and since its performance was "good enough" for the application, it also provided a *lower cost per unit of performance*. That differentiation allowed mini-mills to enjoy fabulous growth as the integrated producers were *disrupted from beneath*. The mini-mills then were powerfully motivated to improve their quality further to extend their capability to angle irons, disrupting the integrated producers from beneath yet again. Continued innovations up the value chain ultimately destroyed the value-creation potential of the integrated producers.

The mini-mill is a disruptive example of selling a "good enough" product at a lower cost per unit of product (in this case, dollars per pound of re-bar). There is, however, another form of disruption: selling a product/service at a lower cost per unit of performance (in the eyes of the customer) but at a higher price per unit of product/service. This approach, too, can result in spectacular growth in shareholder value.

This broadening of disruption to include anything that offers a lower cost per unit of performance demonstrates the universal validity of the power of disruptive innovations.[20]

The Most Important Disruptive Innovation of the 20th Century

In 1955, all computers used vacuum tubes as their basic digital switching device, and computers were the third-largest and fastest-growing market for vacuum tubes. In 1956, IBM decided to convert their largest business computer, the IBM 709, from vacuum tubes to germanium transistors (which switched much faster), and renamed the computer the IBM 7090. The transistors cost $17 each and replaced $3-per-unit vacuum tubes.[21] But the IBM 7090 processing speed was *six times* faster than the 709![22] The cost of the transistors only amounted to about 5% of the total computer cost and hence only slightly increased the cost of the system.

Here is an instance of a product (the transistors) disrupting another product (vacuum tubes) on the basis of lower cost per unit of performance rather than lower cost per unit of product. And rational customers care about performance. The advent of transistors opened up a win-win situation in which transistor suppliers enjoyed huge revenue growth and generated 70% gross profit margins, as did IBM on computers!

In summary:

- Disruptive growth at high margins is the result of lower price per unit of performance
- Disruptive growth from a lower price per unit of product/service requires a lower-cost process (e.g., mini-mill) or lower-cost process/business model (what Dell has done, as we'll discuss on p. 80)

Both can create and sustain above-average growth in shareholder returns if they are defended against all comers.

The vacuum tube business continued to go through several cycles of disruption by semiconductors. For example, military applications were the second-largest market for vacuum tube electronics in the 1960s. Military applications required operation at 125°C, too hot for germanium transistors—giving vacuum tube producers a protected and highly profitable niche market with sustained profits and the illusion of safety.

However, as in the case of the mini-mill, semiconductor manufacturers were *powerfully motivated* to solve this problem—and solve it they did! Silicon transistors, invented in 1956, could withstand 125°C and could operate faster and with greater reliability in high-vibration airborne and missile environments. The price of silicon transistors ranged from $10 for small signal devices to $200 for high-power devices while vacuum tubes cost $3! But the increased speed and performance offset the higher price, and silicon transistors disrupted the vacuum tube market on a cost per unit of performance (think about the magnitude of the cost of an inoperable vacuum tube for a radar, missile or fire control system?).

The final chapter for the vacuum tube was written in the bastion they tried to defend: high-end consumer electronics. Companies like Scott and Fisher produced ultra-high-quality audio equipment, and refused to use transistors because of the audio "hiss" caused by the electrical current leakage. This cheered the manufacturers of vacuum tubes, and they fought back against the transistor manufacturers with the vacuum tube "compactron" solution (*see* sidebar, next page).

But the producers of transistors were *powerfully motivated* to create an innovation to solve the hiss problem—and solve it they did. Jean Hoerni of Fairchild[24] innovated the Planar transistor technology which reduced the hiss to inaudible levels. Soon, the principal manufacturer of vacuum tubes was, fittingly, the stumbling Soviet empire. Texas Instruments, Fairchild, and the latter's offspring, Intel, went on to build enormous electronic empires, consigning the mighty tube divisions of giants like GE and RCA to the dustbin of history.

The story of semiconductor disruption does not end with the demise of vacuum tubes. The next step is the invention of the integrated circuit (IC) in 1959. ICs were first applied to the guidance of the Minuteman II missile, replacing the silicon transistor computer. The initial price of a Minuteman II logic gate was $200 per unit vs. about $40 for the equivalent gate in discrete silicon transistors. The first mammoth order for ICs was for the Minuteman II guidance computer. It replaced the Minuteman I discrete transistor guidance computer. Replacing discrete transistors with integrated circuits reduced the physical size of the computer by 75% and the weight by 67%, while doubling guidance accuracy.[25]

The cost of the IC guidance system, while more expensive than transistors, was a small fraction of missile cost. Apart from the volume, power supply and weight advantages, in principle it took half as many missiles to destroy a target, so here again we see a product disrupting a market based on a cost per unit of performance. Manufacturers of discrete transistors were caught flat-footed on this gigantic procurement, which effectively funded future IC development. Most of the transistor incumbents (e.g., Bogue Electric, Transitron, Pacific Semiconductors, RCA, GE, Sylvania, Raytheon, Amelco) did not create viable IC businesses. Within five years, the cost of an IC gate was well below that of the cheapest discrete silicon transistor gate.

The dangers of *good* management and core competencies

Why didn't the giants like RCA and GE immediately react to the transistor revolution with a large-scale effort? Remember, in 1956 the vacuum tube business was very big, with predictable investment returns, and transistors were small and unknown in terms of volume, investment returns, and the technology involved. Instead, the tube manufacturers invested heavily in sustaining innovations, attempting to make vacuum tubes competitive with transistors, and making subscale investments on the unknown, emerging transistor technology:[23]

> In the early 1960s, tube designers still had a few tricks up their sleeves. GE's Owensboro, Kentucky, engineers introduced the "Compactron," multifunction vacuum tubes that used diodes, triodes, and pentodes in various combinations, and that were designed to reduce the size of and component counts in entertainment and industrial devices. Several metallurgical advances enabled GE engineers to claim a 40% reduction in heater power. GE engineers claimed a two-Compactron radio could replace seven transistors needed for the same performance.

These vacuum tube managers and engineers were intellectual captives of their core competencies, watching helplessly as the electron tube volumes sank to nothing, first in computers, then in military applications, and finally in consumer electronics. RCA's feeble efforts to jump on the transistors bandwagon were no more effective than if it had done nothing.

Overcoming resistance to disruption

The failed "Compactron strategy" discussed in the sidebar is in fact *the way* incumbent managers have historically reacted to a disruptive innovation. Psychologist Elisabeth Kübler-Ross has discovered that the human mind cycles through five distinct phases as it deals with trauma and other undesired information: denial, anger, bargaining, depression, and finally acceptance. In the case of business, acceptance generally comes too late to prevent serious loss of shareholder value of the entity, and often bankruptcy.

James Utterback[26] of Harvard Business School has compiled compelling data which shows that what Kübler-Ross calls the "denial" reaction, takes the form of counterattacking with their existing core competency rather than accepting the disruptive innovation itself. He proves this with dozens of examples: The 19th century Boston ice cutters innovating new cutting and transport methods rather than accepting the disruptive innovation of mechanical refrigeration, the gas lighting industry creating the high-efficiency Welsbach mantle and mounting legal challenges rather than accepting the disruptive innovation of the electric light, and dozens more examples up to the present. Looked at individually, each case might be dismissed as a bizarre instance of poor management. But the cumulative weight of the cases shows that a powerful and fundamental force is at work that makes companies especially vulnerable to disruptive innovations from other companies. The blinders we all wear can potentially destroy the shareholder value of *our* companies unless we react to incorporate the new disruption. Part II will discuss this powerful force in more detail, including recommendations for how to overcome it (including designation of a new Chief Innovation Officer position to purposefully pursue disruptive opportunities).

Join the Winning 10%: Being disruptive (even if based on sustaining innovations)

Many companies are created based on some high-risk product, service, market definition or business model innovation. As the company matures, the goal of profitable execution focuses management on predictable extensions of their offerings to sustain growth, and soon the company is locked into a pattern of sustaining innovations to avoid the uncertainty of disruptive innovations. But sustaining innovations are quickly commoditized, so margins decline and thereafter the innovation earns only the cost of capital and creates no shareholder return. At best they grow revenue at GDP rates, which relegates them to being among the 90% of companies that cannot maintain above-average returns. Worse yet, they may be utterly destroyed by a company that executes a disruptive strategy.

This leaves us with three basic strategies for disruptive innovation:

1. Create a Fast Innovation process that can consistently launch a new sustaining innovation before competition can commoditize existing products or services (*see* Figure 2-07). This is an example of a disruptive process innovation protecting a sustaining product innovation.

Figure 2-07: Disrupting the Market with Sustaining Innovations

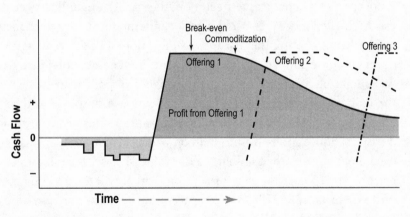

In developing a process to reliably produce new innovations rapidly, you gain the ability to constantly bombard the market with attractive offerings.

2. Create a process for quickly embracing and exploiting disruptive product/service innovations.

3. Create disruptive innovations with fast operational processes, new business models, or new definitions of your market (*see* Chapter 4).

Companies should always pursue option 1 and create a process to continually probe for options 2 and 3.

Conclusion

CEOs or business unit managers must confront the brutal statistic we've cited before: all companies try, but 90% of companies can't maintain above-average growth and shareholder returns! The three engines that provide the propulsive power to maintain above-average growth in revenue and shareholder returns are:

- Differentiation = Successful innovations

- Fast time-to-market = High margins

- Probing for disruptions = Obsoleting the competition

The fact that 90% of companies do not presently achieve these goals means that the current approach to innovation requires significant change... we can't get different results tomorrow by using the process of today.

Significant change in a corporate environment can be accomplished only if there is a burning platform issue clearly enunciated by the CEO and each P&L manager that defines how much more growth in revenue, margins, and shareholder value will occur if the company embraces an innovation process that increases differentiation, reduces time-to-market, and gives them an opportunity to obsolete the competition.

The first step is to estimate where your company currently operates. Is it in the early-to-market, high-margin area of the Fast Innovation curve (Figure 1-03) or in the commoditized area? More specifically:

Fast Questions: What does the specific recent data tell you about your time-to-market performance versus the competition? Using the parameters of your business, what would be the impact of reducing time-to-market by 50% and increasing the height of the margins through differentiation? What is a day/week/month of improvement worth?

> **Differentiation Questions:** When do you get customer input on your new innovations? How deep is the input? Remember that if you are not getting beyond typical survey/interview/focus group data, you are probably missing 95% of the picture! What would significant differentiation do to your prices and/or market share?
>
> **Disruption Questions:** Is a competitor working to disrupt your market? Could you disrupt your own market or an adjacent market? Are you currently pursuing a "compactron" strategy?

What impact would these changes have? Using historical data and reasonable projections, usually the answer is that a company can double shareholder value. That kind of burning platform provides the impetus for learning about Fast Innovation and how to reduce time-to-market, increase differentiation, and become a disruptive force in your industry.

Endnotes

16 Used with permission of the authors.
17 Stefan Thomke, Paul Pospisil, Ashok Nimgade, "Eli Lilly and Co.: Drug Development Strategy," HBR 9-698-010, rev. September 2003.
18 *ibid.*
19 *See*, for example, *Wall Street Journal*, Jan 12,2005, p. B4.
20 Private communications, Christensen/George.
21 Private communication with Richard J. Hanschen, former vice president of Texas Instruments.
22 *See* http://www-03. ibm.com/ibm/history/exhibits/mainframe/mainframe_PP7090.html
23 *See* http://hhscott. com/cc/compactrons.htm
24 *See* http://www.ideafinder.com/history/inventions/integratedcircuit.htm
25 *See* http://ed-thelen.org/comp-hist/BRL64-m. html
26 James M. Utterback, *Mastering the Dynamics of Innovation* (Boston: Harvard Business School Press, 1996).

SPOTLIGHT ON

Customers and Differentiation

We want to create a value breakaway—a compelling, competitive advantage—that is perceivable by the customer.

—Pete Buca, Parker Hannifin

The economic stakes in creating products and services that can command premiums in the marketplace were spelled out in Figure 2-02, which showed that highly differentiated offerings (from the customers' perspective) had an 82% success rate and increased market share by 54%. Those offerings that were moderately advantaged succeeded 58% of the time but only increased market share by 34%. Offerings perceived as me-too succeeded 18% of the time but increased market share by only 12%.

If you are going to get out and stay out of what Jeff Immelt called "commodity hell," you need to be highly or at least noticeably differentiated. If you fail in these areas you are in commodity hell: price is the king and your profit is the pawn of market supply and demand. Buffett eloquently describes this situation:

> *Producers of undifferentiated products... must earn inadequate returns except under conditions of tight supply or real shortage. As long as excess capacity exists, prices tend to reflect operating costs rather than capital employed.*

> Berkshire Hathaway Annual Report, 1978

In other words, ROIC of undifferentiated offerings will at best just cover current operating expenses and the cost of capital, and will create no shareholder value—and that assumes you are excellent operationally. Buffett assumes that every supplier has about the same cost and that improvements require capital investment that can be copied. However, differentiation applies to processes, not just products. If you are in a commodity business, and there is really no scope for differentiation in the offering, then you must create differentiation in the process and business model as have Dell, Southwest Airlines, Wal-Mart, etc. If differentiation in the offering is possible, then, as discussed in Chapter 2, the goal of differentiation is to create an offering with a lower cost *per unit of performance rather than per unit of product*—which can create huge value for your customer—value that your competitors likely cannot match. This form of offering differentiation focuses customers on your value proposition rather than on your price.

It is therefore essential to find out what is highly differentiated or will provide a unique service level or functionality—what will generate a level of performance that customers will highly value—at the very start of the development process (*before* any significant investment). Companies who cannot achieve this goal have to rely solely on process innovation to achieve lowest cost per unit of product.

How good are companies at identifying differentiation? Every company we've worked with or studied thinks they are in pursuit of differentiation, that they are "already doing Voice of the Customer." What does that mean? Consider a 2002 survey by the Confederation of British Industry, which had over 400 company respondents. Here is how the companies gathered data to drive their innovation process:

- Surveys (65% of respondents)
- Ideas meetings (53%)
- Service or product testing (50%)
- Formal observation of customers (18%)

There are two fatal flaws with this state of affairs if your purpose is to create highly differentiated offerings:

- Surveys, internal brainstorms, and testing are unreliable sources of customer information, even for the purpose of identifying sustaining innovations, and they will virtually never lead to a disruptive innovation. Among other things, current customers may try to quash disruptive innovations that they think are distracting you from what *they* think is important.

- Most companies aren't using even these traditional methods as much as they think they are. Pushed for details, most managers we have worked with will describe doing a survey once or twice a year, or say they get customer input only when testing a completely developed prototype (far too late in the design process to have a significant impact). We frequently find that even if a company is collecting useful customer data, functional silos prevent it from being used. Most likely such data is either on a bookshelf or in someone's head, and very often is not communicated or even provided to the people who need it to create innovative products or services.

Perhaps more important, in recent years, increasing numbers of designers have come to see that traditional VOC methods are inadequate for innovation for one simple reason:

> *Customers can't articulate everything they'd like in a product or service.*

Part of the problem is that in asking customers to react to product or service ideas, we are asking them to play with only half the information: they can't know our near-term or future capabilities, and rarely if ever can express their voice about a highly differentiated, potentially disruptive offering. The truth is that customers can't or won't tell you everything that is important to them that might relate to your product or service innovation. As Henry Ford said:

> *If I had asked my customers what they wanted, they'd have asked for a faster horse.*

The hidden gem in this statement is that it is true, because customers could not have known the capability presented by the internal combustion engine—only a prototype could have created a considered response. It simply isn't fair to expect customers to have sufficient imagination. What's different in companies that have built a reputation for being creatively brilliant is something we've come to label as **understanding the Heart of the Customer.** These companies go well beyond what customers *say* (the "Voice of the Customer") to explore customers' experience in their daily lives (personal or professional) or what it takes to make them successful. These companies push deep to uncover customers' wants, needs, hopes, and fears.

To illustrate what we mean, we'll look at some important lessons in becoming a master of the Heart of the Customer.

Understanding the Heart of the Customer

To become a master of customer understanding, you have to increase both the quality and quantity of your VOC processes. Three important strategies are:

1. Develop strong links to both the core *and* the fringes of your market

2. Use ethnography (the application of principles of anthropology to study the behavior of customers to gain new insights)

3. Include customers and customer knowledge throughout the design process (from identifying opportunities to delivery using the Innovation Blitz process where possible)

Let's look at each of these issues in more depth.

Strategy #1: Develop strong links to both the core and fringes of your market

Not long ago, a current customer asked Parker Hannifin (a global manufacturer based in Cleveland) to help develop the specifications for incorporating a new technology into the wing design of aircraft. (Eighty percent of these specs were defined in a four-day Blitz, an intensive session we'll describe in detail in Part III.) As a result, Parker ended up developing a new technology that will open new markets currently untapped by any other company in the world.

In this case, a potentially market-dominating innovation came about because Parker had close ties with its current customers. Parker was able to show the customer some new technology it was developing, which was unknown to the world and precisely solved what had been an unknown customer need. This interaction created a win-win: Parker could deliver new, differentiated offerings on a value-basis rather than a price-basis and will likely attain segment dominance. The customer could not have created the specifications for this product on their own because they were unaware that the perfect technology existed, let alone that Parker could deliver it, i.e., the customer would have asked for a faster horse! And vice versa, Parker could not have defined a new market for this technology on their own because they had a solution in search of a problem.

Talk to lead users and troublesome or peripheral customers

While the Parker example shows the importance of maintaining close ties with current customers, they and all truly innovative companies don't stop there. Peripheral vision is essential to avoid being blindsided by a competitor's disruptive innovation. We all need to work hard to identify and exploit opportunities that exist at the fringes of our current market or even outside our current customer base. Here are a few examples of how to do that.

In all likelihood, a few of your customers are doing something new and different with your product or service. Some of these are lead users, customers who really need your product or service and who are eager to push it to the boundaries. Others are just oddballs (in terms of product/service use!)—people or companies who like to experiment. Lead users and oddballs are generally delighted to have a company adopt their ideas because they're more interested in results than royalties.

The founding of McDonald's is perhaps one of the most famous stories in this category. Ray Kroc, a purveyor of milkshake machines, happened to notice an oddball customer in San Bernardino who was using far more machines than the market would justify. Kroc visited the company, saw a highly successful hamburger business, and the genesis of the McDonald's franchise was created!

IBM has a similar origin: After Thomas Watson, Sr., was fired from NCR, he took over a faltering punch-card business whose primary customers were the railroads and the Census Bureau. Watson learned that a few troublesome customers had tried unsuccessfully to apply the tabulating machines to accounting, so he focused R&D on those applications. The resulting business for accounting eclipsed the previous applications and made the Depression era a golden age for IBM, while laying the foundation for a stellar future!

For 3M, the Cleveland Clinic turned out to be a very valuable oddball user. The Clinic was looking for ways to reduce skin infections during surgery. They had tried spraying adhesive onto Saran Wrap, then applying the sticky plastic to patients' skin prior to incision. The Clinic thought that the temporary kind of adhesive used in Post-It™ notes would work much better for their purpose, so they approached 3M. The result was a substantial and profitable business for 3M.

All of these customers could have been considered oddities, or dismissed as troublesome low-volume customers out of the mainstream business.

Observe non-consumers

Most readers of this book will probably be too young to remember the days when the only portable radios had vacuum tubes and lasted eight hours at best. When Bell Labs developed the germanium transistor, some people thought it would be a good idea to use the new technology in inexpensive portable radios. Unfortunately for them, the dominant suppliers (Philco, Zenith, and RCA) tested this new idea of transistor radios with *existing* customers: mostly middle-aged adults and seniors who simply couldn't understand why anyone would put up with the poor sound quality of these cheap new radios when they could get much better sound out of a vacuum tube radio.

As Clay Christensen has pointed out, in *hindsight*, it seems obvious where to look for a huge audience for smaller, cheaper, low-quality radios: teenagers, who were at that time non-consumers of any radio. But the incumbent companies at the time relied solely on what their current valued customers were telling them: Forget the cheap stuff. Stay with vacuum tube radios. High-end audio companies (like Scott) thought the then-prevalent transistor hiss precluded its replacement of vacuum tubes, and so passed on the market opportunity as well.

Into the void stepped a fringe company, IDEA Corporation, which teamed up with Texas Instruments to build the first transistor radios in 1954. In 1957 another then-unknown company named Sony also bet its little business on the transistor radio. These initiatives eventually brought the semiconductor revolution to the masses. When IBM decided to replace vacuum tubes with transistors in its computers, TI's reputation for low-cost production won it the business. Sony's success has been even more stellar. And where are Philco, Zenith and RCA today?

Study novice users

New users of your products or services approach the experience with much lower performance expectations than veteran customers. They are therefore much more likely to experience frustrations and notice missing features or options that could help them. And you have to be there to watch their initial interactions with your product or service so you can see what goes smoothly and what causes them to fumble (which can provide the inspiration for improving or adding design options). The topic of observing customers leads to our next lesson....

Strategy #2: Use ethnography to understand customer needs better than anyone else

Everybody in the market has access to the same customers as you do. The precondition for getting to the market first with superior differentiated offerings is understanding those customers and their needs better than your competitors do. Developing this level of understanding demands capabilities well beyond traditional VOC techniques (interviews, surveys, etc.) because customers usually cannot tell you about needs or wishes that would lead to innovative or disruptive products and services. Why? There are a lot of reasons:

- In his book, *How Customers Think*, Gerald Zaltman states, "At least 95% of all cognition occurs below awareness in the shadows of the mind while, at most, 5% occurs in higher order consciousness."[27] So even if customers wanted to tell you what they thought, they may not really understand it themselves consciously!

- They don't know your capabilities as well as you do—so it doesn't occur to them that you may be able to help them solve a problem with anything other than a "faster horse."

- Current customers' creativity is more likely to be focused on *their* jobs than on your products/services, and they may dismiss an innovation not related to their goals.

- Few customers have a strategic view of *your* marketplace.

- People are better at reacting to specific prototypes than at coming up with insights on their own (as discussed earlier in this chapter).

- It is often tempting to lie during preview tests as a way to avoid hurting someone's feelings, or to blow off an interviewer to avoid an argument.

The lesson is that you have to be a lot more creative about VOC if you want to find highly differentiated offerings to fuel your innovation process. It isn't enough to ask customers what they like or don't like about current products or services. And if you're investing in radically new technology or service capability, customers may not express interest simply because they don't understand the potential. For example, Warner & Swazey was once one of the largest makers of machine tools in America. When the general purpose computer-controlled machine tools came over the horizon, W&S asked its large automotive customers if they were interested. No, they said, they preferred special purpose, dedicated machine tools, the kind they'd been buying from W&S for decades. But general purpose machines *were* of interest to peripheral customers, low-volume machine shops. Once they got a foothold, general purpose machines quickly became the standard in all applications, including automotive. W&S's reliance on input from current big customers effectively created an opening for the Japanese and signaled the demise of the American machine tool industry.

Microsoft nearly fell into this trap by asking customers to attend a focus group, use their software for a few hours, and answer questions interactively.[28] It went something like this:

> *Question*: Did you like the product?
> *Answer*: "Yep!"

> *Question*: Any features you don't like or want to add?
> *Answer*: "Nope!"

Based on these answers, you'd think that Microsoft had a winner right out of the gate. But Microsoft found that they could not rely on these VOC responses alone. The developers began recording keystrokes, and, with subject permission, videotaped what turned out to be a wide range of negative customer reactions (grimaces, hesitations, etc.). They concluded that they needed to incorporate better VOC methods in their development processes.

This takes us back to the mantra introduced earlier in this Spotlight:

> *Customers cannot articulate everything they'd like in a*
> *product or service.*

(They are, in fact, far better at reacting to prototypes and telling you what they don't like.)

If asking customers what they like doesn't work, what will? The answer: incorporating close, detailed observation of customer behavior into your design work. The epitome of this trend is the emerging field of **customer ethnography**, where you find ways to "live with" selected customers to get an in-depth understanding of their needs. Ethnography is a discipline built on the principles of social anthropology, studying people as they interact with their native habitats.

We define ethnography as:

> *A descriptive, qualitative market research methodology for*
> *studying the customer in relation to his or her environment.*
> *Researchers spend time in the field observing customers and*
> *their environment to acquire a deep understanding of the*
> *lifestyles or cultures as a basis for better understanding their*
> *needs and problems.*[29]

At its simplest level, ethnography includes any direct observation of customers with an eye towards identifying things that could make their lives easier. For example, an Intel ethnographer noticed that people in Indonesia were troubled five times a day finding the precise direction of Mecca for their prayers. This kind of observation could trigger a new product offering: using a GPS signal to create an arrow pointing to Mecca on a laptop!

While watching his wife pay bills, Scott Cook noticed how time-consuming and repetitive the process was. This was the birth of his idea to develop Quicken—which grew into the billion-dollar company Intuit. The practice of observing customer behavior has continued, now alive in Intuit's "Follow Me Home" program designed to gather what we're calling ethnographic customer data. Because of that continued emphasis on understanding customer lives, Quicken and other Intuit software products are consistently rated by consumers as among the easiest to use.

The purpose of ethnography is to generate the kind of deep and intuitive understanding of customer needs and frustrations that can't help but inspire creative insights. The ethnography process frequently discovers opportunities for differentiation that the customer could never have enunciated in a questionnaire, a survey, or a focus group. Purely from the standpoint of time and cash outlay, ethnography can be more expensive than those methods, but you have to evaluate this investment in the context of the value and ROI of delivering a highly differentiated offering to the market. Ethnography may also provide a corrective check on offering or design options that your designers love but that have no customer resonance.

The ethnographic process

A company will select a handful or two of customers or potential customers to observe; while other VOC methods are concerned with information *quantity*, ethnography focuses on *quality*. A team of **trained observers** is sent to watch the customers. Their goals are to:

- Develop a holistic view of customer needs: look at all the behaviors associated with a particular need, not just a single task, including all the activities that surround your offering

- Expose and record "tribal knowledge"—the things that people do automatically, that they don't consciously think about

- Identify customer frustrations and areas of less-than-optimal efficiency, whether related to the product/service or not

An ethnographic study generates a deep understanding of human needs, what it's like for your customers to try to do their jobs or live their lives every day. The limitations of ethnography are that it can be time- and labor-intensive.

Yet the experiences of the people you choose to observe in-depth may be a great source of inspiration and may provide the starting point for your next-generation products and services. The ethnographic findings can be validated on a larger scale using more traditional VOC methods (focus groups, phone interviews, etc.) as well as additional customer observation throughout the design process.

The term ethnography is not widely used yet, though some famous companies have used the close-observation approach to help design products, services, and even workspaces. There are many examples available in the literature and on the internet. Some of the most instructive examples come from two design firms whose approach is built around the ethnographic approach:

- The story of Palo Alto-based IDEO is told in the highly readable book *The Art of Innovation* by Tom Kelley. IDEO's experience demonstrates that ethnography works in any context, from developing high-tech equipment (such as when they observed hospital staff using a particular medical device), to redesigning consumer products (they were involved in converting the old-style mouses into the trackballs of today), to reshaping services (they helped furniture maker Steelcase redesign a key showroom).

- Ideas Bazaar is a British firm. As they explain on their website, "The richness and nuance that ethnographic research delivers brings people and their environments alive. It leads to new insights and perspectives, and provides a solid understanding from which our researchers and clients can work together to achieve a project's strategic objectives."

In traditional design, firms often delegate the work of understanding customer needs to marketing or engineering, usually without a structured process for capturing the Heart of the Customer. That results in a limited perspective that seldom provides the breakthrough insight they need. Leading-edge companies, on the other hand, are working hard to develop ethnographic expertise internally, or develop relationships with outside interviewers/ethnographers (outsiders can sometimes notice more than insiders because they have few preconceptions about what they're looking for).

Ethnography can inform the path to differentiation of offerings you have in mind, and it can suggest opportunities to create additional products that surround your existing offerings but that speak to customer needs or frustrations, which is the subject of the next chapter.

What's Really Different?

Most companies are doing some VOC capture now, but the majority we've talked to spend more energy talking about customer needs with internal marketing and design staff than directly with customers. It's true that the Heart of the Customer capture process laid out in these three lessons may require two to three times more investment than what's made by most companies today. Think of it as the price that must be paid for highly differentiated products, services, or processes that really capture the unarticulated customer need that may create disruptive growth, as depicted in Figure SP1-01 (next page).

Pushing for highly differentiated products, services, and processes is what drives the height of this curve, which shows a positive cash flow and operating margin much higher than if you just earned the cost of capital. The combination of high margins and fast time to first customer capture is what creates the enormous area of positive cash flow (above the dashed line) that is not available to me-too offerings. Differentiation without speed misses the market entirely; speed without differentiation just returns cost of capital. Both are required, and you need high-performance VOC systems to take advantage of the differentiation side of the equation.

Figure SP1-01: Cost and Benefits of Differentiation

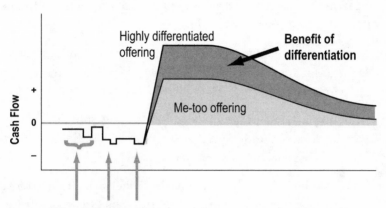

Costs of differentiation
- Improved market vigilance (includes Open Innovation costs)
- Improved investment in gaining customer knowledge (ethnography, Blitz, etc.) upfront
- Improved cycles of testing/learning during development

Slow innovation saves some initial costs (little investment in market vigilance or customer knowledge), but is likely to end up in me-too offerings. With Fast Innovation, the effort prior to development is shorter but about three times deeper reflecting early investment in market vigilance and Open Innovation plus the additional expenses of checking design concepts and prototypes with customers (those are the specific "bumps" downward in the curve). Such checks are necessary for shaping performance specifications prior to the final freeze (Chapter 10). The benefit of these added investments is a greater chance of getting a highly differentiated offering.

A Look Ahead

As noted above, it doesn't matter how fast you are to market if you're not offering something that is differentiated in customers' eyes. Exploring the fringes of your customer base (and beyond) can provide the spark that will lead to innovation; so can getting to know your customers better than anyone else, and using that knowledge to define what differentiation means to them. The basic requirement is being willing to allocate time and resources for ethnographic studies at the start of a development effort.

Other ways to incorporate customer needs into the design process are introduced in the next chapter, with implementation details to follow in Parts II and III. Key concepts you'll find are:

- Involving customers in Innovation Blitzes: including them in intense, focused design sessions where key design requirements are worked out

- Adopting a rapid prototype mindset: testing subsets of features with customers throughout the design process rather than waiting until you have a complete product or service design

- Using Design for Lean Six Sigma techniques (including Flexible Performance Target Design) to find the right balance of features, time-to-market, and price

Endnotes

27 Gerald Zaltman, *How Customers Think: Essential Insights into the Mind of the Market* (Boston: Harvard Business School Press, 2003), p. 50.

28 Michael A. Cusumano and Richard W. Selby, *Microsoft Secrets: How the World's Most Powerful Software Company Creates Technology, Shapes Markets, and Manages People* (New York: Free Press, 1998).

29 http://www.google.com/search?hl=en&lr=&oi=defmore&q=define:Ethnography,def 7

CHAPTER 3

How to Become Fast

We think the pace of innovation has roughly doubled in the past 10 years. So when we make an innovation and bring it to the marketplace, it has a much shorter market life than what it had previously. We need to be moving to upgrade our brands even more frequently.

Gilbert Cloyd, Chief Technical Officer
Procter & Gamble[30]

*Products and services commoditize at such a rapid rate that in the end, the only competitive advantage you have is **speed**, talent, and brand.*

John Chambers, CEO, Cisco

Fast Innovation consists of strategies that either contribute to speeding up the innovation process from initial insight to delivery and/or to significantly increasing the level of differentiation. The "fast" aspect comes from two prerequisites for sustained growth in revenue and value you'll need to pursue simultaneously:

Prerequisite 1: Attacking the causes of long innovation lead time. A critical flaw in traditional approaches to innovation is failure to understand the two principal causes of long lead time—what is *really* adding time into the process. We will identify these causes and provide a quantitative means for you to dramatically reduce lead time of innovation by 50% to 80%.

Prerequisite 2: Rapid learning and differentiation. Many traditional innovation techniques are inherently slow in capturing information needed for differentiation or converting that information into products, services, or processes. VOC data is not captured quickly or reliably up front, performance targets are frozen early, customer interaction during development is minimal. The result: crucial differentiators are missed, and the offering fails to generate the potential margins or volumes. In contrast, Fast Innovation is built around a mantra of rapid learning: "How can we get the knowledge we need faster and reliably create powerfully differentiated offerings?"

Figure 3-01: Innovation Prerequisites

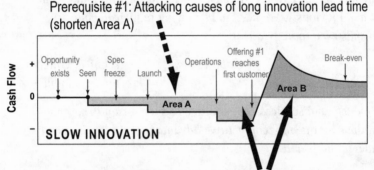

"Fast" primarily comes from...

Prerequisite #1: Attacking causes of long innovation lead time (shorten Area A)

Prerequisite #2: Rapid learning (getting better and faster at differentiation in Area A makes Area B higher and sooner)

The transformational effect of the two prerequisites is shown in the figure above:

Prerequisite 1 (dashed line): Drives down the time to develop a new offering and service, and allows you to create more innovations per year (compare to Fast Innovation figure, F1-03). Allows more differentiated features, increasing margins.

Prerequisite 2 (solid line): Drives down the time and improves the quality of VOC capture, and provides input on "customer delighter" differentiation, enabling higher margins.

This chapter covers the key elements of both of these prerequisites. Details on implementation are in Parts II and III.

Prerequisite 1: Attacking the biggest drivers of innovation lead time

Recall that time and cost overruns are at the top of the list of CEO frustrations with the current innovation processes. Consequently, the subject of how to reduce the lead time of innovation has long been a subject of intense interest. The laws that govern planetary motions, pendulum, and so on, were unknown before Newton. Once his laws were in hand, all motions could be predicted and designed to meet a desired outcome.

Similarly, there are two laws that govern the lead time of innovation—the **Law of Lead Time (Little's Law)** and the **Law of Innovation Variation**—that have only recently been understood.[31] Here is an overview of both laws and how they can be used to dramatically speed up innovation lead time.

The Law of Lead Time

Just as a satellite is governed by Newton's Second Law, the lead time of any process is governed by the **Law of Lead Time**, also known as **Little's Law** (after the mathematician who first proved it in 1961).[32] The law is expressed by a simple equation:

Little's Law Equation

$$\text{Average Lead Time of Any Process} = \frac{\text{Number of Things-in-Process}}{\text{Average Completion Rate}}$$

What varies from application to application is what you use for things-in-process. In manufacturing it's the number of units of work-in-process (aka WIP). In services, it can be the number of work items in process (job requests, files, purchase order requests, invoices, job applications, etc.). In product development, it is the number of projects-in-process. For any single innovator, it's the number of *tasks-in-process*. The average completion rate is simply how many of the tasks-in-process the employee can complete per week or month on average.

For our purposes in this book, the important aspect of Law of Lead Time is depicted in Figure 3-02: **there is a simple linear relationship between the number of active projects (or tasks) in process and lead time.** That is, the more active projects (projects-in-process) you have, the longer it will take for *all* projects to be completed.

Figure 3-02: Relationship Between Projects-in-Process and Lead Time

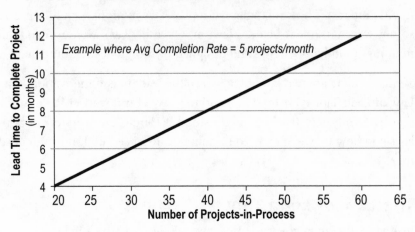

There is a simple linear relationship between the number of active development projects (what we call projects-in-process in this book) and how long it takes to get any project done. The more projects you have, the longer ALL projects will take. The converse is one secret of Fast Innovation: the *fewer* active projects you have, the *faster* the development process can flow.

You might challenge the Law of Lead Time by saying, "Wait a minute— some tasks take a long time and some a short time." True, but the lead time is driven solely by the *average* completion rate. If a quick project is stuck behind a slow one, it is still stuck, it still has to wait in line. And it is the average completion rate that governs the lead time of the process. This simplicity is the power of the Law of Lead Time and why it is so easy to apply in practice.

What the equation and graph also tell us is that:

*if we have no control over the number of projects-in-process,
we have no control over the lead time*

Most companies don't have a metric on the number of tasks- or projects-in-process or on the average completion rate. But even so, some leading companies are recognizing the importance of slashing the number of projects-in-process:[33]

- 3M was stalled at about $16 billion revenue for four years, only breaking through $18B in 2003–04. Their CEO credits this gain to Six Sigma as well as to what they call 3M Acceleration: improving the pace of product development by focusing resources on the right projects. 3M culled 1,500 projects down to the 75 projects they believed represented the greatest opportunities.

- Here's what CEO Jeff Immelt said about GE's famed research facility in Schenectady, NY: "We were running a high-tech job shop, with about 1,000 projects. We cut that to 20 core projects that are meaningful to the company three to five years out."

Why executives must take the lead in reducing projects-in-process

The logic and empirical truth of the Law of Lead Time (Little's Law) cannot be denied. Deceptively simple, the Law of Lead Time explains why development projects are so often late.

Yet one of the hardest tasks that innovation leaders have is convincing executives that the best way to get faster lead times to market from their development work is to put fewer projects into the pipeline!

With the Law of Lead Time to draw on, executives can use data to drive both change and choice:

To attain a given lead time for innovation that is required for market success, what projects can be launched, and which must be removed or delayed to satisfy the Law of Lead Time?

The Law of Lead Time is implemented using a FastGate process (see Chapter 14) that gates new work into the development process only if its impact is such that *all* active projects will still meet time-to-market windows as defined by the CEO or P&L manager. Implementing the Law of Lead Time and using the FastGate process are the essential first steps in controlling lead time, because it puts an absolute control on the number of projects injected into each step of the innovation process.

Even without knowing the average completion rate at these companies, the Law of Lead Time tells us they have just cut the average lead time of their innovation processes 10- to 20-fold! Most of us will be have data on that we can use to calculate average completion rate in our companies. By plugging that figure into the Law of Lead Time, we can quantitatively *predict* the effect of cutting down the number of active projects in our companies—and determine exactly how many projects need to be cut so that we can meet time-to-market targets.

The Astounding Impact of Variation

Using the Law of Lead Time is the first step in controlling the lead time because we learn how to release projects into development at a rate that will not slow down the whole process. But that calculation alone doesn't tell you what happens to a project after it is released. Anyone familiar with the innovation process knows that, at some point in the process, some work goes quickly and other work takes a lot more time than anyone could have forecast. And new tasks just keep coming! This causes a bunching-up of tasks-in-process, which causes time delay at that point in the process, and creates what we will refer to as a Critical Resource (*see* p. 57). The Law of Innovation Variation allows us to predict how much bunching-up will occur on average. More important, this law, coupled with the Law of Lead Time, tells us how we can significantly reduce the bunching-up problem and dramatically reduce innovation lead times.

To begin, let's look at how variation in innovation task time affects the process. Suppose that midway through one project, an innovator runs into a problem he or she can't solve. Time starts slipping away… new work continues to come in per the project management schedule, resulting in a pileup or *queue* of tasks-in-process. This innovator's average completion rate has just fallen: not only is the first task taking longer than expected, but all the other work in the queue is getting behind as well. According to the Law of Lead Time, the lead time of every project that innovator is or should be working on is jeopardized.

The Law of Innovation Variation

High variation is an intrinsic part of the innovation process, and we will show how we can overcome its effect on lead time in this and the next two chapters. Trouble is, most developers are scheduled at very high utilization rates, and that's where lead times can explode. Figure 3-03 graphically depicts the relationship between percent utilization and the schedule delay time of tasks just sitting in queue. This graph was generated for a situation where on average it takes innovators 5 days per design task; the average time for your innovators may be shorter or longer, but the basic shape will look the same in every situation.

Figure 3-03: The Impact of Innovation Variation

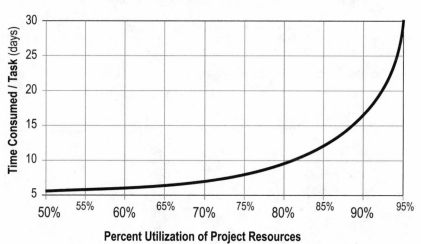

Percent Utilization of Project Resources

If you load innovators to 95% capacity utilization, on average the resulting queues will cause the lead time of the innovators' tasks to increase four times above the level if the innovators are scheduled at only 65% utilization.

The figure shows that given a 5-day average completion rate, if the innovators work at 65% of capacity—they are scheduled to complete a task in 8 days before given a new task—the average task will spend only 6 days in queue. However, if the innovators are loaded to 95% capacity (allowing 5.5 days to complete the average 5-day task), most tasks will spend 30 days in queue! Why? Because when the innovators run into trouble, as they inevitably will do, the tasks will just start piling up!

You can see the potentially catastrophic impact of loading a development team to 100% of capacity. That strategy can explosively increase lead time! Almost everyone who sees the chart says something like…

> *Now I understand why our development projects take twice as long as planned. We **deliberately** schedule designers at close to 100% capacity.*

The Sources of Project Delays

Delays in any process are in fact governed by three major factors, the effects of which interact (*see* Figure 3-04):

- Variation in task time (higher means more delays)

- % utilization of resources (higher means more delays if a Critical Resource is involved; *see* sidebar next page)

- Availability of cross-trained resources to adjust for changes in the first two factors (more resources = shorter delays)

Figure 3-04: Causes of Delays

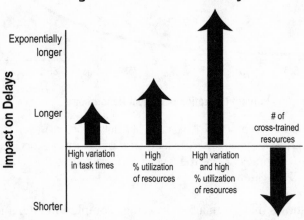

Innovation differs from almost every other business process in terms of the huge variation in task times. Innovation is an incredibly creative and uncertain process by its nature, and as a result, variation is much higher in an innovation process than, for example, in manufacturing or customer service. That's why we call this effect the Law of Innovation Variation. The exact form of the is defined by queuing theory; we won't go into details here, but you can get an overview on p. 61 and details in Appendix 1.[34] The key point is that there are three factors that affect the lead time once a task is "in process":

The percent of utilization of resources, ρ: How much of the available time for a task is scheduled. If you estimate a task will take two months and you assign three months, a 2/3rds (= 66%) utilization rate, incorporating a 50% buffer. More on buffers in Appendix 2.

The amount of variation in task time, C: It is notoriously difficult to predict innovation task time with any accuracy. "C," the coefficient of variation, indicates the amount of variation around a mean task time. For "from scratch" innovations, C about 50% of the mean time, compared to just 10% for manufacturing.

The number of cross-trained resources, N: Having cross-trained resources who can step in and pick up some of the lesser challenges for a Critical Resource that is falling behind can cut queue time by half or more.

Who is a Critical Resource?

Every innovation process will have one or more Critical Resources (CRs) for each project. The CR is the person or workstation on the Critical Path with the largest amount of task time queued up (meaning the largest number of tasks and/or tasks that require the most development time). This CR is therefore inserting the longest lead time in the project. The resource is critical due to one or more of the following characteristics:

- It has the lowest effective average completion rate (e.g., because the work is challenging, or they are multi-tasking, or there is little flexibility in who or what performs the work), or ...

- It has the largest number of tasks-in-process (e.g., because many projects require that kind of work hence it is a shared resource), or...

- It has a lot of variation in the time needed to perform the tasks and thus is prone to having long queues of tasks

CRs are often difficult to predict and may move around, hence we discuss *feedback* loops to get early warning of a buildup of delay time.

The three factors interact with each other, meaning the impact of any one factor is affected by what's going on with the other factors. For example, Figure 3-03 shows that variation in task time has very little impact IF utilization is around 65%. But if utilization is high (above 90%), delay times will explode. As we'll see later in this chapter, cross-training can greatly reduce the impact of variation on queue time. Also, the next chapter shows how to greatly reduce the intrinsic variation, which allows you to operate with utilization of 80% and still have short lead times. (In the actual mathematical equation we can show that the impact of variation on innovation lead time is at least 25 times greater than, say, on manufacturing processes which have far less variation. *See* Appendix 1.)

Delays to the process as a whole are most likely to occur at the **Critical Resources**: the innovators whose tasks lie on the critical path and who tackle the most challenging design tasks (those that require new knowledge or extraordinary creativity—which are the tasks that inherently will have the most variation).

Meeting Project Schedules Despite Task-Time Variation

That I may recognize what holds the world together
in its inmost essence,
Behold the driving force and source of everything
and rummage no more in empty words

Goethe, Faust

Your development managers probably have historical data and experience which they use to estimate how long it takes innovation staff to do particular tasks. They probably add up all the tasks down a critical path for a given project in order to estimate the lead time for that project. The problem? This approach fails to calculate the queue time as a function of %utilization, and hence has very little chance of ever being correct—the predictions of project lead times are "empty words." However, by assigning buffer time to their historical estimates using the Law of Innovation Variation, they will likely meet their critical path schedules, but not at 100% utilization!

Data from many companies shows that most innovation tasks spend more than two-thirds of their time in queue—wasted time caused in large part by scheduling 100% utilization or beyond, and then being savaged by variation in task times driving long queue time. If we can't eliminate variation in innovation development task times to the same extent that we can in operational processes, what can we do? There are a number of ways to minimize the impact of variation upon a desired project schedule. Tactics for cutting lead time by 50% include:

The Seven Imperatives of the Law of Innovation Variation

1. Identify Critical Resources, the innovators facing high-risk tasks on the critical path

2. Load them to no more than 65% utilization with schedule buffers

3. Identify meeting their daily needs as critical goals for upstream providers (the internal suppliers of the Critical Resources)

4. Install feedback loops to report tasks-in-queue at each Critical Resource

5. Cross-train backup personnel to work routine tasks at the Critical Resources (*see* next page)

6. Reduce variation by adopting the Religion of Re-use (Chapter 6) and Open Innovation (Chapter 5)

7. Dedicate Critical Resources to a single task at a time (prevent multi-tasking and reduce non-value-add time)

Some people argue that they "can't always predict our Critical Resources," and we agree. That is why we install feedback loops where Critical Resources are likely, so that a manager can get a daily input without having to attend a meeting or depend on individual initiative, which is a very slow feedback loop. (More information on these initiatives in Appendix 1.)

Managers are often worried about the cost of cutting the utilization of innovation resources down to 65% of capacity. In Chapter 13, we will show how average utilization can be increased to 80% while still reducing lead time by 80%.

The benefits of cross-training

Here's an example of how cross-training can improve management of innovation resources. At International Power Machines, which we'll discuss in more detail on p. 117, only one engineer knew how to design transformers. When a very challenging new design for air core inductors was required "yesterday," all the requirements for a new 60Hz transformer that IPM was developing had to wait. The original transformer designer had become the Critical Resource.

The solution to preventing a repetition of this problem was to train a green engineer on how to design the simpler transformers in addition to his other duties. Having a cross-trained second engineer gave IPM the flexibility to draw on that resource when an urgent task arose that required the first engineer's expertise. This strategy works because the probability that both engineers would simultaneously be tied up on technically challenging work (with a lot of variation) was very small.

The outcome? The queue time for the original engineer was cut in half (*see* Appendix 1). The formal process of cross-training staff to support Critical Resources is an inexpensive means of cutting queue time without adding additional people.

Figure 3-05: Benefits of Cross-Training

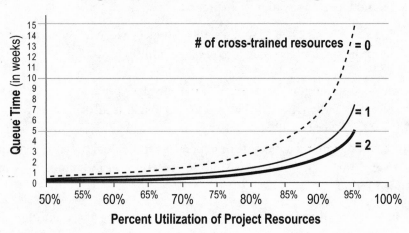

Having cross-trained resources can help you control queue time (delays), an impact that is most dramatic when resources have high utilization levels. (See quantification of this curve in Appendix 1.)

Queuing Theory and the Law of Innovation Variation (for Mathphiles only)

The Law of Innovation Variation is an equation developed by two eminent mathematicians, Polaczek and Khintchine, that computes the number of projects, tasks, jobs, etc., in queue. The first of three factors shows the effect of the percent utilization, ρ. If utilization % (ρ) goes up, process delays increase rapidly. More importantly, as utilization approaches 100%, this term grows very large.

$$\text{Effect of \%utilization on \# of jobs in queue} = \frac{\rho^2}{1-\rho}$$

The second factor shows the effect of the variation in task times. If the mean time to perform a task is μ and about 70% of the tasks fall in the range of $\mu \pm \sigma$ (one sigma above and below the mean), then we adjust by the coefficient of variation (right). And the first and second factor in the equation is shown to the right:

$$\text{Coefficient of Variation} = C = \frac{\sigma}{\mu}$$

This is the curve that is plotted as the Law of Lead Time.

$$\text{Effect of \%util. and variation on \# of jobs in queue} = \left(\frac{\rho^2}{1-\rho}\right)C^2$$

In product development, massive amounts of data indicate that C = 50%, and most people find there is about 50% variation of task times around the mean. Therefore, $C^2 = 0.25$. If you divide by the average completion rate, you get the amount of lead time delay at each activity in the process. In contrast, the variation in task time in manufacturing is much lower—typically C < 0.1—hence $C^2 < 0.01$. Comparing the two C^2 figures tells us that variation in task time has 25 times the effect on innovation lead times as it does on manufacturing lead times.

The final factor adjusts for cross-training. If you can cross-train one or two persons to perform some of the simpler tasks of a Critical Resource, then the number of jobs in queue is cut down approximately by that factor. Thus the final Law of Innovation Variation, accounting for N backup people trained to help out at a Critical Resource, is:

$$\text{Law of Innovation Variation (\# of Jobs in Queue w/ Cross-Training)} = \left(\frac{1}{N+1}\right)\left(\frac{\rho^2}{1-\rho}\right)C^2$$

This equation is graphed in Figure 3-05 for various values of N, the number of people cross-trained to back up the Critical Resource.

Using buffers

Another simple way to deal with variation in innovation task times is to build buffers into the schedule. According to our data, the majority of innovation tasks typically run 50% longer or shorter than the average time. So if an innovator runs into trouble on one task, and he or she is already scheduled to work on a new task, the new work just sits there. And the more jobs that sit in queue, the longer the lead time.

If, however, you give the innovator a time buffer of about 50% of the average time before the next task arrives, he or she will be on schedule. Thus if the innovator should finish a task in about two weeks, you assign him or her one extra week (three weeks total), so the innovator is utilized at about two-thirds of average capacity, and the project will be on time. The buffer time prevents a bunching-up of tasks in a project.

Many companies are using some of these strategies already. For example, Microsoft empirically ran into the need for buffers:

> *Convincing traditional project managers of the need for lots of buffer time can be difficult amid pressures to shorten product development times. I don't know what it's going to be needed for, but time and time again, I know it's needed... So, if you have two months, you'd allocate one month for buffer. A fifty percent buffer rule turns out to be accurate. **I can't always explain why.** [emph ours]*

> *Microsoft Secrets*, p. 205[35]

Microsoft empirically found that there was a relationship between lead time and percent utilization. Their rule of thumb leads them to assign three months of schedule time to accomplish an estimated two months of work. That means the innovator is loaded at two-thirds or 66% of capacity (what we call 66% utilization in this book).

Preview: How much time do innovators spend innovating?

The cynic may have read some of the recommendations so far and said: "Well, it sounds like you are just making an argument to add more resources." The good news is that in general we do not have to add resources. The Law of Lead Time says that if you could double your average completion rate, you would cut the average lead time in half. Thus if you could double the time you spend on actual innovation effort, as opposed to interruptions, attending interminable meetings, etc., you could cut your lead time in half. Is this possible? The answer is definitely yes. For example, Figure 3-06 shows data collected by Texas Instruments on how some of their innovators spent their time.

Figure 3-06: How Innovators Typically Spend Their Time

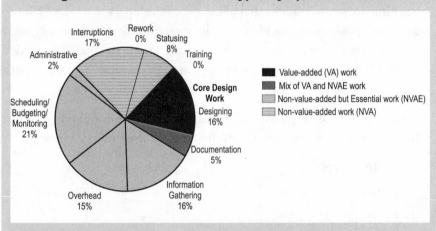

This data comes from innovators who were assigned to multiple projects at one time (what we call multi-tasking in this book). As you can see, there is a lot of opportunity here: these innovators spent only 16% of their time on core design work. Further, evidence from Theresa Amabile of Harvard indicates that creativity in multi-tasking may fall 40%!

As it happens, TI also gathered comparable data on innovators who were single-tasked, and the results are dramatic—raising core design work to 33%. We'll show the full results in Chapter 13 and discuss further the merits of single-tasking and how to effectively add capacity (especially at critical points in the development path). For now, just be aware that there are undoubtedly utilization issues in your innovation teams with a lot of time locked up in non-value-add work. Solutions to that problem are built into Fast Innovation.

Prerequisite 2: Rapid cycles of learning creates differentiation

The previous discussion focused on the biggest drivers of long innovation lead time. The other aspect of becoming Fast is to more quickly and reliably capture the Voice of the Customer, and create "customer delighter" differentiation opportunities for development. For example, in the Innovation Blitz Spotlight (p. 277), we'll give you details on a development project shared with us by Pete Buca of Parker Hannifin where 80% of the specs for an innovative new product (which may well corner a whole new market) were completed in just four days—work that normally would have taken nine months! The key principle is **rapid learning**, using techniques that allow your developers to explore a lot of different options and quickly reach the level of understanding they need to make design decisions. In effect, Parker sped up the value-added creative work: finding differentiators and translating the needs into workable designs.

You'll find the principle of rapid learning woven throughout the Fast Innovation process; we'll highlight just four of the strategies here.

A) Ethnography

B) Rapid prototyping

C) The Innovation Blitz

D) Flexible Performance Target Design

A. Ethnography

We have all experienced that terrible day during development when marketing informs us that the customer has a "new" requirement and we must make major changes in scope. This happens for one of two reasons:

1) The development cycle is so long that the market demand has changed long after the "final freeze" of specifications or design requirements. The Fast Innovation process shortens lead times and delays the final freeze, making a such a change extremely unlikely.

2) The real needs of the customer were not captured prior to development. The slow capture of true customer needs is largely prevented by ethnography on the front end as discussed on p. 41, and with iterations of Rapid Prototyping, discussed next.

B. Rapid Prototyping

The principle behind this concept is to work in small steps. Typically, nothing in development is taken to customers until the product or service is almost full-blown. That gives you only one late, expensive, and possibly fatal cycle of feedback from the market. Instead, you are better off developing a series of single-feature or single-functionality prototypes, get customer reactions to each—ethnographically watching (not just asking for) their reactions—doing more creative design work, then coming back to customers again with revised prototypes. This generates many iterative feedback cycles during the process of defining what differentiation is required by the customer *before* a lot of money has been spent. Small, quick cycles of ...

observation—> brainstorm concept—> prototype—>customer feedback

... has an important advantage: it allows the company to remain flexible as it develops new innovations. Since time is relative depending on the industry, the flexibility to adapt is paramount. A flexible design process can introduce a design change with little impact on the overall lead time. The key theme in the optimal pattern is what's known as **rapid prototyping** in the early phases:

- Doing lots of little tests/customer interactions on a few features at a time rather than a few big tests with complete products

- Using quick cycles to ethnographically test *ideas* (not full solutions) with customers

- Checking ideas while they are still raw; not waiting until everything is set in stone

- Observing customer reactions very closely (the ethnographic approach, described on p. 41)

Here is an example of rapid prototyping that relied on direct observation of customer behavior: Developers who were designing the flight software for the space shuttle came up with 19 different sets of screens they felt the astronauts would need in flight. However, systems engineers (the Department of Defense equivalent of ethnographers) intercepted development, and had the developers build mock-ups of how these screens would look when they came up on computer screens, delaying the actual writing of the hundreds of thousands of lines of source code needed to generate the real thing. The astronauts' reaction to the screen mock-ups was immediate and intense: "Whoever designed these screens has obviously never flown!"

When the developers heard about these reactions, *their* first reactions were not charitable ("These guys don't understand what we're trying to accomplish"). But they agreed to meet with the astronauts. Together the two groups went through several iterations of screen mock-ups before a single line of code was written. The result was win-win all around: enormous time savings to the engineering company and much more intuitive screens for the astronauts.

As Tom Kelley of IDEO, one of the premier design firms in the U.S., says in *The Art of Innovation:*

> *Prototyping is both a step in the innovation process and a philosophy about moving continuously forward, even when some variables are still undefined. And brainstorming … is not just a valuable creative tool at the fuzzy front end of projects. It's also a pervasive cultural influence for making sure that individuals don't waste too much energy spinning their wheels on a tough problem when the collective wisdom of the team can get them "unstuck" in less than an hour. [p. 5]*

> *We believe in that great old saying, a picture is worth a thousand words. Only at IDEO, we've found that a **good prototype is worth a thousand pictures**. Somehow you up the data rate. Give people two or three very concrete choices. [p. 112]*

And these two or three concrete choices may well prove to be the "customer delighter" and the "customer satisfier" which you will want development to explore before the final freeze of performance specs.

How much is ethnography worth in terms of dollars and cents? Commercial companies obviously will not disclose this information, but we have data from systems engineering experience, the government equivalent of design and ethnography.

For example, in a 2003 published survey, 90% of NASA respondents indicated that systems engineering is most effective when applied very early in a project. They have recognized the high value of developing and acting on intimate customer knowledge early to influence the design when incurred costs are low and design changes are easy. There is significant empirical evidence demonstrating the positive cost and schedule impact resulting from adequately investing in the definition of user intent. Werner Gruhl, of the NASA comptroller's office, studied the relationship between the dollars invested in upfront definition compared with the total percent program cost overrun for 32 programs such as STS (shuttle), Pioneer/Venture, Venus probes, etc. Figure 3-07 shows the results of his analysis, with program cost overruns being reduced by an average of more than two-thirds when 10% to 20% definition investments are made, compared with those with 5% or less.

Figure 3-07: Reduction of Cost Overruns

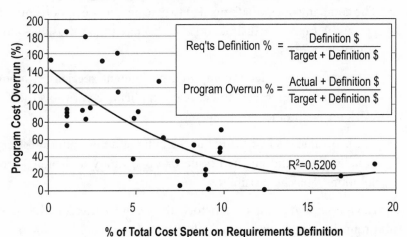

% of Total Cost Spent on Requirements Definition

Most commercial companies spend less than 5% of the innovation project costs on upfront definition issues. You can expect your ethnographic studies to add a cost equal to your present efforts, i.e., the definition phase of innovation will increase to about 10% of total innovation costs.

However, even the data above indicates a four- or five-to-one payback just on a cost basis, to say nothing of the differentiation advantages that result from ethnographic studies. And in the commercial world, this investment may well provide a differentiation advantage that spells the difference between success and failure.

C. The Innovation Blitz

The rapid prototyping process can be further accelerated and made more effective whenever key or representative customers or suppliers are eager to participate in a win-win-win effort. The Innovation Blitz is a four- or five-day event where all the developers on a project meet with customers and suppliers **and work only on the targeted project**. A Blitz works best when ...

- The purpose is carefully selected and narrowly defined. Often, they are focused on a specific customer (a hungry lead user) with a particular need that is congruent with a high-priority business target.

- The company does what's needed to give people the opportunity to get away from the distractions of the day-to-day business and completely focus.

- A cross-functional team composed of different specialties (along with representative customers and suppliers) comes together to work on the problem or challenge.

- The session starts by having the customer and the team think very broadly about the targeted issue or opportunity and brainstorm solutions, *ignoring* feasibility.

- Having explored all the territory, the team focuses on the most promising areas, presenting solutions using capabilities, many of which are not known by the customer, and getting feedback from customers and suppliers.

- The team finishes its work by preparing specific deliverables and debriefing management.

Clearly, to achieve these aims, the Blitz must be led by an innovation expert with excellent skills in the innovation process, customer observations, creative design, and facilitation.

This Blitz approach has only recently started gaining popularity in the innovation world. Its biggest advantage over traditional development models is the speed of results. In addition, the Blitz:

- Exposes the customer to new performance capability that they could not have asked for (in an RFP, for example) because they didn't know it existed.

- Eliminates major design iterations caused by concept errors that arise from a lack of interaction with the customer and with internal thought leaders.

- Avoids the problem of having specifications change during the development cycle (a lot more can change in a year-long project than in a four-day project!).

- Allows focus. Successful innovators and "delighted" customers will tell you that finding the most creative solution possible requires an initial concentrated effort with a small but talented cross-functional team.

- Develops a high-energy environment with direct customer and supplier participation. Suppliers are encouraged to take on portions of the development process as part of the Open Innovation Model discussed in Chapter 5.

- Is extremely useful for identifying both *customer satisfiers* and *customer delighters* (which can be incorporated in flexible design strategies, as we'll discuss next).

You can read more about the Innovation Blitz in the Spotlight on p. 277.

D. Flexible Performance Target Design

In traditional development models, there is usually a fervently held goal to freeze performance specifications before development begins. That goal is very dangerous, and is entirely at odds with the following statement:

> *The spec should always be incomplete, and you always, as a developer, want it to be incomplete. We've seen in IBM the horrors of writing directly to a spec, because nobody is that smart!*

> *Microsoft Secrets, pp. 208-219*

If you try to freeze performance specs before development begins, or very early in a project, you close yourself to learning that occurs *during* the development process, and practically guarantee schedule overrun, me-too offerings, and/or rework loops somewhere down the line. During the innovation process, designers often learn that they can develop a customer delighter much more easily than they could have predicted at the outset. Alternatively, they may be trying to develop a frozen customer delighter that they subsequently find is far more difficult than could have been estimated. A lot of schedule time can be burned before anybody dares broach the subject of changing the frozen spec, with gut-wrenching discussions with marketing and key customers.

Recall Figure 2-02 (p. 16), which showed that me-too offerings succeed only 18% of the time, compared with delighters that succeed more than 80% of the time. Freezing target performance at the outset of a project gives us the worst of all possible worlds: We either end up with me-too customer satisfiers that won't win in the market, likely missing opportunities for creating a delighter along the way. Or, if we're focused only on a delighter and it turns out to be difficult to achieve, we may be too late to the market to reap the rewards.

Thus, where possible, it's best to equip each innovator with, minimally, two targets around each design or performance feature—a customer satisfier and a customer delighter—and freeze the performance level only after sufficient exploratory effort has been expended. That's what we mean by **Flexible Performance Target Design**. This approach is used by companies like Toyota and Microsoft, where performance specifications aren't frozen until as late in the development process as schedule allows. The purpose of maintaining flexibility during design is simple: to recognize the potential for outstanding creativity and to increase the odds of achieving enough customer delighters to have an 80% chance of success, which is the level at which the economic impact is substantial. In Appendix 2, we show how we give more time to Critical Resource innovators to increase the probability of differentiation without compromising schedule.

Conclusion

Of all the tactics described in this book, it is easy to argue that applying the Laws of Lead Time and of Innovation Variation are the most critical for compressing time-to-market, capturing high operating margins, and protecting both sustaining and disruptive innovations from commoditization. The best way to keep your schedule from exploding is to:

1) Reduce the number of projects-in-process (consistent with the Law of Lead Time)

2) Manage the Critical Resources according to the Seven Imperatives of the Law of Innovation Variation

With these actions, *you* will be the master, not the victim, of innovation lead time.

The imperative of maintaining growth through "customer delighter" differentiation is the product of Fast Innovation techniques that are inherently quicker than traditional methods. This includes a number of tactics covered in more detail in Parts II and III of this book. Here we highlighted just four of them: ethnography, rapid prototyping, the Innovation Blitz, and Flexible Performance Target Designing.

These two prerequisites—reducing the drivers of long lead time and using inherently fast techniques—will compress innovation lead time and let you create winning differentiation. And those are the most powerful engines of customer attraction and growth, and can set most companies on the path to doubling value.

Endnotes

30 *Business Week* online, Oct 11, 2004.

31 The first discussion of these laws known to us appeared in "Getting the Most out of your Product Development Process," *Harvard Business Review,* Mar-Apr 1996, and was inserted by Avi Mandelbaum. Though we like to give credit to the people who discovered the laws, we prefer to use names that tell what the laws do as reinforcement for the reader.

32 John D. C. Little, "A proof of the queuing formula $L = \lambda W$," *Operations Research,* 9 (1961), pp. 383-387. Little is a professor at MIT. For those trained in statistics, one of the reasons this seemingly obvious equation becomes a Law is that it is distribution independent, that is, if material arrived in an exponential distribution and departs in a Gaussian distribution Little's Law still is valid.

33 A report by the National Defense University called "The 3M Company: Sharpening the Business Edge and Implications for the DOD" (David W. Ziegler, Col. USAF) cites these figures, taken from an article published internally at 3M ("Picking Up the Pace," *3M Stemwinder,* 26 June - 16 July 2001).

The Immelt quote comes from his presentation at the Emerging Technology Conference in September 2003 (*See* http://www.technologyreview.com/articles/03/09/wo_bender092603.asp).

34 The Law of Innovation Variation is our name for the Polaczek-Khintchine equation.

35 We have all noticed Microsoft's improvement over the last 10 years, and certainly this "rule of thumb" approach is helpful.... but management does not always "get it" (Steve McConnell, *Rapid Development,* Redmond, WA: Microsoft Press, 1996). While improving, there is still a lot of potential. As an example *see* "Start Your Search Engine," *Time,* July 12, 2004 ("The new search engine will be in beta test for a year... ").

36 Adrian Slywotzky and Richard Wise, *How to Grow When Markets Don't* (New York: Warner Business Books, 2004), pp. 5–7.

CHAPTER 4

The Value of Thinking in Three Dimensions

So far we have outlined the critical issues on how to innovate faster and with more differentiation. Here, we return to the broader issue of where you should focus your innovation strategically, and introduce the powerful concept of the Three Dimensions of Innovation and multidimensional innovation.

In the past, most companies thought of innovation as a significant change in a product or service based on some new technology, but in recent years it's become clear that definition is too restrictive and that other kinds of innovation can contribute to maintain long-term growth in shareholder value. This chapter aims to make the case that there are three dimensions of innovation, and if you are not engaged in innovations along all three dimensions, you are missing significant growth and revenue opportunities.

Broadly speaking, innovation is defined as creating new and better ways of doing the things that your customers value and that create value for your shareholders. This leads to a three-dimensional model of innovation (*see* Figure 4-01):

- **Product/service innovation:** "Building a better mousetrap." Most things that people would name as innovations would fall into this category, such as the Apple iPod and iTunes

Figure 4-01: Three Dimensions of Innovation

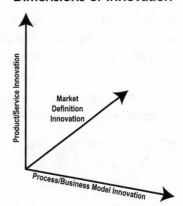

73

- **Market definition innovation:** Developing new offerings that surround an existing product or service, such as GE Aircraft Engines Segment "wing to wing" services

- **Process/Business model innovation:** Creating significantly lower costs, higher quality, faster innovation and operational lead times that often enable a new model of how a company does business, such as Dell and Wal-Mart have done

(We will provide case studies below to show how these companies have innovated.)

In this chapter, we'll look at what each of these dimensions can bring to an innovation effort, and why it is to your advantage to pursue innovations along two or more dimensions simultaneously whenever possible.

Dimension 1: New Product/Service Innovation

When most people think about innovation, chances are they're thinking of the product/service dimension. They may have thought of something that represented a new technology (the light bulb, transistors, airplanes), or new capabilities that grew from new technologies (Microsoft Windows, Voice-over-Internet-Protocol telephony). Or perhaps they thought of some extension to an existing product or service, such as adding fax capability to copiers, getting financial counseling from the bank, or adding competitor's data to service quotes (such as Progressive Insurance has done).

Figure 4-02: Product/Service Innovation

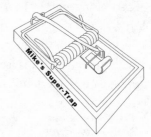

Building a better mousetrap

While these products and services are the cornerstone of most innovation programs, the key point for our purposes is that they are just one dimension of innovation. And no matter how good a product or service innovation is, there are often bigger opportunities in other dimensions, as we'll see next.

Dimension 2: Market Definition Innovation

The market definition dimension reflects (1) the leverage we can get from existing relationships with customers who have received good performance by offering additional products and services that surround existing offerings, or (2) finding entirely new market segments for existing offerings. This includes:

Figure 4-03:
Market Definition Innovation

Surrounding the core product or service with related offerings

- Understanding the frustrations that customers have in using your product or service, and finding ways to make them more successful in their own businesses

- Filling needs that surround but are not part of your current portfolio

Market definition innovation is often the strongest way to leverage the brand you have created within a spectrum of important customers. In the product arena, for example, most new consumer products are serving ever-smaller niche markets and fighting for space on increasingly crowded shelves. Between 1980 and 1998, the number of new food products introduced in the United States each year grew *fivefold*, to nearly 11,000.[36] (This proliferation in products has in fact created hidden costs of complexity, the attack upon which is discussed on p. 165). As a result, traditional product/service innovation has, in many industries, hit diminishing returns, as have the chances of creating a sustainable competitive advantage through superior technology.

To counteract this threat, many companies are creating new growth and value by addressing the hassles and issues that *surround* their existing product/service rather than by introducing new offerings or improving current offerings. To improve returns, they use their market position and customer satisfaction as a starting point from which to do new things for customers that solve their biggest problems. Market definition innovation is built on an undervalued truth: the sale of a product or service may be the culmination of your effort but it marks the *beginning* of the customer's experience.

Market Definition Innovator #1: GE Transportation, Aircraft Engine Segment

Most people familiar with jet engines recognize GE as a leader in this industry. Product innovations, like internally air-cooled turbine blades and high-G designs that improved F14 performance, are typical of the long legacy of product innovations that created important differentiation. However, it can be argued that GE's innovations in the market definition dimension are of comparable or greater importance. Some of GE's customers—the airline companies—face severe credit, cash and management challenges. The goal of GE is to provide services that allow airlines to focus on their core business, transporting satisfied customers. GE continually looks at all the challenges surrounding jet engines that its customers face, and has created diverse services such as:

- Complete overhaul management
- Materials and spares management
- Cash and asset management
- Fixed maintenance costs that transfer risk to GE
- Fixed price per engine flight hour
- Fixed material cost (spares) by the flight hour
- 24/7 on-wing support (shop repairs now last hours instead of weeks)
- Engine leasing

This expansion in the market definition dimension has had a significant impact at GE: 45% of the revenue from the Aircraft Engines segment of GE Transportation is from *services* provided to commercial engine customers; only 20% is from the *engines* themselves. The bottom line is that GE strives to offer all these services at a cost and performance level that is a better value for the customers than doing those things for themselves.

It is interesting that the most successful airline, Southwest, subcontracts all its maintenance to GE, whereas most other airlines maintain internal maintenance operations. If you had to point to one of Jack Welch's legacies, it was to move GE's center of gravity toward services and away from products. The emphasis on innovation by GE's new CEO, Jeff Immelt, is already accelerating the growth of GE after a couple of flat years. The range of services offered by GE Transportation shows just how important market definition innovation can be in generating profits with less invested capital, and most important, with high customer preference. Despite 9/11, the SARS virus, the airline industry meltdown, the slowdown in some military airframes, and vigorous competition, Aircraft Engines turned in year-after-year growth in revenue on the strong annuity stream built within its service enterprise.

Market Definition Innovator #2: Home Depot

Home Depot has two basic types of customers: contractors and the general public. The company discovered that, compared with the public, contractors typically shop more frequently, buy in larger quantities, and have a higher volume of repeat purchases. This meant that the inconvenience of navigating the big store and waiting in line for checkout weighed more heavily on them than on the homeowner customer. Contractors also tend to shop early in the morning to prepare for a day on the job site, and they use short-term credit heavily to cope with uncertain cash flow.

Home Depot applied the ethnography concept, actually putting themselves in the shoes of contractors and observing their daily frustrations and activities. The result is the Pro Initiative: contractors can phone orders into Home Depot so everything they need will be ready when they arrive at the store; they qualify for bulk discounts and new revolving credit programs; and they can take advantage of special customized services such as tool rental, set-aside checkout areas, and help with truck loading and deliveries. Home Depot even began to experiment with adding Dunkin' Donuts outlets to their stores, attempting to make Home Depot *the* stop for contractors in the morning.

Most Home Depot stores have incorporated this Pro Initiative offerings, and participating stores had sales-per-square-foot 12% higher than the average Home Depot store.[37] Given the high fixed costs of running a store, this represents a disproportionate growth in store profitability.

Dimension 3: Process/Business Model Innovation

> *I contend that process innovation is the most important growth strategy of all in terms of both growth rate and value creation. Even in companies where new products represent 35% of revenue per year, there is still 65% left to impact with process innovation. The cost and risk to create process innovation is lower, and it is harder to imitate. Therefore, I believe it is an undervalued strategy in most businesses. It generates profits quickly, giving you even greater resources to invest in development, etc.*
>
> Lou Giuliano, Chairman, President and CEO,
> ITT Industries (retired 2004)

Companies such as Dell, Southwest Airlines, and Wal-Mart are good examples of innovation in the process/business model dimension. What do they have in common? They've improved the speed, cost and quality of how they develop and deliver a commodity product or service to better serve the customer. Process innovations often enable business model innovations—that is, a company discovers it can operate in a fundamentally different way

**Figure 4-04:
Process/Business Model
Innovation**

**Custom
Mouse Traps**
*Delivered direct
Overnight service*

1-888-mice-r-us

Inventing a better way to build
and/or deliver mousetraps

thanks to improved process lead time, process quality, or process cost. Business model innovation typically involves radical innovation in the company's operational architecture and processes.

Process/business model innovations are remarkable in that the resulting competitive advantage lasts longer than that from sustaining product or service innovations. Competitors often quickly copy related product and service innovations, but are very slow to copy process innovations. In that sense, radical process/business model innovations are more often disruptive because the competitor is caught flat-footed and fails to respond. For example, the Toyota Production System (known as Lean in the U.S.) enabled significant quality, cost and lead time advantages, yet it took decades for the Big 3 to begin copying it corporate-wide.

Let's look at two examples of business model innovation enabled by process innovation.

Process innovator #1: ITT Inhdustries

Companies in industries with dominant designs produced by several competitors potentially face "commodity hell" (to borrow Jeff Immelt's term). But such companies can still grow value dramatically if they aggressively innovate along the process dimension ahead of competitors. Recall, too, the comment of Lou Giuliano about the importance of process innovation. Here is how he applied his convictions.

ITT is a diversified company with 2004 sales of $6.8 billion (in pumps, electronic connectors, high-tech defense, etc.) that has made significant investments in Lean Six Sigma to drive process improvement change. Since 1999, ITT has cut the lead time of many operations by more than 50%, and slashed costs for products that have lost their differentiation (become commoditized). For example, ITT determined that it needed to cut costs on a particular pump by 17% to generate a 5% increase in Economic Profit (net of cost of capital). An innovative targeted design session resulted in changes that cut costs by more than 25%!

The market for pumps declined dramatically during the 2000–04 recession, but ITT suffered far less than competitors because its performance allowed it to greatly increase its share of a much smaller market.

Similarly, because of the telecom meltdown of 2001, sales of ITT's electronic connectors went into free-fall, but again process improvement staved off a disaster to shareholder value. One major UK customer said that because ITT's delivery performance was so good, they gave ITT 100% of their business instead of 50%! When the goin' gets tough, the tough get goin'.

Leveraging more than 500 trained Black Belts, ITT has driven step-change gains in lead time reduction and product cost reduction that have generated hundreds of millions more in operating profit. Current sales growth in 2004 was 21% compared with 6% for the industry. ROIC is 17.4% vs. 3.4% for the industry, and was reflected in the share price (*see* Figure 4-05). Given the conditions in half their markets, the company should have *under-performed* the S&P 500 during the recession of 2000-04, and investor relations could no doubt have ginned up a plausible explanation. But this was a time for deeds, not words!

Figure 4-05: ITT Price History

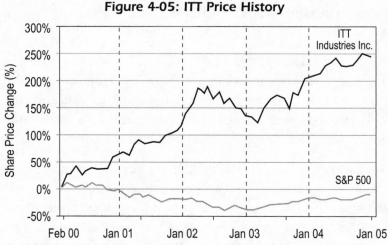

Process/business model innovator #2: Dell

Dell is one of the best-known examples of process and business model innovation. The PC market was founded by IBM, but product innovations allowed Compaq to take over industry leadership. Dell entered the PC market as an attacker, with a disruptive innovation that aimed at achieving lower cost per unit of product. Dell created an operational architecture that dramatically compressed the lead time (order-to-production completion) approaching one day compared with more than two *weeks* for Compaq and other competitors. Dell's progress on lead time reduction can be calculated by their increased work-in-process inventory turns (Figure 4-06). Obviously if you can turn inventory 365 times per year you can start *any new product configuration* and ship it in about a day.

Figure 4-06: Dell and Compaq Inventory Turns

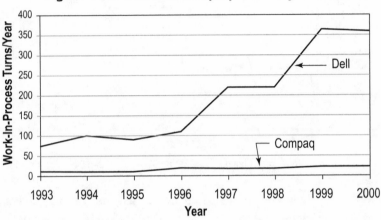

These data came from 10K registrations. We could only go through FY2000 because that's when Compaq was acquired by Hewlett-Packard.

Why is process innovation like this so important? As the number of PC options increased and lifecycles shortened in the industry, the related cost of complexity and overhead cost drove up Compaq's internal operational costs. In addition, the dealers and distributors cost Compaq a substantial markup. These costs are all non-value-add costs, because the customer is happy to purchase the product without them.

In contrast, with its lead time approaching one day, Dell dramatically reduced most of the internal operational complexity, overhead, and obsolescence costs. The *process innovation* of achieving a one-day lead time allowed them to create a new *business model* by shipping preconfigured products directly to customers, eliminating the distribution costs. The disruptive Dell business model allowed them to operate at roughly 60% to 70% of the cost structure of Compaq. In addition, because Dell collects cash from customers before its bills are due to suppliers, it has an A/R of $3.6 billion and an A/P of $7.3 billion, creating a negative working capital impact and an ROIC of 47.7%. Dell's relative stock performance speaks for itself (Figure 4-07).

Figure 4-07: Dell Price History

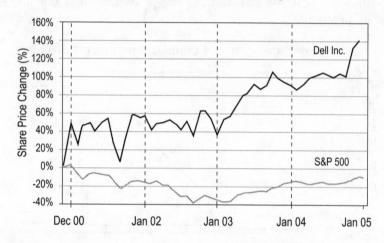

It should be pointed out that Dell created a Fast Innovation process that allowed it to quickly match Compaq's and IBM's *product innovations*, and due to fast operational lead times, bring them to market only slightly behind Compaq. In the words of a former Dell VP, "this allowed us to give Compaq a spanking with their own innovation." This is a case where the process/business model innovator destroyed the shareholder value of the product innovators: Compaq was improvidently purchased by HP; the money-losing $12 billion IBM division was sold for about $1 billion. Dell's process/business model innovation was entirely disruptive because neither Compaq nor IBM copied the Dell process; rather they stood flat-footed with their product innovation strategy despite all the public information available.

The Strong Advantage of Multidimensional Innovation

> *Breakthrough innovations rarely occur within a technical discipline, or within a market, but almost always where you create a novel intersection.*
>
> Clay Christensen[38]

We have spoken of the power of each of the three dimensions of innovation—but the whole is almost certainly greater than the sum of the parts. If you can innovate along more than one dimension, it is far less likely that a competitor can respond. It is one thing for a competitor to copy a product or service innovation, another to copy a process innovation that is delivering that product or service faster and cheaper or that is protected by being part of a market definition array of products and services. Each initiative complements the strength of the other. Thus the ability to maintain above-average shareholder returns is greatly enhanced by simultaneous innovation along more than one dimension. You should therefore continually probe every dimension of innovation to achieve the complementary strength of a multidimensional innovator.

Multidimensional innovator #1: Wal-Mart

Wal-Mart started out with a very simple yet powerful business model: entering rural markets that no major discounters already served (the **market definition** dimension) with much wider selection and lower prices due to volume (**process innovation**). Because the rural markets were individually small, they could not support more than one mass merchant. Wal-Mart's rural expansion strategy thus locked out competitors in each market it entered. Everyday low pricing was enabled by process innovations, such as investment in sophisticated information and satellite communication systems, which allowed Wal-Mart to achieve predictable, near-Just-In-Time supply chain replenishment—which in turn allowed it to reduce investment in inventory and distribution systems and slash the cost of markdowns and obsolescence. Information systems provided centralized data for buyers to help them exert greater purchasing leverage on suppliers. More predictable and leveled demand schedules allowed suppliers to cut prices further. Local store managers used the systems to adjust pricing and selection to meet local needs and flex to local competition.

Wal-Mart management soon realized that if it clustered stores into regions served by highly efficient central distribution centers, it could achieve economies of scales and logistics far superior to its more urban competitors. This insight led Wal-Mart to pioneer what became disruptive innovations in its operational architecture, standardizing its stores and distribution centers with common processes, systems, and support to create nearly carbon-copy stores and distribution systems (**process/business model** innovation). In fact they were able to replicate 26 carbon-copy distribution centers in less than four years. The more dense the stores, the lower the logistics costs and the greater their advantage. Wal-Mart has quickly grown into the largest and most successful retailer (and corporation!) in the world by simultaneously applying market definition and process/business model innovations to support low prices of products that are in fact commodities.

Multidimensional innovator #2: Apple

What led Apple to develop the hugely successful iPod? Apple started with the market definition dimension of innovation in extending from computers to the broader category of lifestyle electronics. In doing so, Apple brought along a ready-made market well beyond the die-hard Mac lovers it had hitherto relied upon, but which had shriveled to less than 2% of the home computer market. With the introduction of the iPod, Apple created an innovation along the product dimension that was completely different from the average MP3 music player. Highly intuitive, with a high storage capacity, the iPod allowed customers to carry entire, extensive music collections around in their pockets. (They did not repeat their previous mistake of having a "pocket device"—the Newton PDA—that was too large for a pocket.)

Ask users why they love their iPods and many probably won't be able to explain it in words. But watch them and you'll see their iPods are with them constantly, as prevalent as a cell phone. And it is not just young people. Many of you who have iPods probably did what co-author Mike

George did: he recently attached an iPod to his car radio so he could avoid the broadcast channels and the tyranny of being limited to five CDs. He now has everything from the Beatles to Beethoven's 32 piano sonatas at his command—the kind of diversity that iPod users relish! Apple has sold 10 million units since the iPod's debut in October 2001— over 4.5 million of them in the fourth quarter of 2004 alone! (And their stock price reflects that fact, *see* Figure 4-08.)

Figure 4-08: Apple Stock Performance

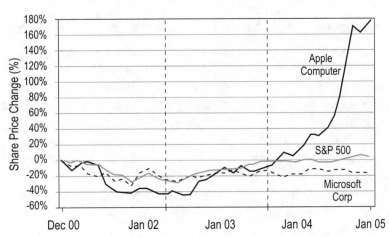

But having an iPod satisfies only one customer need. Consumers still need a source of music. Apple then extended into the process/business model dimension of innovation with iTunes, a direct attack on the traditional method of selling whole sets of songs in the form of a CD. In the same way that Dell bypasses the costs of warehouses and middlemen, Apple's iTunes bypasses the need for warehouses of CDs and for music sellers. iTunes offers music by the song and allows you to *pick and choose* only those songs you want to include in your digital music collection. From the customer's viewpoint, this is in sharp contrast to buying a damageable CD, 80% of whose content may be of no interest. With an iPod and iTunes, music lovers need never buy another CD if they choose.

As of January 25, 2005, iTunes is selling 1.25 million songs per day at 99 cents each! Many of us had written off Apple as a company whose place in *history* was far more secure than its place in the *future*. For the moment, Apple is using sustaining innovations to continue its iPod advantage, increasing high-end memory products, cutting the price of lower-end iPods, improving battery life, etc. If they continue their string of multidimensional innovations, they *may* be able to sustain above-average shareholder returns for more than a decade. As a result of this multidimensional innovation, Apple is now *the* leading online music retailer. This is a truly astounding innovation, one that we would have expected Microsoft to quickly jump on given their need for growth in recent years.

Multidimensional innovation and market shifts

Microsoft has experienced disappointing growth in the last few years. Does this mean that the software markets are slowing down? No, it means that the major growth opportunities shifted from the product dimension to the market definition dimension of innovation, as represented by the stunning growth of the Apple iPod and Google (take it from us, Google is the writer's best research assistant!). Microsoft has thus far failed to respond adequately to the iPod or Google, and has not applied its enormous cash and technical resources to this dimension of innovation—a failure noted by financial analysts.[39] Shareholders prefer revenue growth with above-market shareholder returns to dividends.

Multidimensional innovator #3: Southwest Airlines

For years, Southwest has achieved price leadership with far lower costs and has enjoyed consistent profitability while much of the rest of the airline industry has faced escalating costs and bankruptcy. How? By exploiting all three dimensions of innovation to great advantage:

- **Market definition innovation**: Southwest started out by defining its competition as the automobile and bus rather than existing airlines (the market definition dimension). Routes were picked that would support high volume.

- **Product/service innovation**: Recognizing that it had to provide air travel at extremely low cost to substitute for driving, Southwest pioneered the low-price, no-frills, commodity transportation model of service, which challenged the prevailing glamour model service of the airline industry.

- **Process/business model innovation**: To drive costs below the competition, Southwest had to build an entirely new process model. They operate just one class of airplane, the 737, while other airlines operate as many as 14 different models, leading to enormous savings from reduced complexity in training, pilot certification, repair stocks, mechanics training, and so on.[40] They focused on rapid turns at the gate, making two more flights per day on average than their competition, resulting in lower capital investment and higher ROIC. They pioneered the point-to-point model in high-demand markets, flying in the face of the hub-and-spoke industry paradigm.

When the airline industry came under extreme pressure after 9/11 and with escalating fuel prices, who could have believed that an airline could outperform the S&P 500 by 150%. (*See* Figure 4-09.) The process innovator will always weather a downturn better and recover faster than a high-overhead competitor. Even after a decade of intense cost cutting, other airlines have not been able to match Southwest's cost-per-available-passenger-mile. Innovation along all three dimensions has built a moat around Southwest's economic castle.

Figure 4-09: Southwest Share Price History vs. American Airlines

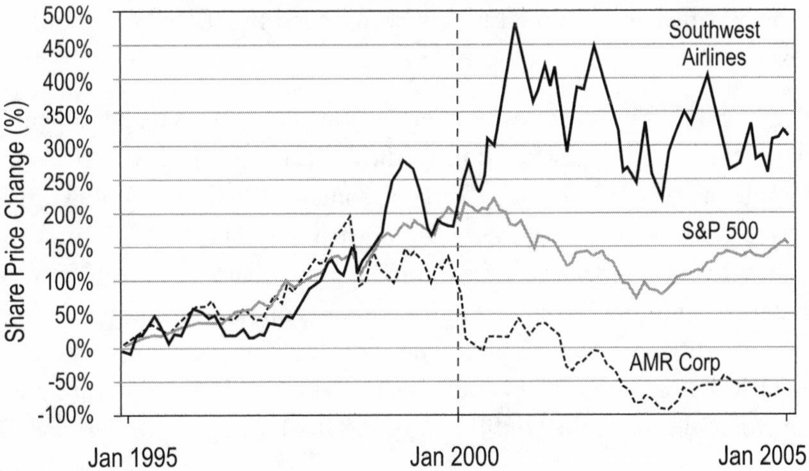

Multidimensional innovator #4: Capital One

Capital One was formed by disrupters: two young men who decided that the credit card business was a knowledge business, not a banking business. After a lot of early frustration in finding a platform on which to try their ideas, they were able innovate along all three dimensions.

When they started, nearly all credit cards offered the same undifferentiated interest rate of 19.8% APR. Capital One built its business entirely around the insight that all consumers are not created equal (the **market definition** dimension) and that they could use credit bureau information supplemented by proprietary in-house algorithms to predict consumer propensity to pay back unsecured credit card debt. This meant they could provide a card with lower interest rates (the **product** dimension) to better (less risky) customers and offer new credit to some higher-risk consumers who had limited or damaged credit records.

To operationalize what they called an Information Based Strategy (IBS), Capital One developed an entirely new business model (the **process/business model** dimension). They run over 40,000 market tests a year to refine statistical models and strategies, and offer a myriad of different products to different consumer segments. Capital One's IBS business model allowed it to grow revenue 40% per year with the industry's lowest default rates and best stock performance compared with even their best-managed competitors, who watched flat-footed for about five years.

The capabilities that allowed Capital One to grow so phenomenally stood them in good stead during the hard times. By 2002, the sheer complexity of Capital One's offerings, some well-publicized blowups by newer competitors, and creaking infrastructure and controls resulting from years of rampant growth, led industry regulators to place an informal memorandum of understanding on the company. After a 40% stock price crash in one day, Capital One quickly deployed process improvement initiatives to get the company's processes and infrastructure under control and restore the confidence of the stock market (*see* Figure 4-10, next page).

Figure 4-10: Capital One Share advantage

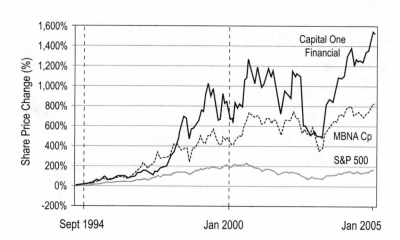

Conclusion

In most people's minds, the word innovation conjures up images of Edison creating the light bulb, Bardeen inventing the transistor, Kilby creating the integrated circuit, Steinmetz creating the AC electrical industry for GE, or, in the service sector, Bezos creating Amazon, etc. To many, innovation *means* new products or services. But as the examples in this chapter have shown, there are many companies that have maintained above-average growth without innovating a single new product or service but rather by exploiting the market definition, or process/business model dimensions of innovation.

The examples also included companies that pursued simultaneous initiatives along more than one dimension of innovation—a strategy that can increase the probability of success and reduce the risk of being commoditized. Working in two or three dimensions significantly increases the probability of maintaining above-average growth beyond what is possible with just one dimension. Moreover, a Fast Innovation process can maintain superior returns by protecting the margins of sustaining product/service innovations.

We've cited statistics that show 90% of companies cannot sustain above-average growth for more than a decade, providing a strong impetus for having every company review each of its business units to assess its innovation efforts along all three dimensions. Management should:

- Map the innovations delivered and planned across each of the three dimensions

- Determine % revenue in each dimension for the last three years

- Evaluate the potential competitive advantage of expanding into more dimensions

- Identify opportunities to extend currently planned innovations by marrying with another dimension
    - Determine how these initiatives will make customers more successful

- Estimate potential margin enhancements to sustaining innovations by adopting Fast Innovation approaches

- Estimate the potential revenue and operating profit to be gained by all new innovation efforts
    - Include the potential increases in ROIC, cash flow, and share price through more successful innovation

We suggest that you facilitate an executive meeting (perhaps conducted in the Blitz format, p. 277) to make a first approximation of the size of the opportunity in your sectors. Use the case studies as examples and a potential guide to stimulate your thinking. Be sure to look beyond the obvious: the results of multidimensional innovation in particular are often non-intuitive. You will find that the process is stimulating and will likely inform your strategic planning process.

A key message is that if your business will not allow a disruptive breakthrough on the product/service dimension, you must operate on the process/business model or market definition dimension, but all three dimensions should be explored. Jim Collins[41] has persuasively argued:

If you cannot be the best in the world at your core business,
then your core business absolutely cannot form the basis of a
great company.

This goal necessarily creates significant discomfort with the status quo within your company. For example, a retailer might decide on a goal to create a new store concept with service that rivals that of Ritz Carlton. When Jack Welch announced that every business in GE would become #1 or #2 in its market or be sold, every business had a new urgency approaching a crisis mentality to innovate and change to become the best or be sold. This was followed by process improvement to further enhance the strength of the survivors. Andy Grove clearly saw that Intel could never again be the best in the world at memories, and he refocused the business on microprocessors where that goal could be met. Gordon Moore commented at the time that this change would make the company programming-centric rather than just process-centric, and result in a major turnover of management. But as Churchill once said: *"The King's First Minister is not called upon to make easy decisions."*

The next chapter will debunk yet another widespread image of innovation: that it is conducted by a small team of inventors working in splendid isolation. In the new world, the whole planet is the laboratory for innovation, and learning to exploit the *whole intellect of the planet* can help you accelerate the speed and differentiation of innovation.

Endnotes

37 Adrian Slywotzky and Richard Wise, *How to Grow When Markets Don't* (New York: Warner Business Books, 2004), pp. 302-4.
38 *Consulting Magazine*, Jan-Feb 2005, p. 22.
39 "The Big Sleep," *Barrons*, Jan 3, 2005.
40 Details on how Southwest has achieved low complexity are in *Conquering Complexity in Your Business* (Michael L. George and Stephen A. Wilson; New York: McGraw-Hill, 2004).
41 Jim Collins, *Good to Great: Why Some Companies Make the Leap... And Others Don't* (New York: HarperBusiness, 2001), p. 13.

CHAPTER 5

Open Innovation

Applying the Intellect of the Planet

No man is an island, entire of itself.

John Donne,Meditation XVII

W hat is the probability that your company has all of the best talent on the planet that applies to a specific innovation challenge? Obviously the answer is near zero. Historically, most companies had to exclusively look internally for insight, creativity, and innovation capability as there was no process to tap the resources of the planet. That's what we call the Closed Innovation Model.

In contrast, companies as diverse as P&G, Eli Lilly, and Intel believe that somebody out there in the world has either already solved their innovation problems or has a vital piece of knowledge that they can use to more quickly find the solution with less risk and generally at a fraction of the cost of reinventing the wheel. With the new capabilities provided by the internet, finding the person with the exact knowledge you need is now within the realm of feasibility for most companies. This looking beyond your own corporate borders is the **Open Innovation Model**.

Besides the obvious contrasts between closed and open innovation (based on the internet), there are powerful differences in *approach* that have a direct bearing on whether you can achieve the power of Fast Innovation:

- **Closed innovation** is knowledge creation done for its own sake, and frequently fails to forge links to commercialization, or misses an entirely new piece of external knowledge.

- **Open innovation** focuses internal development resources on creating only that new knowledge that can be commercialized to support business strategy, and only that new knowledge that *cannot be found outside* the company.

This chapter explores the differences between closed innovation and open innovation, and, more importantly, shows that the Open Innovation Model has become the prerequisite for a company which depends on innovation to maintain above-average growth in revenue and shareholder returns.

A Quick Look at the Closed Innovation Model

For a prime example of closed innovation, we need look no further than Bell Labs/Lucent. Bell Labs boasted scientists like John Bardeen, the *only* person in history to win the Nobel Prize in Physics twice. Bardeen studied the motion of electrons and holes in crystals and invented the transistor. It was this new knowledge that *happened* to create one of the most fabulous wealth-generation engines (and which we referred to as *"The Most Important Disruptive Innovation in the 20th Century"* on p. 28).

Note the phrase "happened to create": the vast majority of Bell Labs discoveries, including the transistor, provided little or no economic benefit for the company. They created enormous wealth for other companies and for society at large. The Bell Labs system of innovation invested in new scientific knowledge creation that *might* apply to its products. It's the epitome of closed innovation: the company gambles on getting high margins from highly differentiated products for a long time because it owns all the knowledge that went into them (and that is ideally protected by patents). Bell Labs has generated more than 28,000 patents since 1925 and has either invented or led the development of many ground-breaking innovations, including digital networking and signal processing, lasers and fiber-optic communications systems, communications satellites, cell phones, electronic switching, touch-tone, modems, information theory, solar cells, Unix, Big Bang radiation, and on and on. In fact, Bell Labs' inventions led to six Nobel Prizes in physics.

This record of brilliant achievement with closed innovation is probably unrivaled in world history. But once telecommunications was deregulated, the exclusively internal and technical focus of innovation was poorly attuned to capture the Voice of the Customer. For example, Bell Labs/Lucent listened primarily to its major customers, the Baby Bells, who, for example, owned copper lines and had little initial interest in fiber optics. Despite the dazzling technological successes of its closed innovation model, Lucent missed the markets (later exploited by Cisco), and nearly went bankrupt.

Another smaller-scale example of closed innovation is Texas Instruments. TI was the first company to create silicon transistors by inventing a technique to purify silicon to a level previously thought impossible. TI was also the first (according to awards by the patent office and the Nobel Prize committee) to create the integrated circuit. These earth-shaking innovations were the badge of honor of the closed innovation model and conferred enormous competitive advantage for TI, who had compounded revenue growth of 30% per year and earnings growth of 27% for more than a decade.[42] But despite this dazzling success, pride in accomplishment did not cloud the insight of TI's president, Pat Haggerty, who in 1964 foresaw a different future for innovation:

> The sum total of exploratory R&D done in other industrial organizations, research institutes, and universities is so much greater than our own organization can perform that it seems almost inevitable that most of our strategic programs must evolve from exploratory research done outside.[43]

The corollary to this statement is that a model of innovation based solely on the closed internal development of all necessary knowledge, science, and technology is *doomed to failure*. It is bound to miss some vital piece of external knowledge that is critical to its customers and markets, products and services, present or virtual. Haggerty's revolutionary 1964 prediction was confirmed by the collapse of the closed R&D model of IBM, Bell Labs, Xerox, and others in the 1990s.

The deadly mindset of closed innovation

One of the biggest problems with a closed model of innovation is that it creates powerful internal constituencies that want to keep control over the budgets and nourish their own research projects. Given that mindset, all innovations created outside are viewed as competition, which is the origin of the pejorative term NIH (Not Invented Here). Dave Dorman, the current CEO of AT&T, quipped at the 2004 Fortune Innovation conference:

> At Bell Labs we say that the phrase "Not Invented Here" was invented here!

Fortunately, there is an entirely new view at AT&T, born of a near-death experience. Hossein Eslambolchi, Chief Technology Officer of AT&T, has said: "*Our mantra was technology for technology's sake. Now it is focused on real business problems.*" In other words, commercialization of technology *that supports business strategy* now drives innovation.

What do the following innovations all have in common?

- personal computers
- bit-mapped image
- PostScript
- laser printing
- the Windows concept

- graphical user interface (GUI)
- ethernet
- semiconductor diode lasers
- the computer mouse

All these disruptive innovations were created by Xerox's Palo Alto Research Center (PARC). However, each required additional, expensive product development, which in the eyes of Xerox's incumbent business operations would have diverted resources away from established product lines. They saw a lot more potential for sustaining innovations congruent with current business strategy and existing customers than with those potentially disruptive offerings.[44] This is just further evidence supporting Clay Christensen's thesis: disruptive innovation is most often killed by *good* rather than bad management decisions.

You probably know the outcome. Each of these developments was picked off by other firms or venture capitalists, or was spun off by Xerox for modest benefit. In effect these innovations lost the battle over management time and capital allocation within Xerox. Yet once outside Xerox they ultimately generated billions of dollars in value for other companies.

Many of the PARC innovations that resulted from purely exploratory research, which, in perception if not in fact, did not fit Xerox at all, but they did absorb development funding. The PARC experience shows that **if closed innovations are *not* exploited by *your* business, they will almost certainly benefit someone else's business.** This phenomenon is true of all closed innovation firms—including Bell Labs/Lucent, Xerox PARC, and IBM—which have created billions of dollars of value for other companies while their own "core" businesses melted down. Which brings us back to what Peter Drucker declared long ago:

> *Contrary to almost universal belief, new knowledge—and especially new scientific knowledge—is not the most reliable or most predictable source of successful innovations.*[45]

It has taken many companies, and their gifted scientists, a long time to realize that new scientific knowledge which is not protected by patents gets commoditized very quickly.

Funding Disruptive Innovations

Closed innovation is undertaken in the belief that it *may* end up being useful *sometime* in the future to *someone*. With that criteria, there is no basis for killing a project—and Bell Labs virtually never did.

In today's economic environment, this kind of approach destroys shareholder value. When funding disruptive innovation efforts, you need to have a way to kill a project if the cost of going to the next development milestone is more than your company can support. Metrics like Net Present Value are irrelevant because there is no rational way of arriving at a discount rate. The better questions are how much do you have to pay to get to the next milestone and retain your option, and what alternative investments might look better at that point. This is the Real Options Theory[46] approach to funding, which is discussed in more detail in Part II, p. 188.

Open Innovation Model

In stark contrast to Bell Labs, Cisco exemplifies the **open innovation** paradigm, whose CEO declares that:

Most innovation will occur outside the company.

Cisco began by selling routers, but early on adopted the philosophy of being customer-driven, rather than technology-driven like Lucent. Cisco set a goal to become a one-stop shopping place for networking, and then set out to acquire the technology it needed to achieve that very broad customer-driven goal. Cisco's core competency was in making and integrating acquisitions, and in creating the IOS software platform to tie all the hardware together, thereby avoiding perhaps the single biggest customer fear: incompatibility (an issue with which Lucent failed to grapple). Cisco's business model depends on acquiring companies with

---

Isn't open innovation just a veiled approach to outsourcing?

Emphatically no! All the companies of whom we have direct knowledge have held R&D spending levels constant at a minimum, and some have increased it. Remember the daunting challenge with which Fast Innovation grapples:

To sustain above-average shareholder returns and growth for more than a decade—a feat that has eluded 90% of the companies on the S&P 500.

The Open Innovation Model allows us to leverage unique internal knowledge with external knowledge to our advantage and get *more* innovation done faster. This in turn results in more highly differentiated products, services, and processes, which is what drives sustained, above-average growth in revenues, margins, and ROIC.

The *distribution* of internal investment in innovation may change as a result of open innovation to focus more on unique internal knowledge capability and less on reinventing wheels. Further, the numbers of people involved in innovation may increase as you work on more dimensions of the 3D Model (though many of the new innovators may be outside traditional R&D job descriptions). Remember, the goal is beating that horrible statistic, that 90% of companies fail to maintain above-average returns for more than a decade, which is simply not possible using a closed model of innovation or by cutting investment in innovation.

promising technology and building internal expertise around market intelligence, due diligence, and post-close integration.

In contrast, Bell Labs/Lucent changed, but very slowly and only with the specter of bankruptcy hanging over its head. However, the financial markets move much faster than do inwardly focused companies like Lucent, and their shareholder value has plummeted as a consequence. Cisco is one of those few companies that deliberately try to innovate, create, and destroy businesses *faster* than the financial markets. Even during the telecom boom of the late 1990s, Cisco's book value was rewarded with a multiple of ten compared to Lucent. During the subsequent industry meltdown, Cisco's 10-year appreciation fell from 8,000% to 1,000% but still outperformed the S&P 500's appreciation of 140% despite "exaggerated reports of its demise." (*See* Figure 5-01.)

Figure 5-01: Lucent vs. Cisco Stock Performance

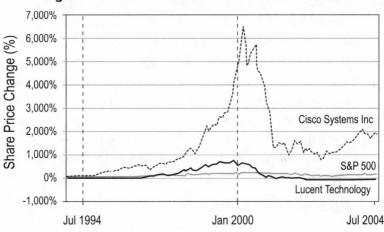

Open Innovation Case #1: Eli Lilly's web-based InnoCentive

Besides Cisco, the new open model of innovation is also being pursued in some form by Merck, Procter & Gamble, Intel, Microsoft, Sun, Oracle, Dow, BASF, Nestle, Genentech, Amgen, Genzyme, and numerous others. To understand how the Open Innovation Model resolves the weaknesses of the closed model, let's look at the market forces at work that drive most companies today, beginning with Eli Lilly.

The pharmaceutical industry succeeds by solving important medical problems through drugs whose development involves great expense and technical expertise. Just to give you a feel for the enormous numbers involved, the pharmaceutical industry invested about $30 billion in research in 2004, which amounts to about 70% of their profits.[47] The success rate is quite low, perhaps 10% at best. The extremely high risk makes the Open Innovation Model attractive, because it allows pharmaceutical companies to offload some of the risk to the institution or person on the planet who has the unique expertise needed.

The internet is the enabling technology for open innovation because it makes all technological earthlings only a few clicks away. At Eli Lilly, Open Innovation started when Alph Bingham, who was in charge of R&D strategy, sat down with Aaron Schacht and a group of R&D personnel to brainstorm how the company could benefit from the internet in general and the collective wisdom of the planet in particular. Lilly's chairman later created a task force of 17 execs who studied how the company could adapt to the new internet world. They recommended, and in 2000 he created, a venture arm they called e.Lilly. Among other accomplishments, e.Lilly incubated and built an internet-based innovation collaborative called InnoCentive, which, in Lilly's own words, is "the first online company that allows world-class scientists and science-based companies to collaborate in a global scientific community. Seeker-companies post scientific problems as InnoCentive Challenges on the InnoCentive Web site, where Solver-scientists worldwide register to solve them."

This approach effectively does for technology seekers and solvers what eBay does for buyers and sellers. When it was led by Newt Crenshaw, e.Lilly also advocated a venture fund so that Lilly could have a seat at the table as new potentially disruptive technologies were fledged. The chairman approved that move and the fund was created in late 2000. The process links traditional and non-traditional intellectual resources (*see* list below and Figure 5-02).

Traditional pools
U.S. and EU first-tier academics
Contract labs (FTE)
Individual networks

Opportunity pools

    Academics at second-tier and non-U.S./EU universities and colleges

    Researchers in less-developed countries (e.g., Russia, India)

    Scientists in other industries

    Excess capacity at contract labs

    Retirees

Technical service organizations, such as…

    Edison Welding Institute

    Ohio Aerospace Institute[48]

Figure 5-02: Global Reach of InnoCentive

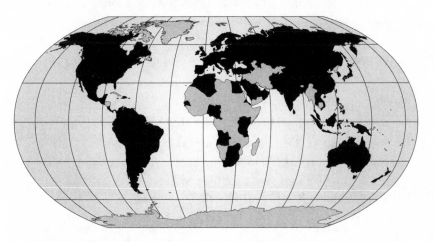

The black-shaded areas show all the regions of the world represented by innovators who have contributed to Eli Lilly's InnoCentive program. See why we call it harvesting the intellect of the planet?

In the past, most corporations and the government relied on *first-tier* U.S. universities for outstanding technical expertise. When Howard Hughes wanted to create a defense electronics business, he hired Dean Wooldridge and Simon Ramo, among the best minds associated with Caltech. When the Air Force wanted help with a Lean aircraft initiative, it went to MIT. But notice something unique about the InnoCentive model: the number of potential solvers grows exponentially through access to non-traditional sources, such as *second-tier* universities, and to the best minds everywhere in the world. This greatly increases the odds of finding a "solver" with the unique knowledge needed. We will see some examples of this below. Alph Bingham, VP of the e.Lilly R&D strategy, explains:

The magic is when the question is posed to a broad base of focused minds and the eureka effect that produces. Finding the well-prepared mind that sees something others don't see. Sometimes there are one or two persons on the planet who know the answer because they already did this research and didn't publish it. But more often we find those one or two minds that enter the "solution space" adjacent to the answer, see it and go, "Aha! someone is looking for that!"

In the more traditional approach, you'd enter a solution space for a given problem at some remote location and brutally hack and chew your way to one of the answers that were already living out there. That "hack and chew" skill is the one we tend to identify with "being a scientist."

The Open Innovation Model is similar to the Wild West, with the company filling the role of sheriff. Rather than take all the risk personally, the risk is offloaded to bounty hunters. They assess their own risk profile, skills, knowledge, etc., weigh the bounty against that, and take the risk themselves. Basically, a lot of business risk is shifted to the market place.

Rewards in the Open Innovation Model flow to outcomes, whereas the closed model rewards the flow of effort (read: steady paychecks and promotions) with a less-direct coupling to outcomes. Many firms have signed up to use the InnoCentive website including Procter and Gamble, Boeing, Dow, Grace, and Nestle. Companies ("seekers") can also place problems on InnoCentive anonymously so that competitors do not know what projects they are pursuing.

Let's take a look at an InnoCentive model example from by Eli Lilly. Dr. Chris Schmid and his group were already too busy to take on the project of designing a new synthesis for the intermediate compound in the quantities they needed. Schmid decided to post his team's synthesis problem on InnoCentive. "I figured we could at least put the problem out there and see what happened," he said. "If we received a solution, great. If not, we were no worse off than before."

Three months later, Schmid's team had its solution, and an InnoCentive Solver scientist received the $25,000 Challenge award.

Figure 5-03: InnoCentive Website

More than 70,000 people have signed up at the InnoCentive website to be Solvers. They can earn cash prizes if they solve one of the posted challenges. Past awards have gone to the head of an Indian research institute, a retired chemist at Hoechst in Germany, an unemployed protein crystallographer, a Russian scientist, and an Oxford researcher. Rather than creating a website yourself, it makes more sense to post on an existing site like InnoCentive, as P&G and 25 other companies now do. It's the same logic that makes eBay so successful.

Some key lessons we need to reinforce: This open model does *not* generate knowledge for its own sake. Companies themselves create very little new knowledge and very few innovations that do not fit directly into their corporate strategies. If a market opportunity happens to be identified that is outside the corporate strategy, the open model uses a venture-capital or Real Options Theory funding approach to protect the large but ill-defined revenue growth opportunity from being destroyed by the capital allocation and management time allocation processes of the core business (which is properly focused on sustaining growth in known markets).

This new open innovation paradigm inspires companies to find the most appropriate business model to commercialize a new idea—whether that model exists within the firm or through external licensing, partnering, or venturing. Open innovation companies use licensing extensively to create and extend markets for their technology. And the faster the technology gets out of the lab, the sooner the researchers will learn new ways to apply, leverage, and integrate that technology into new offerings.

Open Innovation Case #2: Procter & Gamble

Procter & Gamble was the first firm to join Eli Lilly on the InnoCentive website as part of their open innovation initiative. The Chairman and CEO, AG Lafley, actively supports open innovation as a key component of P&G's growth strategy. He has set an ambitious goal of sourcing 50% of new products from outside P&G's development process. The P&G effort was described at the *Fortune Magazine CEO Innovation Summit* in December 2004 by Larry Huston, VP of Innovation. He began with a thought-provoking question:

> How many Technology and Product Expositions are there per year worldwide? 18, 180, 1,800 or 18,000?

The answer will astound you. There are 18,000 such expositions, at which scores of entrepreneurs offer their ideas! In addition to obtaining products from outside entrepreneurs, P&G has used the InnoCentive website to present "unsolvable" chemical problems that have become obstacles to internal development to the 70,000+ solvers. P&G also has created a network infrastructure to find promising ideas and solutions in every region of the world. P&G is supplementing its R&D infrastructure with an *infostructure* that allows them to spot business-building connections worldwide.

The vision for the future of innovation at P&G is not R&D (research and development) but C&D (connect and develop). Huston is leading the effort to develop a whole new business model of innovation where one aspect is leveraging external innovation assets. The P&G burning platform that supports investment in open innovation is clear:

1. Meeting growth goals: Because of its size, P&G needs $2 billion in new revenue per year to sustain above-average shareholder returns.

2. The current R&D model of most firms is not sustainable because of exploding technologies and low success rates. There is a need to accomplish more with less.

One of the greatest challenges that P&G faces in achieving these goals is common to all companies that adopt the Open Innovation Model: overcoming an internally oriented culture. P&G estimates that there are over 1.5 million scientists and developers worldwide who are talented in applicable specialty areas, and P&G needs to leverage that talent to accomplish its goals. These issues are paramount to any firm that wants to sustain above-average shareholder returns.

Larry Huston emphasized that the Open Innovation Model is not about outsourcing. Rather, it is an attempt to accelerate the pace and effectiveness of innovation by leveraging and insourcing other people's ideas. P&G looks at its existing offerings and tries to find adjacencies that are not currently served (market definition innovation opportunities) and then provides a roadmap of where efforts should be applied to meet those needs. Defining the problem is half the solution. This approach has evolved into the creation of a list of "top 10 needs," that, if met, would drive P&G's brand franchises to greater levels of performance. In evaluating candidate adjacencies to build on, P&G looks at the pedigree of the innovator based on past efforts, and how close the product is to the desired adjacency. An example is P&G's Spin Brush, which uses the technology of a child's rotating lollipop. It is 80% as effective as a $120 electric toothbrush and sells for $6. It was developed by an external entrepreneur, as was P&G's Magic Eraser and Olay Regenerist technology.

Open Innovation Case #3: Intel's problem that required thousands of innovators

The InnoCentive model effectively pays a bounty for a solution. But some problems are solved only through the contributions of thousands of active participants, not by one lucky winner. How can we motivate solvers to voluntarily supply their knowledge free of charge? We need an approach that replaces cash with cooperation. But how is it possible to predict that your cooperative model will be more than wishful thinking about the kindness and generosity of technical people? Napoleon, that arch cynic, supplied the answer:

Men are motivated by two forces: fear and self-interest

We might more properly say that these two forces are more predictable than altruism. Wilfred Pinfold, Technology Director in the Systems Technology Labs at Intel, provides these two examples which illustrate the concept (also check out the Intel websites referred to in the endnotes—they provide a good model for enabling massive collaboration).

A) Computer vision technology

One way to provide for self-interest is to make the results of *all* available to *all*. This provides enormous leverage on the relatively small contribution of each innovator and a powerful *self-interest* to sign on.

As an example, Intel created websites for the *Open Computing Vision Library*[49] where contributors could supply code, test and critique code, and potential Intel customer "users" could make suggestions for problems to solve. Approximately *750,000* potential contributors went to the trouble to download the huge file! And 10,000 potential Intel customer users (including BMW, Boeing, NASA, etc.) contributed problems that they believed needed solutions.

Intel started this huge community by proactively building the core in supplying the first code that they had generated internally. They then went to universities and got more code, hence confronting potential contributors and users with a decision: Do you want to do your development independently or with gain the benefit of getting onboard with us? This effort started out like a snowball rolling downhill, picking up more "innovator mass" as it accelerated. Participants shared their problems and code, and did not have to tell what they were using the code for.

One of the major insights Intel gained was: *"Aha, so that is what is important to users!"* Take anti-distortion algorithms, for example. The lens optics of Computer Vision Systems creates distortion, and by looking through the optics at the output created by a standard test pattern, algorithms can be developed that will correct for the system-specific distortion.[50] These algorithms must be general purpose as they are widely used, must execute swiftly, and are a core requirement of potential Intel user customers. Intel's internal R&D might have *recognized* the importance of these algorithms much later, and Intel could never have had the potential coding capacity of 750,000 contributors to create, code and test algorithms that converge swiftly.[51] Self-interest, the ability to invest a little and get a lot, was the motivating force that drove a lot of people and companies to contribute to the solution.

B) *Keeping revenue growth and Moore's Law[52] alive*

Computer Vision is one application that Intel supports because it encourages the need for increasingly powerful microprocessors, effectively creating new demand. If Intel keeps producing new microprocessors whose speed is not required, the company will be overserving the market and could potentially be disrupted on a cost-per-unit-of-product basis (according to the Christensen model). Hence the need for processing-hungry applications of compelling value.

But more powerful microprocessors require more transistors per chip, which means Intel must continually break barriers to higher transistor density. In 1965, Gordon Moore, the cofounder of Intel, postulated based on *just three years* of data that the density of transistors would double every two years ("Moore's Law," *see* figure at top of next page). He presumed that scientists and engineers would *somehow* continue making the necessary technological breakthroughs. The figure shows that this is exactly what happened.

Figure 5-04: Moore's Law

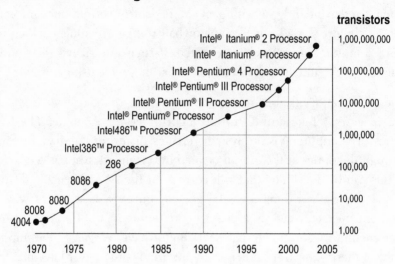

Gordon Moore predicted that the density of transistors would double every two years or so. Actual data matches his prediction.

Recently a new barrier was met: visible light was not fine enough to make the next step in transistor definition. The solution to save the industry's growth and Moore's Law lay in the use of ultraviolet light below 60 nanometers (600Å for older folks). This is about 10 times finer than visible light, and is a domain where glass lenses don't work and reflection optics and diffraction images are used to get the fine detail needed. An enormous investment in both processes and the resulting fabrication equipment was needed to make the higher-density products a reality.

The investment, risk, and need for technical talent are far beyond the resources of any single company, including Intel. Years ago, the industry formed Sematech under government auspices, and under its banner, arch rivals Intel, IBM, AMD, and others cooperated with the likes of Sandia and Livermore Labs to solve many of the UV technical challenges.[53] This provided leverage on each organization's investment, no one was excluded from any result, and the equipment manufacturers were motivated to get onboard quickly.[54] As a result of this and other efforts, Patrick Gelsinger, Chief Technology Officer of Intel, was able to report at the 2004 *Fortune Innovation* conference that Moore's Law is safe until

2012! What would motivate arch rivals to cooperate? In this case, *fear* of being left behind.

The Future of "R" in Corporate R&D

You probably think that Intel has a formidable research capability. They do, but much of it they don't own. While at Fairchild, Intel founders Gordon Moore and Bob Noyce suffered the "glacial swiftness" with which the 600-man R&D operation moved products to production.[55] For example, Fairchild inventors had created a stable MOS (metal oxide semiconductor) product by 1961, yet had not transferred it to production by 1968! And MOS turned out to be the most important technology for the future!

When they founded Intel, Noyce and Moore wanted to eliminate the long delays in transferring new products to production. They solved the problem in part by *eliminating R&D* as a separate entity, instead developing new products *within* production.

While all research departments want to hire the finest graduating PhD students, the environment at Intel is very different. Many new researchers work for six months in manufacturing. Then, if assigned to a development group, they can buy new equipment to develop new chips, but they have to operate that equipment themselves and secure space for it inside an existing production facility.

When Intel has a development or yield problem, it only applies "enough science" internally to solve that specific problem. This is called the **Noyce principle of minimum information**. The approach is to make an intelligent guess at the source of the problem and only develop information that is focused on confirming or denying that hypothesis. If the first hypothesis doesn't work, the learning generally suggests another hypothesis, and the process closes in on the minimum science needed to solve the problem. This approach may not often result in general and profound theories worthy of publication as was the case with Bell Labs; neither does it create a lot of extraneous new business ideas that result in spin-offs. But it solves the immediate need.

In addition to these targeted internal research activities, Intel outsources research by funding university grants (totaling more than $100 million a year) and conducts a variety of activities to promote linkages between its labs and the external research community. Intel assigns employees to interact directly with the students they fund, as well as with the students' professors.

You might wonder what benefit universities can provide Intel, given that semiconductor manufacturing facilities are one of the most capital-intensive processes in the world, costing hundreds of millions of dollars and therefore beyond the investment capabilities of any university. But the R&D process can be parsed into "chunks" of research that can be attacked by the brilliant minds of academia. For example, the plasma etching process can be studied in universities with only modest investments in equipment, and thus can benefit from far more intellectual horsepower than Intel could afford to delegate. The same is true of software development, be it programming parallel processors, RISC studies, or creating design automation software. The company also closely follows the activities of startups in the computer and communications industries through a variety of means that range from informal alliances to corporate venture capital investments. Michael Jensen of Harvard has argued that over the past decade internal research has generally cost more than the value it has created. Management, as stewards of shareholder value, cannot continue this form of investment.

Is the future sounding bleak for pure research? As we've shown, new knowledge created by industrial corporations led to thousands of ground-breaking innovations. Is this vital source of wealth creation irretrievably lost now that companies cannot afford research for research's sake? We are of the judgment that pure knowledge creation for the sake of new knowledge is the purview of universities, research institutions, etc., not for companies that must represent the interests of shareholders. If it is believed that some pure research can potentially benefit the company, then the company ought to contract out the research to a university, institute, or other Open Innovation solver.

The Open Innovation Model leverages, but does not replace, *unique* internal R&D capabilities with the many external sources available through InnoCentive, for example. Internal R&D efforts are freed to focus on disruptive breakthroughs, and on creating exceptional margins and growth rates, without having to shoulder the burden of reinventing every wheel. This is merely process improvement applied to the R&D agenda: redeploying internal investments to unique high-value-add capabilities, and away from what are effectively non-value-add efforts.

Eli Lilly, P&G, and Intel are among the growing number of companies that have come to the conclusion that open innovation provides a strong competitive advantage.

Conclusion

Ask yourself where the next big idea in your industry will come from. If you believe it will come from directed discovery within your company, from your absolutely unique knowledge, then you are well advised to keep your innovation closed, investing in focused internal research activities to increase your chances of finding the next big thing.

If, however, you believe (as we do) that the next big idea is likely to come from the vast world outside your company, then you're better advised to develop the ability to monitor a variety of research sources and to respond quickly to discoveries when and if they arise.[56] Be prepared, however; if your company has a history of closed innovation, making the switch will not be easy for managers, scientists, or developers. Dr. Simon Ramo, who played a central role in the ICBM program, has said:

> Scientists and engineers have a high... preference for attacking each task in an individual, personal way, starting from scratch rather than making use of the results of others.

This preference must be recognized, dealt with constructively, and overcome if the Open Innovation Model is to reach its full potential. It may even mean dropping some lines of research you've begun internally. As fans of Hewlett-Packard, we were thrilled to read an article in the *Wall Street Journal* of August 16, 2004, "Invent Wisely is the New Mantra at Sober H-P." The article revealed that HP had elected to shut down its work on Atomic Resolution Memory.[57] A quick search on Google showed that no fewer than a dozen universities and research institutes were working on similar lines. The probability is very small that HP is uniquely better qualified than the rest of the world to execute this research, and we therefore applaud this difficult decision and hope you'll look to it as a precedent for your own business. The Open Innovation Model is an example of re-use of knowledge created outside your company. In the next chapter we will expand this discussion and conclude that re-use is *the* most powerful engines of Fast Innovation and growth.

Endnotes

42 Patrick Haggerty, *Management Philosophies and Practices of Texas Instruments* (Dallas: Texas Instruments,1965), p. 23.

43 Haggerty, *op. cit.*, p. 56.

44 Moving the operating divisions to Dallas, far away from PARC, and the loss of direct interaction with the prototypes certainly contributed. This move was violently opposed by John Bardeen (the inventor of the transistor) and led to his resignation from the Xerox Board (*see* the book *Genius*).

45 Peter Drucker, *Innovation and Entrepreneurship* (New York: HarperBusiness, 1993), 35.

46 An excellent bibliography on the subject is found at http://www2.sjsu.edu/faculty/watkins/realoptions.htm

47 *Cavuto on Business*, Fox cable news, Jan 8, 2005.

48 http://www.oai.org/pages/Overview.html

49 http://www.intel.com/research/mrl/research/opencv/)

50 http://www.intel.com/technology/computing/sw10021.htm

51 Here is an example of a slow algorithm: do you know what and with a minor tweak of averaging terms, it converges to the same value in 40 terms!

52 http://www.intel.com/research/silicon/mooreslaw.htm

53 ftp://download.intel.com/research/silicon/Chuck%20Gwyn%20Photomask%20Japan%200503.pdf

54 http://www.intel.com/technology/itj/q31998/articles/art_4.htm

55 Richard S. Rosenbloom (ed.) and William J. Spencer (ed.). *Engines of Innovation: U.S. Industrial Research at the End of an Era* (Boston: Harvard Business School Press, 1996), p. 167.

56 Henry Chesbrough, *Open Innovation: The New Imperative for Creating and Profiting from Technology* (Boston: Harvard Business School Press, 2003), pp. 132-33.

57 http://asuaf.org/~joshua/storage/conclusion.html

CHAPTER 6

The Religion of Re-use

Re-use can produce greater schedule and effort savings than any other rapid-development practice. What's more, it can be used by virtually any kind of organization....

Steve McConnell[58]
Rapid Development, Microsoft Series

The Open Innovation Model is an example of the re-use of a capability developed *outside* your company. This chapter will focus on creating a culture where re-using information, designs, processes, etc., *inside* your company is the norm. You will find that Steve McConnell is right: re-use is the most powerful tool to reduce project lead time and effort.

Re-use is an elegant financial contribution to ROIC because it generates a return on intellectual capital that you or someone else already paid for:

> *For example, when P&G decided to move into the home car care business, researchers didn't start from scratch. They looked around P&G for related expertise and struck gold. The company's Pur water filter experts already knew how to de-ionize water, and its Cascade unit knew how to reduce water spots. They used both to create Mr. Clean AutoDry... doubling overall Mr. Clean brand sales.[59]*

Given the advantages conveyed by re-use, it probably comes as no surprise that Toyota is one of its biggest proponents worldwide—which is why they can develop a car in half the time of most other automakers, and with half the resources. Between 60% and 80% of Toyota's designs re-use existing materials, components, assemblies, etc., which dramatically reduces variation in task time as well as the average task time. The Law of Innovation Variation tells us that, with less variation in task time, those innovators can be loaded to a higher utilization rate (recall, it's the tasks with high variation that suffer the most from high utilization rates).

Fred Brooks, project leader of System 360 software development, also discovered the power of re-use, and offers the following cogent advice:

> The most radical solution for constructing software is not to construct it at all. Every day this gets easier... as the PC revolution has created mass markets for software... tools and environments. The re-use of software n times multiplies the productivity of developers by n.[60]

The ability to increase innovator productivity (getting more done in less time) coupled with reduced costs is the reason why re-use is such a valuable tool of Fast Innovation. This chapter looks at what it takes to achieve re-use and what that investment will get you.

Why Re-use?: To become faster and more differentiated

We started the chapter with the powerful assessment from Steve McConnell of Microsoft:

> Re-use can produce greater schedule and effort savings than any other rapid-development practice. What's more, it can be used by virtually any kind of organization....

The Laws of Lead Time and Innovation Variation, introduced in Chapter 3, allows us to estimate how much benefit re-use will yield:

Law of Lead Time: The average completion rate per task is significantly increased if you re-use previous knowledge. If the existing "something" (product, service, programming code, etc.) perfectly suits the new use, the design time for that element will be reduced to near zero. If you have to modify (then test and adjust) the re-used element, the time saved may drop to 50%. The reduction in time per task effectively increases the average completion rate. As shown in the Law of Lead Time:

$$\text{Average Lead Time of Any Process} = \frac{\text{Number of Things-in-Process}}{\text{Average Completion Rate}}$$

If we can double the average completion rate, we will *potentially* cut the average lead time in half. But the savings depend partly on the mix of new vs. re-use design work that occurs. In the data we have on software development, for example, re-use sped up lead time only when less than 25% of the source lines of code needed to be modified. Beyond that point the time savings from re-use were swamped by the extra time needed to modify code. As Steve McConnell points out, people often overestimate the reduction in task time that re-use will effect—but what it will *definitely* do is reduce the upside variation in task time beyond the mean (making it easier to plan for resource use and estimate completion time). Initially, consider any completion rate improvement a bonus. Until you've mastered re-use, we suggest you keep your staffing levels constant and focus on the impact of the reduced variation as we'll discuss next.

Law of Innovation Variation: With re-use, the probability of meeting specs without a significant overrun of the time estimate is very high because you already know it has worked before. In the case of a "from scratch" innovation, you don't really *know* if you can meet specs at all. The benefits of less variation in task time was discussed in Chapter 3.

The re-use perk: more focus on differentiators

Since re-use frees up development time, the natural instinct might be to reduce staffing levels. The better strategy is to apply any extra development energy to creating more "customer delighters" since differentiation or its lack determines the success or doom of an innovation. If you keep staffing levels constant, you can complete projects more quickly and launch the next new project sooner. This is a critical advantage because we want to introduce a new innovation before the competition commoditizes the existing offering, as discussed in Chapter 1.

Even re-using previous designs, there is still a modest amount of variation in the time it takes to integrate the re-used element into the new design. In some of its development efforts, Toyota has reportedly re-used up to 80% of parts from previous products. Achieving the 80% level means that only 20% of any new product (or service) needs to be designed from scratch, and only that 20% will suffer from high levels of variation. The other 80% (built around re-used elements) will have about one-quarter as much variation.

Forcing a high level of re-use gives an overall variation of about 60% less than if everything was done from scratch. At 60% less variation, the equations built into the Law of Innovation Variation (*see* Appendix 1) indicate that overall lead time will thus be cut by about 80%. This agrees with data from Toyota, and it leads to the **80-80-80 Rule**:

> *If an innovation consists of 80% re-use, then*
> *lead time can be cut by 80% at 80% average utilization*

We emphasize the average, because the Critical Resources applied to the 20% of the from-scratch tasks must be utilized at no more than 65% of capacity; the resources applied to the other 80% of the tasks will encounter small variation and can be operated at 85% utilization.

If you cannot get to 80% re-use, don't despair. Many of the other methods described in this book—the use of cross-trained resources, Innovation Blitzes, and Design for Lean Six Sigma techniques—can still help you achieve an 80% reduction in average lead time.

Platforms and Operating Cost Efficiency: An organizing principle for re-use

Re-use can often best be organized as part of **platform design**:

> *A family of different models is generated using a high percentage of common subcomponents. The differences between models is restricted to those elements that create differentiation in the eyes of the customer.*

In addition to reducing the time to develop new extensions of the platform, there are important operating cost advantages to a platform design in terms of replication cost efficiency.

Here's a quick example: Coauthor Mike George was the CEO of International Power Machines, which provided uninterruptible power supply units to protect sensitive equipment like computers from power failures. The company had begun with a 5-kilowatt design, and as customer's loads grew, had added models with seven power ratings between 10kW and 80kW. Each unit had been designed by a different engineer at a different time, and had very few parts in common. As shown in Figure 6-01, the number of different internal part numbers grew in direct proportion to the number of ratings.

Figure 6-01: Explosion of Part Numbers at IPM

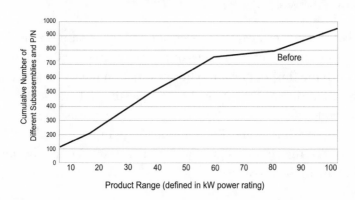

Mike believed that the high number of unique parts (complexity in the designs) was the cause of the company's poor profits and long development times. Consequently, IPM decided to redesign all of these units around common mechanical, electrical wiring and control logic modules. Less than 10% of the components were unique and were related to the power ratings (transformers, filters, thyristors) that the customer valued. The result was much fewer part numbers (*see* lower line on Figure 6-02, next page) and much better financial results.

Figure 6-02: Impact of Platforms at IPM

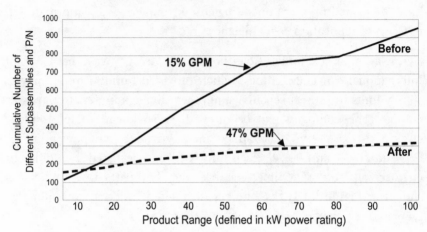

Design commonality reduced part numbers by 67% and increased Gross Profit Margin by 32%.

The platform was created with extension to higher ratings in mind. The engineering effort to create ratings of 100kW, 120kW, 160kW took about one-fourth the time of previous efforts. Variation in task time was significantly reduced, especially in qualification testing… because they started with an offering where 90% of the performance was already proven. Over the next few years, IPM's gross profit more than doubled (*see* Figure 6-02), the company grew at 25% per year, went public, and was acquired by Rolls-Royce.

Many successful companies have embedded platforms into their design mentality, but others have not:

> *On Planet Detroit, automakers used to pride themselves on reinventing the wheel with every model. In 1999, when former Chrysler CEO Bob Eaton introduced the Jeep Grand Cherokee, he proudly held up a bag that he said contained all of the carryover parts. His point was that this Jeep was practically a whole new animal.*[61]

Chrysler did beat all the naysayers last year with the new Hemi engine, the only one of the Big Three to increase market share.[62] But this performance can only be sustained by a rapid repeat of this success. Re-use frees up engineering resources to pursue differentiation, and the problem is not limited to Chrysler. General Motors' slumping revenue is due in large part to "an aging line-up" of cars and trucks, that "are just not good enough to stand out in today's highly competitive market."[63] GM's Bob Lutz has said, "If you don't have exciting, stimulating world class product, you will fail," and we wish him well in saving this American icon.[64]

If you have to design 100% of the car instead of 20%, you have exposure to five times as much variation. With re-use, you win in four ways:

1) You avoid long lead times that would result from the inevitable variation in design tasks

2) You can run a large subset of your development teams *at nearly 80% of capacity* on relatively non-challenging tasks

3) You reduce the average time to develop a new product or service by about 50% (because 80% of the design is already proven or is a modification of an existing design)

4) You can use smaller teams and eliminate communication problems (*see* sidebar, p. 121)

Another example of platform use to improve innovation speed comes from Scania Truck.[65] Although not well known in North America, this Swedish truck manufacturer has leading market share in many parts of the world, including Brazil. Although they have about the same lineup

Avoid the need to tweak

Emery Powell of Texas Instruments offers the following words of caution:

The temptation to tweak reusable modules to "make them just a little better" destroys re-use gains fast. I've seen re-use gains destroyed time after time because an engineer decides to just "slightly tweak" a standard module and thereby creates subsequent problems.

Clay Christensen has noted that this tendency to tweak for maximum performance is often necessary in the early stages of a product, but that as component performance increases, modularity becomes possible, yet the desire to tweak remains.

of trucks as Daimler-Chrysler, they have *half as many* different components because they have practiced the Religion of Re-use for many decades. The Scania archive is essentially a large matrix with components on one axis and end items on the other. Every component is rated by a percentage of re-use across different end items. If a new truck must be designed, and no existing component will serve, effort is made to design a new component such that it back-fits within and obsoletes the nearest functional equivalent. Thanks in part to strategies like this, Scania has compiled a record 43 straight years of profitable operations, unique in their industry.

Overcoming Resistance to Re-use: A case study

Given all the benefits, you would think managers would enthusiastically adopt, not resist, re-use. Such is generally not the case. First of all, most of the benefits of re-use can only be understood if people understand the Laws of Lead Time and Innovation Variation, and these are unknown to most managers. Secondly, the problem of local optimization rears its ugly head with its usual "rational" justification.

Bob Bauer of the Xerox Palo Alto Research Center (PARC) shared the following re-use success story and the resistance that re-use initially faced. Xerox copiers all require a controller and scheduler. At one time, eight different product teams were separately writing their own controller/scheduler software, as was a team in research and another in development (for a total of 10 teams). Some engineers got the idea that they could write most of the code in common modules that could, to varying degrees, be re-used in all 10 products, reducing lead time, cost, and lifecycle maintenance costs.

The engineers on the different product teams were enthusiastic, but when they went back to their managers, the reaction was generally unsupportive. Why? Because each manager had to manage risk against a schedule with limited resources and was not motivated or rewarded to take additional time or resources to work on projects outside of their own scope. If the development of a platform is going to cost their

Mature re-use and the value of small teams

After you have created a re-use database and a re-use retrieval/application process, you will begin seeing significant reductions in mean task time as well as in variation. One of the side benefits of a mature re-use process is that you will need fewer resources to attain a given project lead time. Apart from lower cost, there are important differentiation benefits based on improved communication. The value of having small teams is reinforced by many leading innovation thinkers, who have each stated it in their own way.

Brooks' Law (from the leader of software development at IBM): The delays due to communications rise as the square of the number of people on the team. Adding people to a late project just makes it later.[66]

Bezos' Law of Two Pizzas (from the CEO of Amazon): "To the extent that you can get people in development teams small enough that they can be fed on two pizzas, you'll get a lot more productivity."

Chambers' Law of World Class (from the CEO of Cisco): "I try to hire one engineer who is absolutely world class for a particular business. That one world class individual will attract four more world class engineers. These five will accomplish more than 100 mediocre engineers."

Buca's Law of "Gilligan's Island" (from an innovation enabler at Parker Hannifin): "I try not to have more people on any team than were on Gilligan's Island. That keeps the team small enough that you can work quickly, but diverse enough to have many different viewpoints represented."

budgets more money and time—to the benefit of some other product—they won't support the effort. This is the common and expected reaction. And in fact nearly all the different product team managers refused to allow their engineers to spend any time building the platform.

However, Mark Webster at PARC was determined to drive this effort to a successful conclusion, as were 20 or so of the engineers who knew it was the right thing to do and who decided to use three days of their personal vacation time to meet and begin the platform design. Mark agreed to host the meeting and paid airfare when necessary (some of the product managers refused to pay airfare to Palo Alto), and the 20 engineers got started. The result of this initial effort showed that the premise was correct, common scheduler and controller modules could be designed, and this allowed the engineers to gain the buy-in of their management to spend time designing the platform. The next meeting was attended by 100 engineers, and the next by 150.

Despite the "bootleg" beginnings, the amount of platform controller/scheduler software in any given copier is now as high as 95%, with a minimum of 27%. Now Xerox has an Open Source intranet to share designs. The Xerox story has a happy ending. Re-use became institutionalized in the corporation. Mark Webster comments (Jan 4, 2005):

> *My role has become formalized. In 1997 I became the software architect for the IGen print station. Additional programs were added over the following years until it now includes most of the print stations delivered by the Production Systems Group. We still do architecture the same way—I do not have a formal architecture group reporting to me. Instead, I work with the managers to create short-lived teams of implementers to work on the scheduled feature designs. Because the design teams include implementers from multiple programs, this process has resulted in a common print station architecture with a minimum of program-specific extensions. It has also created a technical ladder, where implementers that show good design skills first participate on the design teams, then lead the simpler design teams, and eventually may end up leading the trickiest designs with impact across the entire Xerox Corporation. Essentially, this is the formalization of the community of practice.*

Given the enormous benefits of re-use, how do we overcome the barriers that Xerox so narrowly surmounted? The structure of most businesses will drive rational business unit managers to focus on their own priorities ahead of those of the broader organization. This focus is often valuable, but often is not. To solve the problem, we encourage clients to create a corporate means of funding the establishment of re-use design elements so that the budgets of individual projects are enhanced rather than penalized by the higher initial costs of re-use. (*See* the discussion of a Chief Innovation Officer in Chapter 8.)

How re-use is shaping the Army's Future Combat System

The U.S. Government and its contractors are very focused on innovation lead time reduction, in large part because the new global security threats require far greater mobility and communication. If you want speed and flexibility, re-use is the way to go.

For example, the Future Combat System (FCS)[67] is the core building block of the future Army's transformation to a modular structure with enhanced lethality, mobility, and agility. This structure will replace the current Brigade structure, which will transform into organizations identified as Units of Action, consisting of FCS capabilities enabled through 18 individual systems networked via a common operating environment, battle command software, intelligence, reconnaissance, and surveillance. The systems include the soldier, ground sensors, unmanned aerial and ground vehicles, armed robotic vehicles, manned ground vehicles, and intelligent munitions systems.

The approach being used by the Army and lead system integrators Boeing and SAIC applies many principles discussed in this book. For example, Claude Bolton, Assistant Secretary of the Army (acquisition, logistics and technology), advised that the software systems will consist of approximately 30 million source lines of code (cf. the software to support *all* systems for the space shuttle was about 25 million lines of code).

Bolton suggested that coauthor Mike George visit Brigadier General Charles Cartwright, whose staff reported that 40% of the code is planned to come from re-use or originate with commercial software. This level of re-use will dramatically reduce the risk to the schedule (per the Laws of Lead Time and Innovation Variation). In addition:

1) The specification and acquisition process is evolutionary, not frozen, and

2) All subcontractors are able to codevelop over the FCS Advanced Collaborative Environment (ACE) through the internet. ACE serves as not only an online repository for program documents but also as the main tool utilized to manage program data and issues.

Using "External" Platforms to Capture Customers

The previous examples have all dealt with *internal* platforms: common design elements that are essentially invisible to the customer, and create a high degree of commonality with product or service lines, yet allow delivery of differentiation desired by the customer. Such internal platforms have their complement in *external* platform designs: product or service architectures that are visible to (and hopefully sought by) customers.

Perhaps the most famous and widely experienced external platform is Microsoft Office, which was one of the first software programs to integrate word processing, spreadsheet, presentation, and other applications. Mike George recalls his amazement when he first used the Office products on Windows 3.0. "Prior to that, I had achieved comparable functionality for my personal needs with three separate programs: Lotus 123, WordPerfect, and Harvard Graphics. Like most CEOs, my computer skills were (and are) rudimentary, and I was always fumbling with the different menus and often had to relearn functions I hazily remembered using. That I could suddenly use common menus and copy portions of one application into another was thrilling!" By bundling all these compatible products together at lower prices, Windows/Office captured 90% of the market by 2000.

Another good example resides in how Intel came to dominate microprocessors. While Intel was first to market with an 8-bit microprocessor, Motorola won the Apple business, and soon Zilog, Fairchild, and TI were far ahead of Intel with a 16-bit microprocessor.

How could Intel counterattack and regain market position? Al Yu relates:

> *The key objective for the task force was to come up with crisp and forceful presentations on Intel's microprocessor strength...*
> *This important marketing program, named the "Crush" campaign, was the most comprehensive marketing campaign that Intel had ever put together. The goal was nothing short of winning the 16-bit microprocessor race....*

Our message was simple: "We have the complete products for you, from chips to development systems to comprehensive support. We have a clear product road map into the future that you can depend on for your new products. We are committed to providing software compatibility of our future microprocessors to protect your investments. We will provide you with leading technology and high quality. Come with us."[68]

Intel put together a road map of all future products, based on a single platform all the way to a 32-bit microprocessor. A former colleague at TI was exasperated that the "inferior" Intel 16-bit microprocessor was beating the TI chip in the marketplace. TI had no platform concept to guide the customer's future! Who at Intel, you ask, could ever forget a monumental come-from-behind victory like that?

However, the commitment to platform thinking must be part of a *formal innovation* training process which we recommend for each generation of manager, engineer and all other innovators. In Chapter 2 we discussed Intel's failure to develop a 64-bit Pentium chip. In fact it was really a failure to remember the powerful lessons of the "crush" campaign. Pentium customers saw 64-bit as an option for the future. They were willing to spend more to get it now so that if they wanted to run 64-bit software *sometime in the life of that platform* it would be there… which of course was the very essence of the "crush." Despite Intel's very existence in the microprocessor market being owed to the platform strategy, the 64-bit Pentium chip was not pursued, and *Intel had to play catch-up* with AMD!

A new generation of engineers at Intel nearly blew another huge technology advantage with Centrino, again by not wanting to use a platform concept. Paul Otellini reports:[69]

We had what was unquestionably the world's best processor for Notebook PCs. But the engineers wanted that chip out there. However, I made a decision early on that we were going to launch this as a platform. That was a business decision that overrode a technical desire. In hindsight, that business decision, at $5 billion of Centrino chips and running, was a good decision.

Rather than just sell a processor, the Centrino platform included a processor, a chipset, a Wi-Fi chip, and often other parts that customers otherwise might have purchased from different manufacturers. As the new CEO, Otellini has reorganized the company into five divisions designed around the platform mandate to serve high-growth markets. Potentially, this reorganization will give Intel an opportunity to sell processors to the cell phone companies that currently buy its flash memory but few microprocessors. Reuters reported that, at the February 2005 Intel Developer's Conference:

> One buzzword certain to make its mark at the show is "platform." Intel executives have begun to use that word at seemingly every occasion to explain the company's new strategy of selling not just single products, but bundles of chips, hardware and software.[70]

This is the kind of response that is a prerequisite to preventing events like that of AMD disrupting Intel in X86 processors.

Conclusion

It is an executive responsibility—preferably a Chief Innovation Officer (p. 177) or similar position—to champion re-use because you will encounter a lot of resistance. For example:

- Re-use in general and platforms in particular do not come free. They exact an incremental upfront cost that any individual developer of the platform cannot afford to pay. Xerox had your best interests in mind when they agreed to share their experience with having to develop re-usable platforms as almost an underground effort because the business unit managers involved were focused on the impact on their individual budgets and timelines. That is the norm, not the exception. We do not fault the individual managers; they are just the doing the job they're paid to do. Rather, it is the job of the CEO or P&L manager to create a way to fund the initial cost of platform design at the corporate level, since it is the corporation that is the biggest winner.

What about scientific innovation in the wild blue?

The last bastion of opposition to re-use usually comes from scientists who honestly believe that they are engaged in the creative unknown. Let us grant them the position that no one on the planet has *specific subject matter* knowledge that can be of assistance. We can then attempt to open their minds to re-use by considering the *process* of a person who is *at least* their intellectual peer, even though the subject matter is different.

A few creative geniuses have told us not only *what* they achieved but also the tortuous process *by which* they achieved it. Foremost among these is the mathematician Leonard Euler (pronounced "Oiler") who meticulously recorded his every blind alley and false start on his road to each discovery.[71] He made so many discoveries that historians started naming his formulas after the *second* person who discovered them! What we find in all of Euler's descriptions of his struggles is a common line of attack which starts with:

- Have I ever seen a problem like this before?
- Have I ever seen a related problem?
- Can I apply that solution if I restate my problem?

Thus Euler was always trying to **re-use a previously solved problem**, a method outlined in the famous little book *How to Solve It* by George Polya. Euler argued that most solutions to problems come from reasoning from analogies from other problems, i.e., re-use!

The point is that even though no one has ever tackled this problem, maybe someone can suggest an analogy! And as Chris Schmid of Eli Lilly said, there is little potential harm in posing the problem anonymously and with suitable cover on the internet.

Historically, the new product/service development mindset has been one of invention (creating new things) rather than of innovation (creating new things that add value to the customer and company). Changing this basic mindset is key to speeding up innovative creativity and to delivering the best new offerings to your customers.

- Individual innovators may be concerned that their professional status or rating will suffer if they divert attention away from creating new knowledge to re-using existing design elements.

The effort needed to overcome this resistance is well worth the effort because re-use can dramatically reduce lead time-to-market (as a result of the Law of Innovation Variation and of Lead Time). The 80-80-80 rule (*see* Figure 6-03)—you can reduce lead times by 80% with 80% re-use and an average utilization of 80%—provides a strong rational motivation to accept re-use. Re-use also helps reduce operational costs.

Figure 6-03: The 80-80-80 Rule

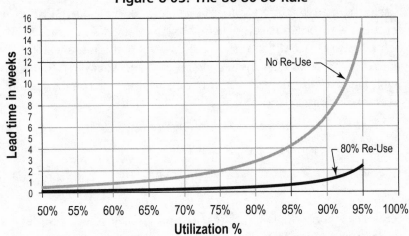

Furthermore, manifestation of re-use in the form of a platform concept has both internal cost and external customer benefits. That a customer can plan their own future, know that their investment is protected, and understand how they can guide their own innovation efforts is a powerful differentiation feature beyond any one performance parameter!

Endnotes

58 Steve McConnell, *Rapid Development* (Redmond, WA: Microsoft Press, 1996), p. 527.

59 "Building an Idea Factory," *Business Week On-Line*, Oct 11, 2004.

60 Frederick P. Brooks, *The Mythical Man-Month: Essays on Software Engineering,20th Anniversary Edition* (Reading, MA: Addison-Wesley Professional, 1995), p. 198.

61 *Fortune*, Feb. 2004, "Detroit Buffs Up."

62 *Barron's*, Mar. 21, 2005, pp. 13 and 20.

63 *Barron's*, Feb, 28, 2005, p. 24.

64 *Barron's*, *ibid.*, p. 27.

65 H. Thomas Johnson and Anders Bröms, *Profit Beyond Measure: Extraordinary Results through Attention to Work and People* (New York: The Free Press, 2000).

66 Brooks, *op. cit.* (*see* note 60).

67 http://www.army.mil/fcs/

68 Albert Yu, *Creating the Digital Future: The Secrets of Consistent Innovation at Intel* (New York: Simon & Schuster,1998), pp. 24-26.

69 *Wall Street Journal*, Jan. 12, 2005, p. B1.

70 http://www.reuters.co.in/locales/ c_newsArticle.jsp?type=technologyNews&localeKey=en_IN&storyID=7749689

71 Euler appears on the Swiss 10 franc note.

SPOTLIGHT ON

Leading Innovation

In the Preface and Chapter 1 we presented statistics that showed that 90% of companies cannot sustain growth in revenue or above-average returns for a decade—despite the fact that innovation-driven growth is at the top of most CEOs' priorities. This contradiction indicates there are powerful forces at work opposing sustained growth and innovation. These forces are both hidden and unconscious—after all, nobody says, "I'm against innovation and growth." So where do these forces come from and how can we overcome them?

In our analysis of growth, we found that obstacles to growth differed depending on which dimension and what type of innovation was in question. Here are the highlights:

(a) Sustaining product/service innovation:

Situation: Sustaining innovations are preferred by incumbent management because they are low risk, have predictable volumes and profits, are sold to existing important customers, and are amenable to NPV analysis.

Problem: Innovation outcomes are unreliable. Process may be too slow, too variable and/or deliver offerings that are quickly commoditized. Any growth and above-average returns will be *temporary and unreliable.*

Solution: Need a Fast Innovation process to create a new innovation just as commoditization attacks the previous innovation (as discussed in Chapter 1).

(b) Disruptive product/service innovation

Situation: Higher risk; volumes and profits not predictable; important current customers may have no interest in the innovation; not amenable to NPV analysis.

Problem: Incumbent managers, in denial about the threat and/or counterattack with existing core competencies, entirely missing the economic profit window. Even if the disruption seems a good idea, there is no mechanism to execute. Process for delivering any innovation to the market is too slow, costly and unreliable.

Solution: Need an alternative way to develop disruptive innovations to prevent any single organizational unit from bearing the financial and resource risks; develop a new structure outside the incumbent organizational funding and operational structures (*see* the discussion of the Real Options funding approach, p. 188). Use Fast Innovation approaches to ensure fast, reliable time-to-market.

(c) Market definition, process/business model innovation

Situation: Innovation thinkers often currently reside within fairly narrow disciplines (R&D, development, etc.).

Problem: As a result, few companies are incorporating these other dimensions as part of the strategic innovation planning.

Solution: Assign resources to study and stimulate cross-functional analysis of multidimensional innovation opportunities.

If you look closely at the three sets of solutions proposed here, you'll see that they have one thing in common: they all will require significant change and a strong leadership engagement to make that change happen. Thus Fast Innovation really must be a *leadership initiative,* coming from and actively supported by the CEO and senior management. It is their responsibility to **enable innovation** within the company, or their company will never reach the goals of long-term above-average returns.

In this Spotlight, we'll look first at a few examples of CEOs and leadership teams who have successfully driven innovation in their companies. We'll then look at what characteristics these executives often display, and specific actions needed to build a strong support system for innovation.

Disruptive Innovations Where CEO Presence Was Necessary

Sometimes the CEO or P&L manager must take a very direct hand in driving a *disruptive* innovation to a successful conclusion. This is always appropriate when the company has an opportunity for a huge increase in growth, and where failure means being crushed by a competitor who succeeds with that innovation. Here are four examples of these cases where hands-on executive action was necessary:

Success case #1: Progressive Insurance and the drive for customer centricity

The leader must drive the rest of the organization to listen to the customer. It is only then that "customer obsession" can begin. Peter Lewis, former CEO of Progressive Insurance, described an interaction with customers that led him to Progressive's famous innovation of providing rate quotes for the competition. Lewis sat with customers and listened to their concerns about the auto insurance market not being competitive. Lewis, who experienced the tough competition every day, said, "You're crazy. There are 350 insurance companies. If we move our price just a little bit, it changes the flow of business dramatically. It is, therefore, competitive. I actually came to the edge of being angry enough to walk out."

But Lewis eventually got the message from his customers: they did not trust that the industry was open and fair about pricing. As a result, Lewis personally drove the new innovation (to provide multiple price quotes from its competitors), despite significant opposition from his team. Do you think this innovation would have ever happened had Lewis not had direct customer knowledge and the determination to overcome obstacles?

Success case #2. Dell and the direct connection to the customer

Before the internet was used commercially, during 1992 and 1993, Michael Dell personally understood the need of his largest customers to be able to have a simple, convenient way to order large numbers of PCs with their own configuration and options. Dell relentlessly drove his marketing and technology teams to find ways to give large customers the ability to place their orders for PCs from their desktops, without having to interact every time with a customer service representative.

The early pre-internet prototypes for "automated ordering" were, in retrospect, truly awful. They required that Dell send a desktop computer to each major customer with the ordering/configurator software loaded. Then, to keep up with pricing, availability and configurations, a new database would have to be shipped each week to the customer on a removable zip drive. When prototypes of the new system were shared with Dell's largest corporate customers, the response was underwhelming at best. At this point the initiative could have lost steam, and in fact more than one key manager tried to kill it. But Michael continued to drive his team to satisfy the customer need. When the internet began to become commercially viable, Dell was ready. With an automated front end and a supply chain that could deliver any product in three days, the cost of the distribution and dealer markup was eliminated, and the process/business model innovations (p. 78) conveyed a 30% cost advantage that led to the toppling of Compaq as industry leader.

Success case #3. Amazon and customer-driven resource allocation

This leadership support, nurturing and protection must extend to the early launch stages of a new innovation. Jeff Bezos of Amazon recognizes the risks of the status quo destroying the new and innovative: "When you have something big—our retail business—and something small—our then-emerging marketplace business—it is hard to get people focused on the little thing, no matter how strategically important it is. People are incredibly busy, and they simply have bigger fish to fry most of the time."

As a testament to Amazon's ability to nurture new innovations, note that the marketplace segment, introduced in 2000, now represents 28% of Amazon's total unit volume. Moreover, Amazon has been able to continue to introduce new categories at a rate of about three per year over the last five years, and for the first time (in Q304), consumer electronics surpassed books as Amazon's largest category. Bezos has made a number of contributions to Amazon's innovation along several dimensions, all enabled by his Law of Two Pizzas (discussed on p. 121), which drives small team size, which in turn increases creativity and enables speed.

Success case #4. "The Most Disruptive Innovation of the 20th Century"

The Minuteman I missile, as discussed on p. 29, used discrete transistors which resulted in a large, heavy, power-hungry guidance system. Texas Instruments, faced with this fabulous new challenge, was awarded an Air Force study contract for finding smaller and lighter alternatives. TI innovator Jack Kilby had conceived of the Integrated Circuit (IC), and based on his study the Air Force had determined that IC would cut the weight and volume of the guidance system by a factor of four and double guidance accuracy. The whole future of the IC therefore depended on entirely satisfying the U.S. Air Force—and a fabulous future for the IC could even then be dimly seen over the horizon.

We now want to discuss the role that the executive (or Chief Innovation Officer surrogate) must be prepared to play in disruptive innovation. The technical challenges of creating ICs were immense and the project was completely stalled! There were five levels of management between Kilby and the TI president, Pat Haggerty. Nevertheless, Haggerty swept everyone out of his way and effectively became the program manager of the effort, focusing enormous talent on unexpected[72] problems that threatened disaster. TI won both the patent for the IC and the huge Minuteman II contract, just barely beating Bob Noyce's technically superior team at Fairchild. Jack Kilby subsequently won the Nobel Prize in Physics for the accomplishment. TI's leadership position in semiconductors was maintained for two decades until the '70s, when Not Invented Here caused them to be late to the MOS revolution, and the mantle of industry leader irrevocably passed to Intel.

Recommendation: We recognize that the CEO is a busy person, often running a mammoth enterprise, and that the level of focus in these case studies is difficult if not dangerous for the business. We therefore recommend the creation of a Chief Innovation Officer, who speaks with the voice of the CEO, and who has the time, the energy and the passion to take on these initiatives, as discussed in Chapter 8.

Characteristics of an Innovation-Enabling Executive

You can find a good description of desired leadership characteristics in Jim Collins' book *Good to Great*. Our own experience with executives over the last 20 years has generally confirmed Collins' insights about what leadership really means. We've built on his work to derive a list of traits that will help managers successfully lead innovation.

The overarching goal is to create a company capable of both sustaining and disruptive innovation. That requires:

Trust: Change involves risk, and risk will be taken only by employees who trust their managers and executives. The innovation-enabling executive nurtures the change process and encourages calculated risk-taking. The innovation-enabling executive creates trust among peers and subordinates that he or she will support and nurture their efforts, will accept good failures, will encourage learning, and will not fear great achievers.

Intellectual curiosity: The courage to experiment and pilot new ideas, giving these seeds the support they need to germinate. The executive must actively fight hubris and the unspoken but universally powerful and malignant force of Not Invented Here. Curiosity extends from exploring the marketplace horizons to continuously pushing to deeply understand the Heart of the Customer.

Integrity: Puts the company's success first, willing to let his or her operation become a cash cow to finance disruptive innovation.

Belief in a better future: Faces reality, can admit that current performance is not good enough, and has the honesty to see that it could be better—a *lot* better. This specifically means cutting innovation lead times by 50% and sustaining twice the growth rate of the markets he or she serves.

A demand for results: Integrates the CEO's burning platform on growth into the reality of operating plans, and creates metrics and a review process to make the plan happen.

Knowledge of the demands of Fast Innovation: Learns the Fast Innovation process, understands the biggest drivers of long time-to-market (per the Law of Lead Time and the Law of Innovation Variation) and supports them by thought, word, deed, and energetic action. (More details on these demands are in Part II.)

When we study the few companies whose innovations and growth strategies have succeeded in sustaining growth rates for more than a decade, we find that these leadership qualities are those that CEOs demand in their management teams.

On the other side of the coin, look at the 90% of companies that have failed to sustain above-average growth in shareholder value for more than a decade. In all cases the failure can be linked to a failure of *one or more* of these leadership qualities. We also find that when successful companies have had a change of command resulting in a violation of these principles, above-average returns swiftly disappear.

This list is really just an innovation-specific version of business integrity, and is reminiscent of Warren Buffett's remarks to the MBA students at Columbia University:

> *A manager must have three qualities:*
> *1. intellect*
> *2. energy*
> *3. integrity*
> *and if he doesn't have the last one, the first two will kill you!*

Defining the Burning Platform

The fact is that the innovation and growth processes are not sustained or healthy in most companies. Like cancer, ineffective innovation silently kills potential revenue growth and operating profit. Ineffective innovators blame irrational customers and competitors for failure, instead of looking at the real culprit: their lack of knowledge of the true causes—lack of leadership, poor capture of the Heart of the Customer, long lead times, lack of differentiation, poor operational innovation and execution, poor lifecyle cost control, or their unwillingness to commit to the difficult task of changing internal mindsets, policies, and processes.

And like cancer, ineffective innovation spreads through the organization unless the business leader steps in and becomes its champion. Ineffective innovation is often diagnosed late, when a catastrophic event suddenly imperils the patient's life. Some companies, like TI, Xerox, Intel (in memory chips), and IBM, fortunately survived their cancer and resurrected the companies—but many have not. Still, experiencing catastrophe, near death, and resurrection is not pleasant for anyone and is certainly not a risk that shareholders deserve.

Fast Innovation involves critical strategic actions that are exclusively in the domain of executives, and often cannot and must not be delegated, any more than can shareholder value. Part II discusses a wide range of specific policies and practices that comprise Fast Innovation, but before you begin to think about implementation, by far the most important leadership issue is defining the burning platform message that explains in simple terms why your company *must* get better at innovation. Recall Jeff Immelt's terse message for GE ("we are just a moment away from commodity hell"). Whirlpool says "Innovation Everywhere and From Everyone."And maybe you've heard that "Apple's DNA is innovation."

There are so many potential and often hidden barriers to strong growth through innovation that we recommend that management teams spend offsite time as a team defining the growth and ROIC rates needed to achieve a significantly higher share price multiple, and then spend another day learning the Fast Innovation process, and finally thinking through the challenges that implementation would encounter in their organization.

Before the meeting, collect data you can share at the retreat:

- Current mix of sustaining vs. disruptive innovations and significant lost opportunities

- Build an innovation dimensions map

- Gap analysis benchmarking organic growth rates and ROIC over the past five years for you, your principal competitors, and the market in general

- Evaluate the percentage of innovation revenue in each of the three dimensions for the last five years, with an estimate of potential opportunity for the future

- Restate your financial performance over the last five years had innovation lead times been reduced by 50% and success rates increased to 80%; indicate which innovation dimensions would have been affected

- Estimate resulting economic profit% of each P&L center

- Roll up restated range of share price performance

> **Getting the right people on the bus**
>
> To the extent that managers or other leaders in your company *cannot* become innovation enablers, it is the duty of the CEO to follow Jim Collins' advice in *Good to Great:*
>
> > get the right people
> > on the bus and
> > the wrong people off

This reflection on the past is not intended to serve as an indictment but rather a chance to consider what could have been and what could be. We are reminded of the great Japanese proverb: *"When is the best time to plant a tree? 20 years ago! When is the second best time to plant a tree? Today!"*

These figures will drive home the lesson that you *can be a lot better* than you have been and are today, and will provide the foundation for your burning platform message. The message should include a metric that everyone can understand, for example: *Our goal is organic growth of 10% per year with ROIC>WACC+5%.*

The alternative is to remain with the 90% of companies who cannot sustain average shareholder returns for more than a decade.

Having created a burning platform message and achieved management buy-in, you are prepared for deployment, which is the subject of Part II of this book.

Endnote

72 As just one example, when the usual Gold bonding wires were used to connect to the Aluminum metallization on the chip, a mysterious high failure rate occurred, which got worse the longer you tested the chip! This "purple plague" slowly grew, could not be detected electrically, but ultimately caused a mechanical failure. The solution required a clever metallurgical solution, and at the time metallurgy was far from a "core competency"!

Recap of Fast Innovation

Most companies today are operating in **slow innovation mode:**

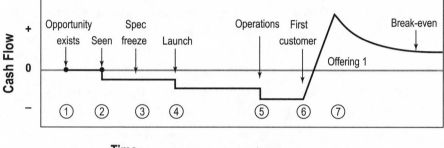

1) Small investment in sales and marketing intelligence, surveys, focus groups is applied, and is usually limited to the product/service dimension of innovation.

2) The opportunity is seen, and a few marketing and technical people, with varying degrees of customer input, write a business case.

3) The business case is accepted and the performance specification is frozen, compromising potential differentiation and potentially lengthening schedule.

4) The project is launched without regard to its impact on the lead time of previously launched innovation projects. Customer feedback in regard to performance changes is not sought during development.

5) The offering is transferred to operations who must make the offering conform to the delivery process, requiring iterations and rework. Marketing may demand late modifications to meet customer demand, requiring more iterations.

6) The offering is delivered to the first customer.

7) Margins are low because the offering is late and commoditization has already set in, and differentiation is not optimal because of the

early freeze and lack of customer corrections of performance during development. Revenue is disappointing because customers are looking at Offering 2.

Disruptive Offerings: Ignored, or attacked with improvements from existing technology or offerings (the Compactron reaction), resulting in failure to enter a new offering segment and potentially destroying operating profit potential.

Fast Innovation changes the equation entirely. Here is a visual depiction of the 10 biggest effects of Fast Innovation.

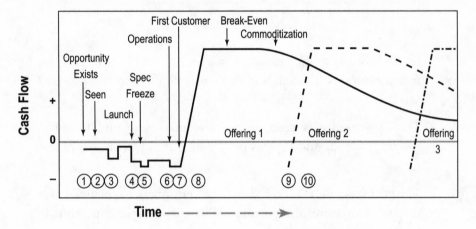

(Fast Innovation tools and concepts in **bold** letters)

1) Investment in **ethnographic** observation of customers, and a focus on **small peripheral and lead users** will detect more opportunities along all **three dimensions** of innovation.

2) Opportunities will be **seen and evaluated earlier** and more reliably than is possible by solely relying on less expensive surveys, focus groups, marketing and sales inputs, valuable though these may be.

3) An **Innovation Blitz** is launched to prove the potential for the Innovation and to reduce lead time and improve accuracy of the business case.

4) The innovation is launched only when the requirements of the **Laws of Lead Time and Utilization,** as implemented in the **FastGate™** process (p. 287), prove that the lead time of projects already in development will not be compromised by the launch of this new project.

5) **Late Specification Freeze:** enhances differentiation through **Flexible Performance Target design,** and through additional **Innovation Blitzes** conducted during development.

6) Development lead time: Reduced 80% due to application of the Laws of Lead Time and Innovation Variation using tools such as **Open Innovation, Religion of Re-use, elimination of multi-tasking, cross-training for Critical Resource support, application of lead time feedback loops.**

7) Time from handoff to operations to reaching the first customer reduced through application of **Design for Lean Six Sigma.**

8) **Higher margins** on Offering A results from being **first or second to market,** sustained until commoditization ensues. Development of Offering B is launched.

9) Commoditization signals that more than half of the offering's life-time operating profits have already been earned, and that a **new, differentiated innovation is required** to preserve margins and growth.

10) First customer for **differentiated Offering B, and offerings from all Three Dimensions of Innovation.**

Plus there is the capability to generate disruptive offerings: Championed by the Chief Innovation Officer, resulting in deeper negative cash flows and longer periods to commoditization.

PART II

Building Corporate Innovation Capacity

Introduction to Part II

Did you notice that many of the Fast Innovation concepts introduced in Part I run counter to current management practices and corporate culture?

1) Good management discipline around the need to serve current customers and focus on improving the quality and timeliness of current offerings causes incumbent business units to almost universally oppose disruptive innovations. History shows this to be a significant cause of corporate decline and failure.

2) Good management practices, such as launching lots of innovation projects and loading innovators to 100%+ of capacity, cause long development time and late arrival to the market, another major destroyer of corporate value for sustaining innovations.

3) Standard management practices that minimize investment in comprehending the Heart and Voice of the Customer, and demand an early freeze of performance specs means that sustaining innovations often lack sufficient differentiation (contributing to market failure) and that the company never discovers opportunities for disruptive innovation.

If management thinks it is following *good* practice, but the effect is *bad*, we clearly have a cultural challenge that should not be underestimated. No blame should attach to current management, because the Fast Innovation process has been practiced in bits and pieces but never presented as an integrated whole. That being said, dedication to shareholder value must lead us to regard those common *good* practices as sins of *commission*. There are additional sins of *omission* in not embracing new strategies that are not part of current practice, including:

- A deliberate drive toward 40% to 80% re-use

- Exploiting the full power of Open Innovation

- Building a strategy applying all three dimensions of innovation

- Heart of the Customer initiatives, such as ethnography, Innovation Blitz, etc.

The fact is that 90% of companies do not sustain above-average growth for more than a decade because they fail to apply Fast Innovation principles. Clearly there is a huge gap between current practice and the needed path forward. Companies that embrace the tenets of Fast Innovation can close that gap and create a large competitive advantage—even the potential to dominate their markets. But as shown by the cases cited in Part I, the vast majority of companies require a cultural and structural change to embrace these principles.

Over the last few decades, industry and government have gained a lot of experience in understanding what is needed to make successful major transformations, and in understanding deployment weaknesses that can cause failure. No matter the initiative, success will result only if the corporation has engaged executives, clear metrics of success, a sound organization, and a plan to support the change. The purpose of Part II is to provide key insights to companies determined to sustain higher growth.

CHAPTER 7

Foundations of
an Innovation Factory

People who have lived through the many incarnations of "business performance improvement"—Value-Based Management, TQM, Lean, empowerment, business process re-engineering, Zero Defects, and Baldrige, to name just a few—know that results were often mixed. Each of these prior approaches were more descriptive systems that told you where you were going, but not prescriptive of how to get there and how to sustain results. Despite their enormous value-creation potential, these initiatives have generally lacked either the leadership engagement or the sustainable infrastructure to make a lasting change to the business. Companies sometimes achieved much higher levels of performance when guided by consultants, but the results were transitory; once the consultants left, benefits frequently declined because capabilities weren't transferred to the client and the business culture hadn't changed to support the new methods.

In contrast, Lean Six Sigma has had continued success since the 1990s because of its *prescription for* leadership engagement and a supporting infrastructure that embeds the necessary principles and systems into a company's culture. Having these prerequisites for success in place leads to greater sustainability of quality, cost, and more lead time improvements than were accomplished under the old models. In brief, Lean Six Sigma shaped the corporate environment in ways that eliminated barriers and made success more likely *and* sustainable.

Fast Innovation has the same need for corporate deployment and sustainability, and therefore should be similarly supported by executive leadership and infrastructure. This chapter looks at three of the most important foundations, including:

1) Leadership courage and engagement

2) Building the capability to deliver innovations and drive operational excellence

3) Goals and metrics: giving *life* to a vision, its objectives, and its strategies

Two additional foundations—the need for a new executive role *dedicated* to championing and leading innovation efforts, and the need to achieve operational effectiveness and control of complexity—require more discussion than we can devote in this chapter, so are treated in a subsequent Spotlight and chapter.

Foundation #1: Leadership courage and engagement

G. Gilbert Cloyd, P&G's Chief Technology Officer, said:

> When you get really big brands that are generating a lot of profit and cash flow, there's a tendency to make changes very carefully. If you do something that your large consumer base doesn't like, it can be a very significant negative financial impact. You've got to be careful, or caution will freeze you in place.

In *Darwin and the Demon*, author Geoffrey Moore warns that:

> To overcome inertia, management must introduce new types of innovation while deconstructing old processes and organizations. The most common mistake executive teams make when they seek to introduce change is leaving legacy structures untouched. Their hope is that the success of the new will draw resources away from the old and allow change to occur organically and painlessly. This approach has little chance to succeed. The way to move forward is to aggressively extract resources from legacy process and organizations and repurpose them to serve the new innovation type, or, if that's not

possible, take them out of the company altogether... So
management must pursue a twofold path of concurrent
construction and deconstruction.

The inertia that Moore discusses is a result of the frameworks that are part of a company's culture. They are often baked into company lore under the rubric of "core competency." The mental model says: *We have always been successful doing XYZ. That is what we're good at. So we need to continue doing that, or something like that.*

The problem is that this inward-looking view has nothing to do with what *customers* want. At that point, sustaining innovations are not the answer. Survival for the buggy-whip manufacturers of a century ago didn't depend on making better buggy-whips (sustaining innovations); it depended on getting into a new business entirely.

But the need for radical change is not always so visible, nor is it easy to move the culture from one heritage to another. Andy Grove in *Only the Paranoid Survive* recounted the moment that Intel "straddled a disconti- nuity"—the era in which it faced and then transcended the commoditi- zation of its core business, memory chips. Intel had a proud heritage of innovation along the production dimension, which history showed was the inappropriate response to the process innovations of the Japanese:

> *We had been losing money on memories for quite some time*
> *while trying to compete with the Japanese producers' high-*
> *quality, low-priced, mass-produced part. But because business*
> *had been so good, we just kept at it, looking for the magical*
> *answer that would give us a premium price.*[1]

Rather than improve their quality by process innovation, Intel had chosen the route of product innovation to solve the quality problem: they designed in redundant cells that were fault tolerant. But this indi- rect approach failed, time passed, and the window of opportunity was closing. As the losses mounted, panic set in.

> *We had meetings and more meetings, bickering and argu-*
> *ments, resulting in nothing but conflicting proposals...*
> *[including] a "go for it" strategy: Let's build a gigantic*
> *factory dedicated to producing memories, and nothing but*
> *memories, and let's take on the Japanese.*[2]

151

(This "gigantic factory" strategy was in fact tried by Texas Instruments and failed.) Others at Intel were considering the idea of producing differentiated "special-purpose memories" (another product innovation) as a means of surviving, but this idea, Grove said, was "an increasingly unlikely possibility as memories became a uniform worldwide commodity." By 1985, he said, "we had lost our bearings."

> I remember… I turned back to Gordon [Moore] and I asked, "If we got kicked out and the board brought in a new CEO, what do you think he would do?" Gordon answered without hesitation that he would get us out of memories. I stared at him, numb, then said, "Why shouldn't you and I walk out the door, come back and do it ourselves?"

Intel was disrupted by innovation along the process dimension to which it failed to effectively respond. The window for such a response had closed irrevocably, and this created the need for a gut-wrenching decision to get out of memories, or go the way of Mostek and others to destruction. You'll find suggestions later in this chapter for how to make detecting and dealing with a disruptive challenge part of your business norm rather than a dreaded happenstance for which management is not prepared.

The ultimate in executive engagement: The Chief Innovation Officer

Because of the cultural challenges and other factors we'll discuss in later chapters, Fast Innovation has to be led at the corporate level. For large companies, we recommend creating an executive position specifically for that purpose (what we call the Chief Innovation Officer). Smaller companies may want to wrap the needed responsibilities into the position of an existing executive who has a passion for the Fast Innovation process. The issue is so critical that we devote an entire chapter to this role and its responsibilities (see Chapter 8).

Building Leadership Engagement

According to Lou Giuliano, recently retired chairman, president, and CEO of ITT Industries, the leadership team needs to grapple with three questions when embarking on a major change such as Fast Innovation:

1. Do we really need to change? There must be a clear and strong burning platform for change that the whole leadership team believes in and embraces.

2. Do we believe that Fast Innovation will work and be a major part of our solution?

3. Are we willing to dedicate the people, resources and attention to follow through and make it happen?

After working with many leadership teams to undertake major changes in how they operate their businesses, we think Lou has the questions exactly right. Consequently, the first step of this journey is to attain leadership engagement by equipping executives with:

- the burning platform issues that make change an imperative for the company

- a clear comprehension of the Fast Innovation process as it relates to their business

- the magnitude of the benefits vs. the investment required

- a model of the deployment process

- an understanding of the management action and commitments required

This knowledge is required before you make a formal decision about whether to go forward with the Fast Innovation process. These meaty issues are of the utmost strategic importance, probably necessitating a significant change in focus or direction for the company. The process we have found most effective in building leadership engagement is the executive retreat.

How to Get There: The executive retreat

It is amazing to observe the power of a senior team that understands the Fast Innovation strategy and has bought into it. But this conversion must be done as a team, and should be the first step of deployment.

We recommend that executive management first go through a process together so they reach a point where they agree on the need for change and understand what barriers each function must break through. One of the most effective venues for that purpose is a carefully facilitated offsite retreat or even boot camp approach—it is essential for the team to physically and mentally step away from the day-to-day fray to gain perspective on the future. The goal is to provide officers with a one- or two-day learning experience in the Fast Innovation process within the context of their business.

During this retreat, the executives should determine strategic direction, focusing on the portions of the business that have the highest value-creation potential, and therefore increase the odds for attaining superior returns (based on the company's current capabilities and its projected capabilities using the Fast Innovation process). The executives should gain a deep and direct view of current challenges in determining what the customer wants and needs in these high-potential businesses. We find that it is valuable to bring in customers or to provide videos of customers discussing the company's services/products.

If the senior executive team concludes that they wish to pursue sustained growth through the Fast Innovation model, the next step is identifying a Chief Innovation Officer whose primary job it will be to press through the organizational inertia and drive the Fast Innovation process (*see* Chapter 8 for a discussion of this role).

The key outcome of the meeting is to have the executive team enunciate a burning platform message that explains why the corporation must proceed with Fast Innovation. This burning platform should include a metric that everyone can understand. For example:

> *"Our goal is organic growth of 8% per year every year"*

> *"To become the market leader in growth in every segment through new value-added innovation"*

Once the leadership has decided to embrace the Fast Innovation approach, key actions and changes are required to make Fast Innovation a way of life for the company, as captured in Table 7-A.

Table 7-A:
Fast Innovation Demands on Executive Leadership

Demands	Management changes required
• A leadership team of innovation enablers (as described in Part I)	• Evaluate the leadership team to be sure "the right people are on the bus"
• Motivated, engaged leadership at all levels of the business	• Lead workshops throughout the business to ensure leaders understand the burning platform and the plan, and have outlined their own actions to engage
• A cross-functional process vs. silo-functional focus	
• Constant/consistent engagement	• Knock down silos and realign organizations to support the innovation process
• An approach to understand and manage complexity of the offering	• Drive full goal deployment through the business; Integrate Fast Innovation goals into operations, reviews, and business metrics
• Resources, people, and attention	• Adopt the analytical tools needed to drive the right balance of innovation and complexity reduction
	• Recognize that if Fast Innovation is to succeed it must be considered an investment (quick returns, but not immediate net profits)

Foundation #2: Business units capable of meeting the demands of Fast Innovation

In many companies today, the functions and responsibilities that drive effective innovation are divided between organizational functions that have only minimal connections with each other. Marketing identifies opportunities; design staff develop the product or service; operations makes the product or delivers the service; sales does the selling. If these separate functions have little interaction along the way, there is a very high probability of a failure in communication or handoffs, or because of a lack of accountability and ownership for the overall design—> development—>delivery system.

In contrast, we recently worked with a big-box retailer that succeeded in designing a new store because they had the courage to assign the project to a small dedicated team of high-level executives that owned the process from beginning to end, from idea to launch. This team accomplished the task with an unprecedented level of creativity, speed, and value creation. Previous attempts had depended on a series of specialized teams of lower-level employees, resulting in unsynchronized handoffs across the silos, long lead time, and low effectiveness.

In fact, barriers to open communication and knowledge sharing are also barriers to Fast Innovation, which requires extensive and fluid cross-functional collaboration. To create a *company* capable of Fast Innovation, you'll need to change how various departments or functions operate. Here is an overview of the demands that Fast Innovation will place on key functions:

1. Design/development groups (R&D)

Current situation: Current home to most development efforts. Inherently focused almost exclusively on the product/service dimension.

Table 7-B: Innovation Demands on R&D

Demands	Changes required
1) Exponentially better knowledge of customer needs to identify potential differentiated "delighters"	1) Endorse and support customer-centric practices (ethnography, customer involvement in Blitzes and throughout design, etc.)
2) Better two-way street with suppliers (transfer your knowledge of customer needs, opportunities, and potential uses of an offering to them and communication about their capabilities to you)	2) Establish mechanisms for cross-functional collaboration between R&D, marketing, and sales to ensure exchange and coordination of knowledge about customer needs
3) Awareness of opportunities in all three dimensions of innovation	3) Nurture partnerships with key suppliers, involving them in development (through Innovation Blitz, for example)
4) Skills, tools and processes to bring operations into the design process (as appropriate) to achieve faster lead times, lower costs, and higher quality	4) R&D resources must become capable in all Fast Innovation processes and tools, and receive expert coaching on their implementation
5) Institutionalization of Open Innovation	5) Company must establish web-based systems for tapping into corporate- and world-wide innovation resources
6) Target of 40%-80% re-use in product/service designs	6) Management must incorporate metrics for re-use in project reviews; corporate should fund the development of platforms and re-use standards, and create a training environment to make re-use commonplace within business units
7) Proactive participation in disruptive innovations	7) Chief Innovation Officer (Chapter 8) should lead development of new funding model that recognizes and champions disruptive innovation opportunities

2. Marketing/Strategy

Current situation: Often in charge of capturing Voice of the Customer data and communicating it to the business.

Table 7-C: Fast Innovation Demands on Marketing

Demands	Changes required
1) Identify opportunities in all three dimensions of innovation (product/service, market definition, business model) and understand the cost of time-to-market	1) Create deep Heart of the Customer capability
2) Develop peripheral vision to find and evaluate disruptive innovation opportunities	2) Give marketing the lead responsibility for identifying 3D opportunities, and, working with Chief Innovation Officer, identifying peripheral opportunities with lead users and new or fringe customers, and to counter trends in low-margin business
3) Nurture deep and genuine connection with development organization to ensure best solutions and opportunities to reduce complexity	3) Help marketing develop the capability to estimate the cost of time-to-market
	4) Involve marketing as champions of complexity reduction

3. Sales/Service

Current situation: Typically has the closest ties to existing customers; aware of opportunities related to existing products/services (rooted in "what is").

Table 7-D: Fast Innovation Demands on Sales/Service

Demands	Changes required
1) Much faster sustaining upgrades to existing offerings (so that speed of innovation can become the disruptive advantage)	1) Create capability to build a pool of sustaining innovation ideas so innovation executives or marketing can launch projects into Fast Innovation as needed to prevent commoditization

Table 7-D: Fast Innovation Demands on Sales/Service (cont.)

Demands	Changes required
2) Ability/willingness to deal with disruptive offerings (to be sold to new customers, in new markets, in new ways) 3) Improved quality of customer input	2) Re-examine sales training and commission/incentive programs to make it attractive for sales staff to spend time promoting and selling high-margin, high-growth innovations 3) Establish mechanisms for bringing sales into Heart of the Customer/ethnography efforts to improve ability to capture valuable customer inputs

4. Operations

Current situation: Most likely already pursuing process improvements; very likely to be burdened with excess complexity in the product/service lines.

Table 7-E: Fast Innovation Demands on Operations

Demands	Changes required
1) Flawless and swift execution to get innovations to market quickly (to maximize early-entrant advantage) 2) Reduced lead time in the chain from suppliers to customers, as well as an intense focus and process for driving out defects and waste	1) Drive implementation of Design for Lean Six Sigma methods so operations can collaborate with development to achieve smooth transition from final design into operations with low-cost, fast operational lead times and high quality. 2) Have operations take a lead role in eliminating value-destroying complexity from the portfolio as a whole and from individual designs. (See sidebar, next page.)

continued on next page

Table 7-E: Fast Innovation Demands on Operations (cont.)

Demands	Changes required
3) Openness to re-thinking production/delivery models (for business model innovation)	3) Implement Lean Six Sigma[3] throughout organization to reduce lead times and cost, and improve quality.
	4) Create the necessary conditions and incentives for operations leadership to drive innovation in design, production, delivery, sales, and service functions.

Dealing with complexity

Successful implementation of Fast Innovation in the product/service dimension will drive rapid growth in your company's offering portfolio. However, unfettered proliferation of products/services causes an exponential increase in overhead costs and time-to-market, which can cripple your economic profitability—obviously not the result we're looking for from innovation.

Every company needs to regularly evaluate the portfolio of offerings at the business unit level, parsed into three types:

1) Offerings that currently generate positive economic profit (recall p. 5)

2) Offerings that generate negative economic profit but can be improved by process improvement, pricing, or redesign

3) Offerings that will always generate negative economic profit

Business unit leadership can usually deal with ways to support type 1 offerings and make the changes necessary to convert type 2 offerings into profit generators. But dealing with type 3 offerings requires executive action. That's why your company's senior leadership needs to deal with the issue of complexity proactively. See the Complexity Spotlight on p. 165 for details.

5. Finance

Current situation: May be contributing to innovation inertia by reinforcing the focus on making the "next quarter" numbers and by adhering to measurement and cost accounting policies that favor "local efficiency rather than global effectiveness" and reinforce the status quo.

Table 7-F: Fast Innovation Demands on Finance

Demands	Changes required
1) Must be able to financially evaluate disruptive innovation opportunities differently than sustaining innovations	1) Replace metrics such as Net Present Value to evaluate the potential of a disruptive opportunity using Real Options Theory (see p. 188)
2) Must have separate mechanism for funding disruptive innovation development	2) Create VC funding/Real Options Theory model with Chief Innovation Officer for both internal and external investment
3) Must understand the need and approach to evaluate the cost of complexity for new innovations	3) Adapt cost-accounting methods to adjust for the true cost of complexity by reviewing overhead allocation methods[4]

Foundation #3: Superior execution capability to deliver innovations

The ultimate goal of Fast Innovation is to fulfill or shape strategy by getting differentiated products, processes, and services out into the marketplace *fast,* either as a first mover or a fast follower. Part I talked about a number of strategies—controlling the number of projects-in-process, monitoring percent utilization, using rapid prototyping, and so on—designed to specifically speed up development work. Your ability to realize the benefits of these and other strategies is determined in large part by your underlying operational excellence (or lack thereof) in getting the offering to the customer.

At a minimum, the operations that provide the product or service to customers must be continuously improved in lead time, quality and cost using Lean Six Sigma (or whatever version your company has adopted). While Fast Innovation is a vital ingredient, its value can be lost unless you have flawless day-to-day execution on the production, delivery, and service of the offerings that your innovation process generates. **It is critical that you protect your speed advantage, not just through the design phase but all the way through execution.**

You can probably think of companies that got the differentiation aspect of innovation right, but fell short on the execution—they created fabulous innovations that made no money and contributed little revenue growth, even if the innovation concept was highly valued by the customer. Compaq, for example, was without question the leader in bringing new innovations to the PC market. But Dell was able to copy any innovation that Compaq announced, and, thanks to high flexibility and short operational lead times, able to get the product into customer hands at about the same time as Compaq. And *even if* Compaq had been able to beat Dell to market, Dell would have quickly eroded Compaq's first-mover advantage through the sheer strength, speed, and cost competitiveness of its supply chain.

Consider the data depicted in Figure 7-01, from Gary Cokins' book on Activity Based Accounting.[5] Look first at the dots connected by the dotted gray line: it shows that originally this company needed about 360 days and $200 million to go from receiving a Request for Quote to getting the product to the customer. After making improvements to the process (darker line), they were able to do the same work in about 225 days at a cost of about $140 million—in getting 38% faster, they dropped costs by 30%. They also had far more flexibility in responding to customers' requests and competitors' aggressions.

This example hit home for a recent client of ours who made heat exchangers. Our client absolutely had the most differentiated, highest-quality product in the market. Unfortunately, their customers needed to be able to order and receive the product in 5 days. When we first analyzed the client's process we found that it took at least 3 days for the client to take the order and get the order to manufacturing. As a result,

Figure 7-01: Reducing Lead Time Reduces Costs

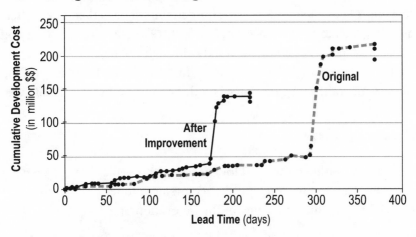

This company cut more than 140 days from its development cycle and saved $70 million as a consequence. That kind of operational speed (and lower costs) is key to the Fast Innovation value proposition of delivering differentiated offerings to the market quickly.

on-time delivery was a lackluster 64%. The company never had a chance! Customers were willing to accept the competition's less-differentiated product because they could get it when they needed it. Fortunately for our client, the story has a happy ending. They deployed a Lean Six Sigma team and cut quotation and order entry time from 3 days to 3 hours during a one-week Blitz project and won back a substantial share of the market.

Another aspect of operational excellence that affects your ability to achieve Fast Innovation is how competent you are in the tools associated with Design for Lean Six Sigma (DfLSS), which ensure robust execution of an innovative idea and make it easier for operations to deliver the product, service, or process with high quality, low cost, and rapid operational lead times. Thus, creation of DfLSS capability is an integral part of delivering on the Fast Innovation value proposition. (You'll find a description of DfLSS tools on p. 202).

A third aspect of operational excellence involves the proliferation of offerings generated through innovation, which falls under the rubric of complexity. The issue is so prevalent and the potential gains so great that we devote a Spotlight (p. 165) to complexity. By way of a preview, the basic message is that a complexity-conquering strategy has three elements: (1) explicit mechanisms for determining whether a new offering can generate positive economic profit, (2) dedication to achieving fast operational lead times (primarily through application of Lean Six Sigma) to deliver high quality quickly, and (3) methods for controlling the costs of complexity. Resources on these topics are readily available.[6]

Conclusion

This chapter outlined the need for executive engagement in shaping and deploying Fast Innovation, and the requirement to have their buy-in on the need for significant change in the innovation process.

The fact is that the Fast Innovation process described in Part I will not deliver its potential benefits if implemented in an organization that does not change its strategic direction, structures, practices, or metrics. There are simply too many ways in which the demands of Fast Innovation run counter to current "good" practices.

The foundations described in this chapter lay out a basic framework that will allow Fast Innovation to thrive. The most important of these is true engagement by senior executives. Changes at lower levels in the company will have limited effect unless there is strong leadership from the top.

Endnotes

1 Andrew S. Grove, *Only the Paranoid Survive: How to identify and exploit the crisis points that challenge every business* (New York: Currency/Doubleday, 1996).

2 This is in fact the approach that Haggerty's successors at Texas Instruments pursued... resulting in a complete mis-allocation of capital and management attention and loss of leadership in semiconductors... and a billion dollar writeoff.

3 Michael George, *Lean Six Sigma* (New York: McGraw-Hill, 2002); Michael George, *Lean Six Sigma for Service* (New York: McGraw-Hill, 2003); Michael George, David Rowlands, Mark Price, John Maxey, *The Lean Six Sigma Pocket Toolbook* (New York: McGraw-Hill, 2004).

4 *See* Michael L. George and Stephen Wilson, *Conquering Complexity in Your Business* (New York: McGraw-Hill, 2004).

5 Gary Cokins, *Activity-based Cost Management, Making it Work: A manager's guide to implementing and sustaining an effective ABC System* (New York: McGraw-Hill, 1996). Used with permission.

6 *See* notes 3 and 4.

SPOTLIGHT ON

Conquering the Cost of Complexity

With Stephen Wilson[7]

Differentiation that does not drive customer preference is a liability.

Geoffrey Moore, author of Crossing the Chasm

We have discussed the need to achieve operational excellence in delivering the output of the Fast Innovation process to customers with fast lead times, low cost, and high quality. Many companies are using approaches like Lean Six Sigma to deliver on those goals.[8] Lean Six Sigma, however, does not explicitly challenge the breadth of the portfolio of offerings and its resulting impact on operational results. In fact, our experience with Lean Six Sigma implementation has shown that there is a formidable impediment to achieving operational excellence, exacerbated by the Fast Innovation process itself: burgeoning complexity in a portfolio of offerings. If a company doubles the number of its offerings, the lead time to deliver those products or services will at least double, all other things being equal.[9] Worse yet, experience shows that the overhead cost per product/service will more than double. Thus the impact of Lean Six Sigma process improvements will be diluted by an ever-growing portfolio.

In and of itself, complexity is neither good nor bad. That evaluation depends on how the complexity is perceived and valued by the customer. In most mature companies, for example, there is normally a significant amount of value-destroying clutter: products, services, options, features, and so on, that do not create positive economic profit. But in becoming a growth-oriented business, we need value-creating complexity: brand extensions in a premium segment that customers want, options or new offerings that create differentiation in the eyes of the customer, etc.

Most companies can deal well with good complexity (the variety or feature choices that customers value), naturally exploiting what is already popular with customers, but have no means of dealing with bad complexity (the proliferation that will never earn positive economic profit). This sets up a dynamic common to many Fortune 1000 companies: Product and service portfolios get increasingly cluttered with low-value offerings, which diffuses attention and resources, impedes processes, and drives up cost. The company is essentially carrying a burden of products, services, options, configurations, etc., that customers do not highly value. And as the pace of commoditization increases, the burden gets heavier. In such a case, complexity becomes a value-destroying phenomenon (cf. Figure 6-02, p. 118). The problem is compounded because managerial accounting assigns too little overhead cost to low-volume products and services. An adjustment needs to be made to understand just how poorly some products are performing.[10]

If you are a fast innovator but ignore complexity, portfolio clutter will build up faster than ever before. And complexity has widespread impact on profits, growth, processes, and customer satisfaction. The irony is that in the pursuit of innovation you may strangle growth.

"Complexity kills innovation," said Eamon Malone, until recently a vice president at Motorola and Motorola Computer Group. He cites two reasons:

- It consumes resources, both financial and human, that could be devoted to innovation. "Any complexity that is not being valued in the marketplace chews up costs and impacts my profitability. It takes away from my capacity for R&D."

- It erodes execution capability.

  "Complexity can drive down quality, increase costs and lengthen lead times," Malone said. "If that's the state you're in, you have poor execution—and you can't innovate your way out of poor execution."

Take a look at his results (Table SP-A). Eamon inherited a business that had been losing money for severl yaers, one with 3,500 different products. The previous solution was a misguided attempt to "build all 3,500 in China" which was reversed. Then Eamon helped champion an effort to eliminate the value-destroying products. As shown in the table, by 2004 most of the products that could *never* generate positive economic profit had been eliminated through end-of-life sales, outsourcing, etc. Operating earnings rose from -6% to +7% of sales, a 13% improvement.

Table SP-A: Reducing Cost of Complexity at Motorola Computer Group

Attribute	Measure	2002	2003	2004
Product Portfolio	#s	3500	2079	499
Product Development Projects	#s	120	22	20
New Products Introduced	#s	0	8	14
Product Development time	Months	N/A	24- 28	12
Repair Throughput	Days	55	30	12
On-Time Delivery	%	70	78	90
Manufacturing Productivity	%	100	224	306
Early Life Failure	DPM (Defects/Million)	8500	2118	225
Customer Satisfaction	%	27	55	90
Revenue (% 2002 baseline)	%	100	125	240
Gross Margin	%	32	35	41
Operating Earnings	%	-6	+3	+7

Notice, too, the balance of active projects vs. new products introduced and development time. In 2002, Eamon's division had 120 active projects, introduced NO new products, and had no control over development time. Just two years later, active products had dropped to just 22, the division was able to introduce 14 new products, and development lead time was a reliable 12 months.

Equally importantly, percent of satisfied customers grew from 27% to over 90%, quality improved dramatically, and revenue more than doubled. By dramatically reducing the portfolio by a factor of seven, process improvements such as Lean Six Sigma could be focused with seven times the effort per offering.

By combining Fast Innovation, lower complexity, and Lean Six Sigma quality, this business was transformed from being one of Motorola's worst divisions to one of its best—showing that conquering complexity and using Fast Innovation are both necessary to cleanse operations of the bad and nourish the good. Profitable operations result from the balance of these two complementary forces.

The (Often Hidden) Impact of Complexity

Let's consider another case study. Assume for the moment that you are Procter and Gamble.[11] You are a fast innovator and have launched thousands of successful products that generated strong premiums when first introduced. You have strong brands and great management. And over time, all this has naturally resulted in a lot of complexity. But what is the impact of the high complexity?

Durk Jager, P&G's CEO, framed the issue this way: "We stand poised for another great leap, another breakthrough in business growth, success and profitability... *If* we dramatically simplify the way we do business in a rapidly emerging global marketplace."[12]

P&G moved beyond *If* and in 1996 launched a targeted reduction in complexity. Over the next three years, P&G reduced the number of SKUs by 20%. How? The company standardized product families and packaging, divested some brands and killed others. It reduced the number of product introductions, but not—we stress *not*—at the expense of product innovation. The cuts in product introductions came from a disciplined rejection of me-too products, the brand extensions that would further clutter the shelves in already crowded supermarkets.

That's what they did. Now let's look at the results.

- **Impact on operational costs**: Before the simplification, operations were inefficient and costs were high. Ralph Drayer, vice president, explained: "The proliferation of product, pricing, labeling and packaging variations necessitated by extensive promotions translated to an explosion of SKU and UPC (Universal Product Code) changes. This further burdened the order, shipping and billing activities throughout the value chain—without producing real value for retail customers or consumers. In addition, the bloating of the supply chain with product, together with the proliferation of product variations relating to promotions, increased manufacturing costs by generating erratic demand patterns."[13]

Reducing the number of SKUs reduced the overall cost of products by $2 per case, accounting for nearly $3 billion in savings. By 1999, complexity reduction had enabled P&G to close 10 plants, yielding annual savings of nearly $1 billion. The company saw $325 million in benefits to the supply chain cost structure and $100 million in cost improvement, by standardizing pricing and promotion policies and reducing the number of price brackets.

Prior to the initiative, more than 27,000 orders taken at P&G each month required manual corrections. Afterward, the order error rate was cut by 80%, bringing $20 million in benefit. Shipping costs were reduced: with fewer SKUs there was a significant increase in full truckloads. Quality also increased as fewer products led to a 25% reduction in damage costs, worth $15 million.

- **Impact on sales**: The fear of losing revenues when you simplify the portfolio is one of the biggest barriers to complexity reduction. But in fact, pruning a cluttered portfolio will often lead to an *increase* in revenues and a dramatic improvement in profitability. In the first five years following its complexity-reduction initiative, P&G's overall market share went from 24.5% to 28%. As an example, the company cut the number of Head & Shoulders Shampoo SKUs by 50%, but the sales per item **more than doubled**.

How does such a counterintuitive result come to pass? For one thing, the smaller product line focuses management attention and provides the opportunity to put more power behind the marketing/sales engine for remaining offerings (more training, more and better advertising/promotion, and so on). Second, in our experience, service levels suffer when a company has a cluttered portfolio. When the portfolio is trimmed, excess process waste can be eliminated, enabling smoother faster service levels on the right offerings.

- **Impact on profitability**: With such huge reductions in cost, and sales holding steady or increasing, the real transformation emerged in the profit margins (and by extension, stock price). In just three years, P&G increased their margins from 6.4% to 9.5%, the highest in nearly half a century. Remember, most of this increase in margins came from simply removing the clutter from the portfolio.

There are plenty of companies benefiting from purging clutter. Clutter tends to creep in over time, eroding profitability and focus almost without anyone noticing. For example, consider the French luxury goods giant, LVMH Moët Hennessy Louis Vuitton. After several years of growing primarily through acquisitions, the company was bloated and management focus was diluted. Following the recession, Bernard Arnault, chief executive, decided it was time to retrench and eliminate the clutter brands and complexity. At the core of this decision was one startling statistic: 60% of LVMH's operating profit was coming from just 1 of their 60 brands. The decision to focus enabled Arnault to concentrate on his star brand, and reportedly he regularly sent 30 to 40 faxes to his staff every Monday morning with ideas generated over a weekend spent reading fashion magazines.[14]

Another example is Heinz, which in recent years shed 40% of its items to concentrate on fast movers such as ketchup in an easy-to-pour upside-down bottle. In fiscal 2003, operating income rose 17.5% to $1.38 billion.[15]

As you can see, this winnowing of a portfolio not only boosts profits but is often the prerequisite for growth, as the company can better focus its resources and management capacity.

The difficulty of diagnosing service complexity

One of the reasons why the complexity examples used here revolve around products is that complexity problems are easier to diagnose in product-centered environments. There, you can at least touch and see much of the *symptoms of complexity* (warehouses, rework, SKU stockpiles). By contrast, in service industries there is nothing tangible, so *the symptoms of complexity are hidden*, which is why service complexity is more likely to go undiagnosed.

Many financial service companies, for example, have witnessed growing revenues but deteriorating profitability in the last five years amid an explosion of service choices. One financial services company noted that for one of its lines of services, there were 5 million potential configurations because of all the options offered to customers.

In fact, increasing complexity is often more insidious in service businesses than in product businesses. One client of ours who provided professional services catalogued and categorized the number of different offerings they were delivering to clients. They found over 200 different offerings. After some analysis, they were startled to find that amongst these many offerings there was so much duplication and non-value-added differences that they really offered only about 20 truly different services. How had this happened? They had created the problem by allowing their creative entrepreneurial people to individually develop and deliver their own service lines or put their own personal spin on an existing offering. (There were nearly as many different offerings as sales people!)

So be on the lookout. In a service business, changes to offerings are often very easy to make yet very rarely governed, resulting in significant complexity creep!

Conquering Complexity Accelerates Innovation

Eamon Malone has told us that many companies tend to focus on the innovation *means*—the resources, the ideas, the process—without stopping to consider the innovation *ends*. "And if you don't get innovation out into the marketplace, it means nothing," he stated. His sentiments echo those of Churchill, who once noted, "However beautiful the strategy, you must look at the results." In fact, in later chapters we will outline the Design for Lean Six Sigma process which provides the bridge to getting the innovation into the market that Eamon talks about, by driving detailed Voice of the Customer information at the project level, and translating that to design concepts which can be seamlessly delivered to the operations organization and launched into the marketplace.

We saw the results of complexity in the story of IPM. Remember Figure 6-02 (repeated in Figure 7-02)? It showed how IPM's costs dropped as it simplified its approach to design.

Figure 7-02: IPM Results

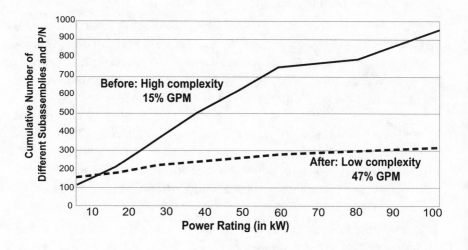

Before driving to reduce design complexity, IPM was trapped into low Gross Profit Margin (GPM) driven by high internal costs. After reducing complexity and enforcing platforms, GPM rose to 47% thanks in large part to much lower internal costs—even though IPM still offered the same variety of product.

In this case, what was the cost of complexity? For one, it is the cost of unique components whose uniqueness is of no value to customers—a cost that arises when each engineer starts with a blank sheet of paper, with no view to leveraging common parts and platforms. It is also the cost of spares, small order sizes, uniquely trained engineers, and a slower learning curve. All of these costs added up to a 32-point difference in gross margins.

But moreover—and more pertinent to our discussion of innovation— a company ends up in one of two very different states, depending on whether it has conquered complexity. For IPM:

- **Original situation**: IPM existed in a state where it struggled to innovate and to compete effectively. Each new model added a whole new wave of cost. The focus on what was *truly* valuable to the customer was absent: the company in this state was considering all invention to be innovation, and we know that not to be true.

- **After a variety of products were built off common platforms**: After inaugurating the Religion of Re-use (Chapter 6), IPM continued to grow and innovate with little impact on its cost structure: it had a *low cost of complexity*. It fully understood the difference between innovation and invention. In this state, the company was still offering a full range of offerings. **Instead of reducing complexity, it reduced the *cost* of complexity.** Understanding and exerting these levers is the key to balancing and optimizing Fast Innovation.

The fundamental difference between the two states is that the former is internally focused (each engineer working independently), while the latter has a customer focus ("What do we do that is of value to our customers?"). At some point there has to be a shift between internal and external or else you run into trouble.

Attacking Complexity

Detailed methods for diagnosing and solving complexity challenges are provided in our previous book, *Conquering Complexity in Your Business*. In brief, there are two paths to addressing complexity issues in your company.

1) Reduce the complexity of your offering portfolio

Our research indicates that one of the biggest drivers of non-value-add cost is the complexity of the portfolio. Why is this so? It costs just as much (if not more) to produce products/services that customers don't want (or won't pay a premium for) as it does to produce those they do. Improving the processes associated with these offerings will do nothing to alter the fact that the product/service is of low customer value and will therefore likely never generate positive economic profit. Or as Peter Drucker puts it:

> *There is nothing so useless as doing efficiently that which should not be done at all.*

2) Reduce the costs of delivering complexity

After you have purged your portfolio of offerings that can never earn an economic profit, how do you reduce the cost of complexity for the remainder? Part of the solution lies in the same methods you'll be using anyway to improve execution: through application of Lean Six Sigma. The other major driver of lower cost comes from creating platforms (the Religion of Re-use) to increase commonality among related offerings in features or components that are transparent to the customer. You want differentiation the customer values, not complexity the customer does not value.

Cloyd of P&G commented: "We've put more emphasis on serving an even broader base of customers. Today, we probably serve about two billion-plus consumers around the globe, but there are six billion customers out there. That has led us to put increased emphasis on low-end markets and in mid- and low-level pricing tiers in developed geographies. That has caused us to put a lot more attention on the cost aspects of our products."[16]

What drives the cost of complexity? Consider Ford's luxury brands. Mark Fields, Ford's executive vice president of Europe and Premier Automotive Group (the senior executive in Europe), was recently quoted in *The Wall Street Journal* as saying that Jaguar has "lots of opportunities" to share more components and technologies with its sister brands in

Ford's Premier Automotive Group. The specific example he gave was Jaguar and Land Rover's practice of outfitting their vehicles with different types of navigation systems and wiring harnesses.

"Does the customer care whether they have a Jaguar navigation system or a Volvo navigation system or a Land Rover navigation system? No," Mr. Fields said. "They care about whether it's a navigation system that can get them from point A to point B with the right amount of functionality and [one] that's easy to use."

If you can reduce your *cost* of complexity and your competitors cannot, you have a differentiating advantage that you can exploit by delivering more products and services (than your competitors) to customers without significantly incurring costs. *You have an advantaged platform for innovation.* If the competitor tries to follow, but with a high cost of complexity, the costs incurred can be fatal. Recall the two lines in Figure 6-02 and imagine for a second that they represent two different companies. You can judge from the difference in gradient how the increase in offerings dramatically increases costs in one, and not in the other.

Endnotes

7 Stephen Wilson is the Director of the Conquering Complexity practice at George Group and coauthor of *Conquering Complexity in Your Business (see* note 10). His experience includes strategy development and execution, Value Based Management, and Lean Six Sigma, in areas including financial services, consumer goods, technology and manufacturing. He holds an MBA in Finance and Strategic Management from The Wharton School.

8 For service applications *see Lean Six Sigma for Service* (McGraw-Hill, 2003); for manufacturing *see Lean Six Sigma* (McGraw-Hill, 2002), both by Michael L. George.

9 This is a result quantified by the Complexity Equation. *See* note 10.

10 *See* Michael L. George and Stephen Wilson, *Conquering Complexity in Your Business* (New York: McGraw-Hill, 2004).

11 Case study excerpted from Steven M. Cristol and Peter Sealey, *Simplicity Marketing: End Brand Complexity, Clutter, and Confusion* (New York: The Free Press, 2000).

12 "Preparing for an Emerging Global Retail Supply Chain," *Forum,* Summer 1999.

13 "Procter and Gamble's Streamlined Logistics Initiatives," *Supply Chain Management Review,* Summer 1999.

14 "Its Closets Full, LVMH Decides to Return to Basics," *The Wall Street Journal,* October 8, 2004.

15 "There Goes the Rainbow Nut Crunch," *BusinessWeek,* July 19, 2004.

16 "Online Extra: At P&G, It's '360-Degree Innovation,'" *BusinessWeek,* October 11, 2004.

CHAPTER 8

The Executive Engine of Fast Innovation

Using a Chief Innovation Officer to Drive Results

Business unit managers have their hands full making the next quarter's revenue and profit numbers, satisfying existing customers with sustaining innovations, and fending off competitors. The Fast Innovation process will help them with all these intense and important goals while ensuring the long-term growth of the incumbent organization, so long as it is not attacked by a disruptive innovation! They must implement the Fast Innovation process in its entirety as described in Part I, except for disruptive innovations, and consistent with the recommendations given above. These managers can implement many of the specific tools discussed in this book, such as the Laws of Lead Time and Variation, the FastGate project review system, and proper resource scheduling. But there are many requirements for Fast Innovation that require leadership or coordination at senior levels because they cross the functional operations and silos or involve disruptive innovations (that rarely survive to implementation at the business unit level).

As we've discussed, the focus that business unit managers need almost always leads to lack of peripheral vision and the "compactron reaction" (p. 30) of denial and anger when a disruptive innovation is thrust upon them by the competition. Since to be effective, these managers must remain focused on sustaining innovations and business operations, how can a firm take advantage of and proactively create the kind of disruptive innovations that will lead to sustained above-average returns?

For companies of sufficient size and scope to warrant it (often over $1B revenue and/or with multiple business units), the answer lies in assigning the responsibilities for implementing Fast Innovation and nurturing potentially disruptive innovations to at least one and perhaps two executives. The title of this executive varies by company: Some, such as H. J. Heinz, Interpublic Group (49,000 employees) and Hain Celestial, call it the Chief Growth Officer. Others, such as Textron, Humana, Coca-Cola, Cargill and Eastman Chemical, call it the Chief Innovation Officer. We prefer the latter name because innovation connotes value to the customer, whereas growth connotes value to the company.

As an aside, a few companies recommend that the role of Chief Information Officer assume all the innovation responsibilities, but many companies (including ours) think this is too big a job.[17] We believe that the competencies needed for the innovation executive role differ from those of a Chief Information Officer. Indeed, some who advocate combining them seem to confuse the internal application of information technology with the external application of, for example, the technology of product development.[18] A company that wishes to combine roles should base the decision on which executive has the passion, the capacity, and the background that qualifies them for attacking these issues—and that might be a marketing, strategy, or manufacturing executive instead of the Chief Information Officer.

The Responsibilities of the Chief Innovation Officer

The Chief Innovation Officer or other executive you put in charge of innovation success has the responsibility to:

- **Drive cross-functional collaboration.** Creating, maintaining, and funding initial links between business units or functions, where no such links currently exist, requires a good deal of relationship building. We gave one example of these links in the case of implementing re-use at Xerox (p. 120), or internal Open Innovation at P&G (p. 104). The links must be supported at the top levels of the company or they will not obtain many crucial benefits of the Fast Innovation process.

- **Champion an ever-deeper understanding of customer needs and disruptive market dynamics.** The absolute heart of innovation is gaining a deep understanding of what the customer wants or may want without yet knowing it. Most businesses are still relying on anecdotes from the sales team, customer complaints, survey methods, or maybe focus groups to decipher customer wants/needs. This lack of depth directly limits a company's ability to innovate. Nor will a once-a-year visit to observe customers do the trick. Deep VOC understanding requires a permanent infrastructure and commitment.

  The specific approach will depend on the markets a company serves and how its customers are divided by business unit. The three avenues recommended in this book are:
  - Drive ethnographic efforts to observe customer needs
  - Sponsor Idea Forums (*see* p. 216)
  - Create infrastructure capability for Innovation Blitz

  Initiatives like these will help you generate ideas for services/products (or shifts in business models or market definition) that may not readily fit within the purview of individual business units.

- **Maintain peripheral vision of disruptive threats and opportunities** and develop plans for responding to these disruptive threats (done in concert with the business unit marketing managers).

- **Nurture disruptive innovation** by working with the CEO to obtain a block of discretionary funding to support disruptive innovation (*see* the funding discussion, p. 186, for details). This may require a special stream of funding within existing operating units, or, as is often the case when existing units have no interest in pursuing the disruptive opportunity, creation of a free-standing entity (possibly with venture capital investment) to undertake the development. This approach is essential because incumbent organizations will have much more data to prove a disruptive innovation will fail than to show it will work or can be made to meet cost and profit goals.

- **Champion an Open Innovation Model**: The Chief Innovation Officer needs to establish mechanisms that allow designers and developers to regularly reach beyond the company for creative ideas or solutions to your specific challenges. If you choose a model like the InnoCentive website described on p. 99, the mechanisms will also require funding for rewards or other incentives. This open model should also include mechanisms to license technology to and from other firms. While research for research's sake is not encouraged, technology may be developed that could be valuable for another market.

- **Institutionalize re-use:** The benefits of re-use are obvious in hindsight—and achieving a high level of re-use is critical to achieving the Fast Innovation value proposition—but its benefits accrue more at the business or corporate level than at the business unit or designer level. So initially you won't find much support for re-use. We already touched on resistance to re-use in Chapter 6 and will go into more detail in Chapter 11, but for now recognize that widespread implementation of re-use won't occur unless there is a strong corporate champion leading the charge.

- **Provide Fast Innovation resources for creating capability within the P&L centers:** The P&L centers must pursue innovations along all three dimensions of innovation by learning and applying the Fast Innovation process. They will need to be taught to apply Fast Innovation tools, and will also require expert coaching in their first implementations. Examples of this capability creation include:
  - implementation of the FastGate process (Chapter 14) for controlling project lead time
  - implementation of ethnography/deep customer data capture
  - implementation of Design for Lean Six Sigma tools and processes to ensure fast and robust execution
  - collection of data on innovation processes
  - creation of common time buffers (Appendix 2)

  Since the purpose is to enhance overall growth of the corporation, the costs for this education should be borne by corporate.

- **Create Fast Innovation metrics for business units to track** (discussion to follow).

Reminder: Why the focus on disruptive innovation?

Recall from Part I that disruptive innovations are much riskier than sustaining innovations, but have a much higher potential for long-term continuous growth. Yet a focus on "core competencies" (what organizations currently do well) prevents market incumbents from accepting the reality of a disruptive innovation. The Chief Innovation Officer must have the peripheral vision and power to champion potentially disruptive innovations that incumbent managers cannot or will not recognize. Kodak recently underwent the disruptive battle as camera film fell victim to the disruptive innovation and growth of digital cameras. As one newspaper reported: *"September 26, 2003: Eastman Kodak Co. slashed its generous dividend by more than 70 percent, its first cut ever, as it scrambles to redirect resources into the fast-growing digital market and away from its conventional film business.*

"The decline that became evident for sure in the second quarter of this year to the historic film-based businesses can be managed," [CEO Daniel] Carp said. "It requires hard work, a different model, heavily driven on cost reduction and then selected investments for growth." Kodak expects its digital businesses, which have yet to turn a profit, to account for half its profit and 60 percent of its sales by 2006, up from 30 percent now. Its traditional businesses, which still anchor its profits and image, will drop from 70 percent to 40 percent of sales, it said."[19]

This is a clear statement of the challenge, and we wish Kodak well in effecting the turnaround. By contrast, competitors have a different story: Canon's year-over-year growth of digital cameras in the fourth quarter is projected at 85%, up from 45% in the third quarter, with camera operating margins of

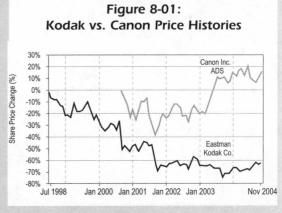

**Figure 8-01:
Kodak vs. Canon Price Histories**

14%.[20] Clearly a company must have the peripheral vision, the organization and the Fast Innovation process to effectively respond to a disruptive innovation and sustain the growth of shareholder value.

Defining Innovation Goals and Metrics

Measures give life to a vision, its objectives, and its strategies. They provide a focused objective that lets each of us know how we contribute to the successes of the company.

Dean Clubb, Chairman
Texas Instruments Quality Leadership Team

As the designated champions of innovation within their companies, Chief Innovation Officers need to work with the executive team to define specific growth goals for innovation. They will also need to define and monitor the metrics that will let them know if their companies are getting there (and how quickly or slowly).

The goals are part of the burning platform, which we already discussed on p. 138. At a high level, key internal metrics should clearly reflect that burning platform and the company's business strategy. For example, if the overall goal is to increase revenue from $20B to $25B with ROIC = WACC+5%, then each division would be responsible for a portion of that objective.

The choice of metrics will vary from business to business. Just as when tracking corporate performance, there is a need to achieve balance (*see* Figure 8-02). For innovation, you also need to pay attention to which dimension(s) of innovation you're pursuing. One issue is that simply measuring current growth is not enough to guarantee *long-term* sustainability of gains from innovation. You also need a way to measure the vitality of that growth.

Figure 8-02: Balancing Metrics

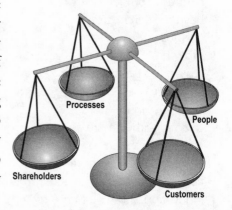

Processes

People

Shareholders

Customers

Too many companies become overly focused on the overall growth number, driving an over-emphasis on growth from acquisitions. Often acquisition-related growth does not drive the level of return that was expected. Companies that drive organic growth rather than acquisitional growth will tend to have greater sustainability. We recommend breaking down financial goals into organic (from innovation) and non-organic components:

A. Organic growth in revenue and ROIC from...
  - Existing products/services
  - Sustaining innovations
  - Disruptive innovations

B. Acquisition performance: attainment of goals for
  - ROIC
  - Growth
  - Complementarity and capability
  - Market share

What financial metric is best?

Every sustaining innovation project should have financial goals that are clearly stated in the project charter, calculated using the primary metric that the business uses to evaluate financial performance (discounted value of economic profit, NPV, IRR, etc.). It should be noted that, of all these metrics, economic profit is the most severe: it asks, "When will this project generate positive cash, less the cost of capital? This metric cannot be manipulated as easily as can NPV or IRR (just pick the discount rate you need!), and is often the acid test on launching a project, measuring the value of an acquisition, etc. This approach does not work with disruptive innovations; use the funding model in Chapter 8.

You will also need corporate-level metrics to understand whether your portfolio of new innovations-in-progress is vital enough to support growth several years into the future. To get a handle on this issue, you'll need to look at operational metrics:

- Anticipated revenue from current and in-development sustaining innovations

- Number of sustaining and disruptive innovations at each stage of your development process

- Average lead-time-to-market

- Failure rates at each stage of the development process

Together, these figures would give you a good idea of how many existing projects are likely to reach completion, how long it will take to complete

---

Using the Y = f[X] format

Some companies like to summarize their goals in the $Y=f[X_1, X_2, \dots]$ format that represents having an output (Y) that is a function of inputs (Xs).

"Best In the World" Output Goals (the Big Ys): An innovation output goal describes *what* it will take to transform a company into the kind of growth engine needed to be among the 10% of companies that sustain above-average shareholder returns for more than a decade. Describing the goal defines what businesses the company should be in, the impact on shareholder value and competitive position, and the role that the Fast Innovation process will play. A "Big Y" for innovation should challenge the organization to achieve greatness and should be set to require disruptive innovations along one or more dimensions.

Input Drivers (the Xs) deal with the process drivers, or *how* the company will become "Best In the World" in its business. Certainly among these drivers are:

X_1 Retaining businesses that can create economic profit

X_2 Eliminating businesses that can never generate positive economic profit

X_3 Implementing a Fast Innovation process

X_4 Implementing a Lean Six Sigma operations process

X_5 Conquering the Cost of Complexity

X_6 Complementary acquisitions and divestitures

X_i and other goals specific to your business

Data on X_1 and X_2 should be distributed at the executive retreat.

---

them, and what kind of revenue impact that will have. You can round out the picture by looking at:

- **Customer metrics:** Typically covers customer satisfaction ratings and/or defect or time data associated with the quality, cost, and lead-time-to-delivery of products or services.

- **Re-use:** Think of re-use as a leading indicator of lead-time-to-market and cost—the more re-use there is, the more likely you can be quick to market and gain the early-entrant advantage.

- **Summarized project-level metrics:** Time-to-market and other metrics for individual projects will be tracked and managed at the functional or business unit level. Combine the data from all business units for review at the executive level. This will help you judge whether the company as a whole is capable of meeting time-to-market goals.

Tracking goals graphically

Critical parameters for any project or initiative can be tracked with scorecards, which are built around the principle of making sure you're looking at diverse metrics.

For example, the balanced scorecard approach is an industry-recognized best practice for aligning activities (work, improvement efforts, metrics, and goals) with strategic objectives (*see* Figure 8-03, next page). It relates past performance (in the form of outcome metrics) to strategic objectives, and integrates them with process improvement initiatives to drive long-term performance. The scorecard is balanced in the sense that it represents both long- and short-term perspectives, leading and lagging indicators of performance, and the perspectives of the three primary stakeholders in a business (customers, employees, and shareholders).

The balanced scorecard method is well documented elsewhere[21] so we won't go into details here on how to develop one. If your executive team is already using something similar, then the key is to either add in several metrics related to your specific innovation goals (revenue from new products/services, average time-to-market, new markets or customer bases established, etc.) or create a separate scorecard just for your innovation efforts.

Figure 8-03: Balanced Scorecard

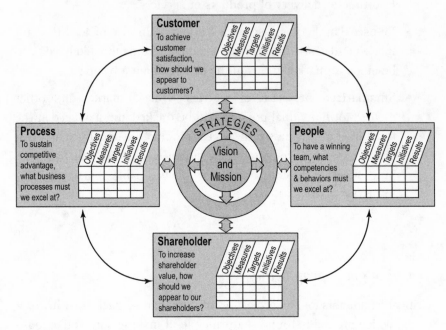

Funding Disruptive Innovation: Real Options Theory

ITT Industries is a company that operates in disparate businesses—defense, pumps, electronic connectors, automotive fluid applications, and associated services—in 14 different countries. Current revenue is $6.36 billion; employment is 39,000 people. The company has generated superior returns for shareholders, sustained through good economies and bad. During the recession of 2000–03 this long-term commitment to process and product innovation allowed the company to outperform both their industry and the S&P 500 by wide margins (*see* Table 8-A and Figure 8-04).

Table 8-A: ITT Industries Stock Performance

Investment Returns *(all figures in percentages)*	ITT	Industry	S&P 500
Return On Equity	20. 6	8. 1	14. 5
Return On Assets	5.8	2. 4	2. 5
Return On Capital	16. 9	5. 0	6. 9
Return On Equity (5-Year Avg.)	23. 4	7. 6	12. 1
Return On Assets (5-Year Avg.)	6. 2	1. 9	2. 0
Return On Capital (5-Year Avg.)	16. 6	5. 7	5. 6

Figure 8-04: ITT vs. S&P 500 Stock Performance

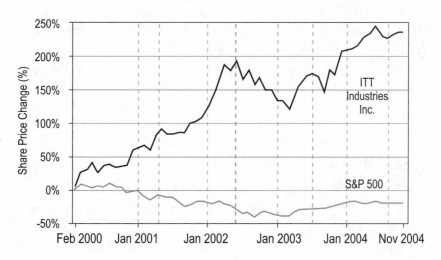

Lou Giuliano, the former CEO of ITT, offers the following insights:

> *Disruptive innovation definitely has to be funded from the top.*
> *To really make this work you have to have a different type of*
> *organization—either funded by you or venture capitalists. It's*
> *very difficult to use existing organizations to disrupt their*
> *own business. You need a different team, energized with a*
> *new mission. It usually takes different types of people with*
> *entirely different skills. I think you need to consider the power*
> *of a senior team that understands the need for disruptive*

innovation and has bought into it. The management of the incumbent organization may be called upon to transform itself into a cash cow to fund the disruptive growth company that will inevitably replace it.

These comments summarize the major points of participating in disruptive innovations. In particular, you need to operate disruptive innovations either as a semi-independent function within your existing corporate structure or as an entirely separate business entity. The second lesson: think about whether you want to fund disruptive innovation yourself or seek support from venture capitalists.

No matter how you structure the disruptive effort, you'll also need a different model for allocating funds to specific projects because traditional models of evaluating Net Present Value do not work. The discount rate is both unknown and unknowable. The answer lies in Real Options Theory.

Real Options Theory

An IBM manager likened sustaining innovations to playing chess—you know how all the chess pieces move, it's just a matter of intellect to create the best strategy. But disruptive innovation, he said, is more like five-card draw poker. You are dealt five cards, and if you get a pretty good hand, you meet the bets to stay in for the next draw, then discard and replace your weaker cards. If you end up with a good hand, you stay in. If, however, the cost to stay in gets too rich compared to your chances of winning, you fold. This poker approach is called the **Real Options Theory model** of funding, and it works well for disruptive innovation where more traditional economic guideposts like Net Present Value have virtually no meaning since we don't have a handle on the risk discount rate.

Applying Real Options Theory to funding innovation means that management endorses a project one phase at a time, with renewed endorsement needed for each phase. At each checkpoint, management needs to answer two simple questions:

- How good is my hand looking right now?
- How much do I have to risk to stay in for the next round?

If they'd have to risk more than they can afford to lose, then they have to either drop out of the investment or find ways to mitigate the risk (get funding from outside). If the odds look good and the risk is tolerable, they stay in for one more round.

This is precisely the mindset and behavior of good venture capitalists who stage investments as a series of bets, each one providing an opportunity to reevaluate the value of the hand. Once they've bet, they suspend judgment until the next investment point.

Impatient for profits

Clayton Christensen has suggested that where disruptive innovation is concerned:

> *You should be patient for revenue growth and impatient for profit.*

The benefit of this mindset is that if you push the managers of a new venture to get profitable fast, they will change the business model as needed to turn the first profit faster, rather than blow a lot of money on an impractical dream.

Here's an example from the personal experience of coauthor Mike George. When Mike left Texas Instruments many years ago, he joined a firm (using the term loosely) that was funded by a venture capitalist, Dick Hanschen, a former VP at TI. At that time, the firm, International Power Machines (IPM), consisted of an engineer/CEO and a technician in a 2,000-square-foot leased space known as "losers row." The developer had a background in building military airborne frequency converters—devices that would transform the 400Hz aircraft power to 60Hz power needed for test equipment. He had adapted a communication technology to power the conversion, one that greatly reduced cost and weight in transformers and filters.

The venture capital firm supporting the development of the new technology set the following milestones:

Milestone	New Funding
Phase 1: Working breadboard	$100K
Phase 2: Initial delivery to key customer	$100K
Phase 3: Profitable sales	$100K

While the developer was working on the converter, Mike scurried around to find the key customer needed for the Phase 2 target. The alleged big business that they had hoped to get from NASA and the Air Force amounted to a mere two converters… with the clock ticking and the till running dry!

While working with NASA, Mike met a sales rep who said that a Shell refinery needed something like this new converter, so together they made a sales call and won the order—and the next round of funding. This sale was the precursor of an emerging and unknown market. Soon other companies like Houston Lighting, engineering firms like Bechtel, Brown and Root, etc., and eventually IBM customers all needed uninterruptible power. So IPM won the third round of financing and was profitable.

Championing the Real Options approach

A venture capital model of funding is very different from typical funding models based on metrics like NPV. But a phased approach to funding is essential to rein in passionate disruptive innovators. It limits the risk of innovation, forces a reevaluation at each milestone, and drives entrepreneurs to quickly evolve a product/service that can deliver early profits—and thus prove the value of the innovation. Even the fabulous innovations that spun out of Xerox's PARC (e.g., 3Comm) actually went through a similar evolution that was necessary to succeed in the market.

Here again we run into an element of Fast Innovation that is unlikely to receive support naturally from traditional business units. And that's why funding disruptive innovations through Real Options lies in the purview of the Chief Innovation Officer.

Conclusion

The principal structural change recommended in this chapter is the creation of an executive position that will oversee your innovation and growth strategies, and champion disruptive innovations (and their funding). Large companies should give weight to creating a new position (the Chief Innovation Officer) especially for this purpose; smaller companies may want to subsume those responsibilities within an existing corporate position.

The need for a dedicated executive position arises from several facts:

- 90% of companies do not sustain growth above S&P average shareholder returns for more than a decade

- The majority of companies fail to participate in disruptive innovations due to current "good" practices

- Sustaining innovations tend to become quickly commoditized so the *next* sustaining innovations must be churned out before margins collapse on the previous innovation

The changes required to overcome these problems are beyond the control of, or may even run counter to, the interests of individual business unit managers, and therefore must be led from the top. The Chief Innovation Officer will play a critical role in the success or failure of your innovation efforts—another fact that dictates that a strong leader occupy that position.

Endnotes

17 *Information Week OnLine*, September 28, 1998.
18 McKinsey's Next Generation CIOs report, http: //www. computerworld. co. nz/news. nsf/0/A2C0EDD39251E9D5CC256F3B000E98BB?OpenDocument
19 http: //www.detnews.com/2003/business/0309/26/b03-281639. htm.
20 http: //www. canon. com/ir/conf2004q3/conf2004q3e.pdf
21 Robert S. Kaplan and David P. Norton, *The Balanced Scorecard: Translating Strategy into Action* (Boston: Harvard Business School Press, 1996).

CHAPTER 9

Becoming Customer Driven

With Anthony Curtis[22]

The ultimate goal of the innovation process is to create offerings, processes, and business models that convey a powerful competitive advantage by delighting customers. The aim is to create a highly differentiated offering that has an 80% probability of success in the marketplace, commands premium prices and/or exceptionally high market share, has low costs (to drive high margins), lowers invested capital per unit of output, and delivers high growth. These parameters, and these alone, are the drivers of high shareholder value.

One of the most powerful tools to really understand the Voice (or Heart) of the Customer is ethnography, the close observation of customers using your offering *and/or* a competitor's offering in their environment. This kind of detailed knowledge is absolutely essential for achieving the "highly" degree of differentiation required for superior returns.

Since we discussed ethnography earlier in the book (*see* p. 41), this chapter will focus on broader issues surrounding VOC in an innovation context. We'll look at why and how VOC information must play a dominant role throughout the design process, then present a case study showing how diverse VOC practices come together in real life, and end with a review of several key tools for translating identified customer needs into economically profitable offerings.

Using Customer Knowledge Throughout the Design Process

Many companies launch product or service design efforts based on existing knowledge about customer needs gained from a range of sources (questionnaires, focus groups, competitors' marketing pieces, the opinions of marketing staff, senior developers, management, etc.). Teams review the existing customer and competitive information, then launch directly into design work. Decisions are often based on opinion or old data rather than on a genuinely deep and up-to-date understanding of what customers really need. After launch, the company has, at best, superficial contact with customers until the product or service is released into the marketplace. (*See* Figure 9-01.)

Figure 9-01: Typical VOC pattern

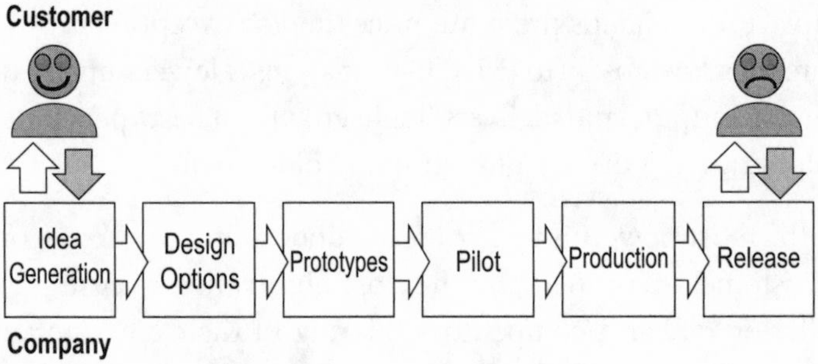

In this model, leaders (or sometimes even non-leaders) have decided that they "know" what the customers want and they are going to give it to them. As you see, customers are never engaged in the development of the ideas or prototyping efforts. Therefore, the first time the customer is even aware that there is a new product or service is when it hits the market. The risks of this non-data-driven approach are evident.

This common approach to VOC has a number of flaws, one being that there is only one feedback cycle from the market, which comes after all development costs have been spent and change is extremely expensive. At this juncture we hear companies say things like, "The customers don't understand all our features... they treat us like a commodity... they don't recognize the value of our differentiation, etc., etc." The fault lies with the company, not with customers.

True masters of the Heart of the Customer incorporate customers and knowledge of customer needs throughout their development processes:

- They conduct ethnographic studies up front (*see* p. 41)

- They always include customer representatives and key suppliers on design teams (particularly during something like the Innovation Blitz, p. 277). This is critical interaction, because customers cannot know your internal capabilities until they *see* a prototype, and this essential knowledge cannot be derived from interviews without that experience. As Henry Ford once remarked:

  > *If I had just asked customers what they wanted,*
  > *it would have been a faster horse!*

- They do a lot of quick cycles back and forth with customers, a few features at a time, throughout the design phases, incorporating detailed customer preference information into the analysis of tradeoff decisions, etc.

- They use the Flexible Performance Target approach (p. 221), presenting customers with a range of possible features and solutions to play with, so through a process of observation and elimination, they find out what customers like and want.

Figure 9-02: Optimal VOC pattern

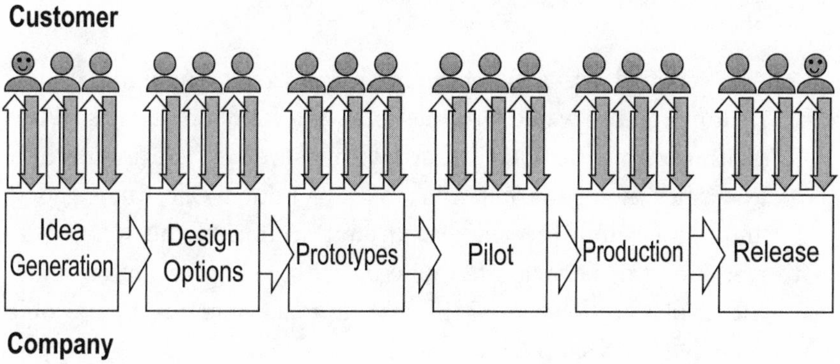

Fast Innovators understand that VOC is ongoing throughout the innovation process. As the diagram shows, customers (external, internal, or both) are engaged after EVERY major process step.

Note that this model is entirely consistent with the rapid prototyping approach discussed earlier. Using this approach to VOC capture/design enables a much faster cycle time to each design decision and ultimately provides a better outcome.

Recall from Part I that perhaps 95% of a customer's thinking and decision process occurs in the subconscious level. So it's not that customers *won't* tell you what they want. More than likely they *cannot*.

Here are few more examples (the first two from Gerald Zaltman's *How Customers Think*):

- The correlation between a customer's statements and actual behavior is low and often negative. Zaltman found that 60% of consumers participating in an at-home test of a new kitchen appliance said they were likely or very likely to buy in the next six months. Yet eight months later, a mere 12% had followed through. (But what number do you think went into the business case for this product?) Worse yet, the ones who didn't follow through on the purchase could not explain their behavior.

- Consumers of over-the-counter medicines insist in interviews and focus groups that they know that generic and brand-named products are exactly the same. But the majority will buy brand over generic when their own symptoms are severe and will almost *always* buy brand for a spouse or child.

- An executive with a major retailer got a personal reminder of why it's important to watch customer behavior for opportunities. While visiting a store, he noticed that many customers were approaching associates asking for directions to find a hot new electronic gadget and were being directed to a distant section of the store. After watching this behavior, he came up with a simple solution: move the display to the front of the store to make sure customers could quickly find what they were looking for.

- Surveys of people entering a supermarket consistently indicate that the majority of consumers prefer lots of fruits, juices, vegetables, whole grain products, less sugar, less saturated fat, etc. But when these same people are ethnographically observed within the supermarket, an entirely different story unfolds. The overwhelming majority purchase highly processed food loaded with saturated fat, processed baked goods, high-fat meats, little fish, a few fruits and fewer vegetables. Similar results are obtained when consumers are asked about consumption of fast food.

We've all heard and have certainly experienced the following truisms: "80% of communication is non-verbal" and "Actions speak louder than words." These lead us to a conclusion about learning about the Heart of the Customer: If a picture is worth a thousand words, then customer observation may be worth a thousand interviews/surveys. What customer behaviors are you missing in your business? What is the financial opportunity if you could understand your customer's behavior?

A Case Study in VOC

To see how the many elements of VOC come together in practice to create differentiated offerings, let's look at the experience of a major national retail chain. As background, remember that various retail stores used to be *destination stores*—meaning that customers would go there when they had a specific need or product in mind (such as televisions, clothes, or books). This has changed in recent years with the growth of online shopping and warehouse stores. Many consumer products have been commoditized as information has become more plentiful, antiquating the model of destination stores with knowledgeable sales staff.

This national retail chain decided to react to these changes. They launched an effort to improve the geographic locations of their stores because many were located in subprime locations. But the other looming question was, "What should the stores look like once they are moved?" They knew they could not stick with the old design—walking into their existing stores was like entering a time warp and going back to the '70s and '80s of retail. While effective in its time, the old store design had changed and a new look was needed.

Given the potential importance of this issue to the company's future, they wanted to make sure the design team was set up for success:

- The team was led by a high-level executive who reported directly to the CEO so the team had a lot of exposure to and interaction with the company's leadership

- Team members included only a handful of very talented, high-profile people (recall the "laws" governing team size on p. 121)

- Team members focused solely on the task of redesign; they were relieved of all other responsibilities

- The team's goal was to understand how they could redesign the stores to give shoppers a more pleasant experience (one that would correlate into sales)

While not directly stated to the rest of the company, it was understood that if this team asked for help, anybody was to quickly assist them—after all, they were designing the future look of the company's stores! To get started, this team:

- Looked at the current state of store layout and design, and assessed how it matched up with what the customer wanted (as much as they knew at that point, at least).

- Reviewed existing quantitative data. Like most good companies, this retail chain had an abundance of market and consumer segmentation studies, market share studies, and business results on hand.

The team used this historical data as a starting point only (many companies will stop here and not go any further, assuming that this data is true and basing all their decisions on it; in fact, such an assumption is *seldom* true). Based on what they learned, they began working on two different fronts: (1) what other companies were doing (benchmarking) and (2) what customers wanted (collecting VOC).

Benchmarking

- They made countless trips to competitors' stores, did subjective evaluations of whether those designs seemed to be working, and looked for design features they could incorporate into their redesign effort.

- Team members traveled to the ends of the earth searching for the newest, hottest store design examples and concepts. For example, they found that certain European retail stores were much more cutting-edge in their fixturing designs.

- The team also looked at designs for many types of stores (not just those in their market), hoping to find inspiration.

VOC collection

- The team recognized that focus groups, surveys, and simple interviews wouldn't cut it for their purposes—those forms of VOC research work better when revising a specific or existing product, not when you're testing a new idea or concept. Their goal was to understand which products and services the store offered were really important in the customers' lives.

- So they went to the customer, on *their* turf, conducting in-home customer visits when they shared the team's preliminary findings, and listened to the concerns and opinions of the consumers.

- They also exploited two direct ethnographic observation techniques common in retail: (1) shop-alongs, going to competing retailers with consumers and observing their actions, asking for clarification on why they did what they did, and capturing detailed notes on consumer reactions, and (2) mystery shoppers, having their own people go to stores as fake customers and interact with the sales associates to see how they were treated, what was offered to them, etc.

Based on the wealth of information they collected, the team moved into the next design phase: prototyping. Though often considered for new product development only, prototyping is critical for all development efforts. This team took its research and ideas and incorporated them into miniature store layouts and designs. For example, to test a completely new design of the music section, they constructed (in open warehouse space) a scaled version of the new fixtures and layout. Then they brought in customers to test out the shopability of the new prototype design. The feedback was immediately implemented into improving the design and establishing a second prototype, which was also tested. The same process was used, a few features at a time, for each department until the store design was finalized.

Now the real test began: the company built a new store based on the complete prototype design. The new design was more expensive to build than one based on the traditional layout, and required a different staffing model than that used in the company's other stores. But the format was visibly differentiated from all existing store designs and contributed to improved sales that more than offset the higher cost. Initial customer reaction was very positive and there were more reports of favorable shopping experiences. Significant changes in the new design included:

- A layout and operational design with lower operating costs. Much of the savings resulted from lower stocking and restocking costs; the new design eliminated the need for a huge warehouse in the back to hold excess product, so actual warehouse space was dramatically reduced. Instead, the plan called for easy changing of floor fixtures so product went right from the truck to the sales floor.

- The new layout was designed to solve customer challenges/frustrations in finding things they wanted. There was a shift to a more functional setup in the store that allowed for cross-selling and experience selling (e.g., if you were planning for your daughter's graduation, everything you needed to videotape it, store the file to a disk, play it on a DVD, watch it on a television, print still frames from a computer, and so on, was all within arm's reach at best, or within eyesight at worst). These layout changes improved customers' range of visibility and ease-of-access through the use of simpler signage (including clear pictograms) to lead customers to the areas of the store they were interested in.

- The new layout, stocking functionality, and other changes freed up staff from much of the mundane work in the store so they could put more time into value-added sales tasks (such as selling complex digital imaging equipment).

As a result of this design effort, this retailer now constructs all new stores in easily changed and transformable fixturing—which minimizes the cost of making changes, and therefore makes the company far more responsive to changing customer needs. They are also more likely to experiment with different layouts or fixtures. This capability means every store can easily accommodate changing markets and different customer tastes. To date, every indication is that the changes are successful. Sales at new stores using some of the new design elements have greatly outperformed the legacy stores in the same or similar markets.

Different retailer, similar results

Another retailer used the same customer-centered approach to redesigning its stores and came up with very similar results:

- The redesigned layout allowed for significant savings in labor costs. In their case, the savings resulted from strategies like shelving items in their original shipping cases with a cutaway for access, and easier shelf maintenance (hanging items were spring-loaded to always have a nice facing).

- They, too, came up with ways to improve customers' use of the store. For example, they moved away from an aisle-dependent layout (which hides most of the products from customers' eyes), instead designing around pods—areas of use focused on customer functions/needs rather than on typical stocking categories. Large pictograms hanging near the pods enabled customers to easily look around the store and see where they needed to go.

- The open-pod design also enabled the retailer to reduce staffing levels for the store. Fewer associates were needed to staff the store because they could see the whole store at once. This enabled better supervision (the store manager could see whole store at once, too) AND reduced shrinkage.

Here's a summary of everything this company did right:

- The level of the team was suitable for the importance of the issue (business-critical project with high executive visibility)

- The team was kept small, which made it easier to move forward quickly

- They looked *outside* themselves—and, in fact, outside their industry—for ideas

- They used historical data *only* as a starting point; actual design decisions were based on new ethnographic customer data

- They got information from a variety of sources

- Up front, they directly observed customers in actual stores (the ethnographic approach), complemented with other means of identifying customer needs

- They got additional VOC input through rapid prototyping—multiple cycles of testing individual ideas on a small scale rather than waiting to do a grand test of everything at the end

VOC Translation Tools (Design for Lean Six Sigma)

It's one thing to come up with design options based on customer needs—quite another to create a design that operations can replicate at low cost, high quality and with fast lead time. The field of study concerned with these issues is called Design for Lean Six Sigma (DfLSS), the design tools used to ensure process speed (Lean) and high quality/low cost (Six Sigma). DfLSS focuses on achieving a flawless launch of new high-value products and services that meet the cost and timing goals of the business while delighting customers.

The essence of DFLSS is to ensure customer focus, design quality, rapid design time, and predictability during the early design phases, and fast operational lead times and flexibility to serve customers quickly and with low cost.

Robustness: The secret of DfLSS

One of the principles built into the DfLSS approach is designing products or services that are "robust to variation"—meaning they will perform to specifications even in the face of natural variation in the environment. This robustness goes a long way towards ensuring a successful launch.

DfLSS also includes a number of tools that prevent errors or delays and hence minimize operational lead time. For example, development teams can deliberately design products and services that require very little or no setup time when changing from one design to another (setup time is a major contributor to process delays). The benefit is more flexibility, shorter lead times, and lower non-value-add and overhead costs. Widespread use of DfLSS tools results in:

- Significantly better alignment of the executed innovation with the Voice of the Customer
- Less design rework and fewer market launch issues
- Better teamwork and communication between innovators, operations and marketing
- Earlier detection of problems and a sound basis for resolution
- Smoother transitions from concept to design to implementation
- Faster operational lead times and greater flexibility
- Higher customer acceptance levels
- Lower design costs (specs focused on critical-to-quality customer needs); lower manufacturing/production costs, fewer product returns, and lower warranty and liability costs

Many tools are available to help in this process. Discussing all the tools indepth is beyond the scope of this book, but here's an overview of the most valuable and therefore most popular tools. (Interested readers can learn more from many sources.)[23] If you're a manager or executive, you don't necessarily have to learn to use these tools yourself, but you need to understand their power and make sure that their use is part of the warp and woof of launching any new innovation.

DfLSS Tools for Translating Customer Requirements

The purpose of these tools is to develop a deep understanding of the Voice of the Customer at the project level:

1) **Analyzing customer statements:** Ever had a product or service that sounded great in the idea-generation phase only to flop in meeting customer needs once it was executed? Tools like Affinity Diagrams and Structure Trees can help you find the pearls of wisdom in customer statements (from observation, interviews, focus groups, etc.). These tools should be used throughout a project to analyze customer input and reactions.

2) **Conjoint Analysis:** If asked, most customers will say that they want every possible feature at the lowest possible cost. Conjoint Analysis is a powerful statistical analysis tool for marketing, to evaluate ideas, compare features, and determine price elasticity. Conjoint studies force the customers to make choices, and let you understand the benefits and potential losses of trade-offs.

3) **House of Quality:** The House of Quality is a matrix at the heart of the Quality Function Deployment (QFD) methodology. It's used to help teams convert imprecise customer statements ("I want a fast car") into tangible, measurable design requirements with specific targets and allowable variability (engine size and power, for example). Creating a House is time-intensive and teams can get bogged down if they dive into too much detail for all aspects of the design. Instead, use the tool broadly at the beginning, and then focus on critical areas.

DfLSS Tools for Exploring Design Alternatives

These tools are designed to help you innovate and explore high-level design concepts.

4) **Analytic Hierarchy Process (AHP):** AHP allows for a weighted comparison of what customers want (Voice of the Customer) with what the business can afford to do in terms of lead time, costs, etc.

(Voice of the Business). The tool allows the team to make subjective comparisons yet get quantitative results that help lead to clear design decisions. AHP provides a critical input for concept selection using the Pugh Matrix (*see* next tool).

5) **Pugh Matrix:** Of the many concepts that a design team has considered, which is best? The Pugh Matrix is a decision matrix that allows teams to select a concept that will best optimize customer needs and business objectives. Use this tool to replace lengthy discussions based on opinions with a fact-based quantitative approach to selecting the best design.

6) **Simulation Modeling:** How do you know without investing any capital that this service or product design is likely to actually work? Simulation Modeling reduces costs and allows for risk mitigation earlier in the design cycle. By prototyping with a simulation, you can check out design scenarios at almost no cost.

7) **Capability Analysis:** Is this design capable of meeting the customer's requirements? Are you sure? Capability Analysis statistically calculates the ability of our product or service to meet both the high-level and detailed specifications.

8) **Statistical Tolerancing:** Lean Six Sigma has taught us the importance of reducing variation. How much variability is allowable in your new products and services? Statistical Tolerancing breaks down the higher-level requirements to the detailed level to ensure overall quality.

DfLSS Tools for Optimizing the Detailed Design

9) **Design of Experiments (DOE):** When is your design good enough? Is it the best it can be in your delivery environment? Have you optimized its ability to meet customer requirements? DOE is used to optimize the design so that it is robust to variability in the environment. By providing a scientific approach to optimizing design variables (vs. traditional trial and error), DOE also allows you to reduce design task time and variation in design task time.

10) **Hypothesis Testing:** Are you really confident that this new service is better than the old one? How strongly do customers prefer it? Data analysis and statistical tools are used throughout the DfLSS process, so that design choices are as fact-based and data-driven as possible.

11) **Failure Modes and Effects Analysis (FMEA):** Ever launched a new offering, only to have production, delivery, or use problems appear later in unexpected and seemingly unrelated areas? FMEA is a tool that helps teams anticipate problems and develop solutions. This kind of risk mitigation begins early and continues throughout the design process at both the conceptual and the detailed design levels. This tool ensures that you address the risks prior to market launch.

12) **Design for Manufacture and Assembly (DFMA):** If your company is like most, the transition from design to manufacturing (or more generically "production" if we include service preparation) is fraught with rework, frustration, non-value-added activities, and avoidable delays. Months of revenue from new offerings are lost due to a poor hand-offs between the design and manufacturing teams. DFMA helps teams design products that will have a smooth

Other tools useful for innovation

DfLSS techniques form the core of an innovation toolbox, but there are others you should include as well, such as:

- Lean Best Practices: Techniques like mistake proofing (poka-yoke), the Four Step Rapid Set-Up Method, and many others are used to ensure that design, development, and delivery processes are truly Lean (operate with maximum speed and minimal cost).

- Cost of Complexity toolset: As discussed earlier in this book, complexity in processes and offerings is a huge drain on cost and efficiency. Since innovation by definition is adding new things (product, services, processes, methods) to a company's repertoire, it behooves us to use the tools for conquering complexity—platform design, commonization, rationalization, modularization, etc.—in parallel with the innovation process itself.

transition to manufacturing, will be environmentally friendly, and that minimize maintenance, serviceability, and other life-cycle costs.

To give you a taste of how these tools help in the design process, we'll go through four of them in action.

Lean QFD / House of Quality

We've already talked a lot about the importance of understanding customers' true wants and needs. In our experience, even companies that do a good job of collecting such data often fail to effectively represent those needs in the final product or service—hence leading to the overall failure of the innovation effort.

The House of Quality tool described earlier is well suited to making the translation from need to product/service. The House is a one-page summary of customer-related information important to the early phases of a development project:

- Which customer needs are most important? How will they be measured?

- How does your company benchmark relative to competitors? How are you doing technically?

- What potential conflicts in design need to be resolved?

If used effectively, the House of Quality analysis can be completed in hours or a few days. The example in Figure 9-03 (next page) took about an hour to prepare. Like any analysis tool, the best results will be achieved with a Lean mindset—focusing on achieving the maximum benefit from the minimum time investment.

Figure 9-03: House of Quality

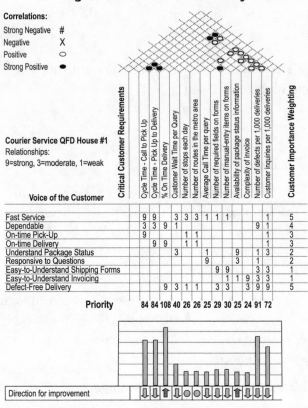

This House of Quality summarizes data gathered through a QFD approach. It displays key metrics that relate to satisfying the Voice of the Customer, and targets for the design process. With this detailed information, the team was on track for a design that truly delighted the customer.

Design of Experiments

Design of Experiments (DOE) is a powerful technique that can be used during the design process to arrive at the best combination of design elements to drive superior performance or value for the product or service you are designing. It is a set of tests that let you evaluate multiple factors at the same time (compare that to the traditional "change one thing at a time" approach). The output from these simultaneous multiple experiments shows you which *set* of input conditions leads to the maximum value of output.

DOE is perfectly suited to companies seeking fast design times because it generates a lot of information *much* faster than traditional experimentation. It can be used in nearly any situation, from evaluating specific designs to screening numerous options. For example, Capital One makes about 40,000 small DOE tests per year to determine the optimal parameters for a given credit card in a given market segment. Similarly, as described in the HBR article, "R&D Comes to Services: Bank of America's Pathbreaking Experiment," BOA has actually set up a prototype banking center that regularly runs designed experiments.[24] The result, according to author Stefan Thomke, is "surges of fresh thinking, improved customer satisfaction, new customers, and deep[er] understanding of service development. The payoff? A crucial edge over less adventurous competitors." The key to success is having the ability to test a lot of different things at once—which not only saves time but also reveals how different factors interact.

DOE will also impact design task times and task time variation. One of our clients was struggling to optimize two very important and conflicting parameters for construction equipment design—the maximum load that the vehicle can lift, and the vehicle's stability. The traditional practice was to delegate the dilemma to a senior design engineer who would spend a few weeks with trial-and-error approaches, ending up with designs often sent back to the drawing board by management who thought the solution wasn't good enough. A model created in one afternoon using DOE optimized the scenario immediately, and was available to be re-used on all future models.

Conjoint Analysis

Conjoint analysis is a variation on DOE that focuses specifically on feature trade-off decisions: What do customers value? How much do they value it? Will they be willing to pay a higher price for exactly what they want? What don't customers value?

Here is one quick example of conjoint analysis to illustrate the principles. During ethnographic observations of the actual use of a medical instrument, a company noticed a very distinct pattern: Nurses used the device much more often than physicians, but used only a few features. Physicians used the device much less often, but when they did, used many more features (*see* Figure 9-04). Yet the front panel of the instrument was cluttered with all the features, which made those used most often by the nurses difficult to access.

Figure 9-04: Feature Usage Input for Conjoint Analysis

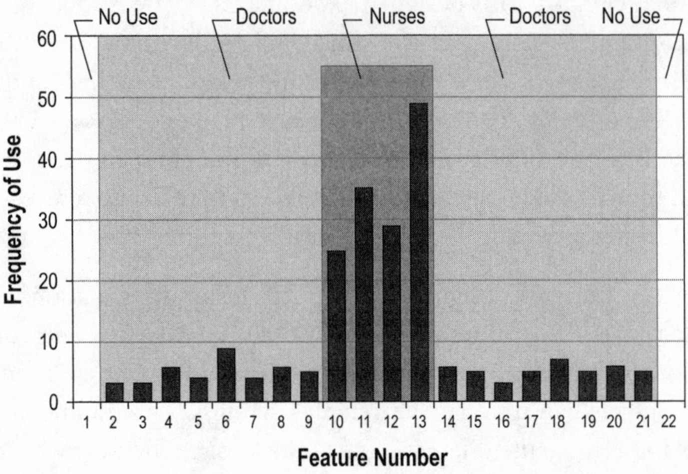

The nurses used only features 10 to 13 very often; physicians used a much broader range of features much less often. Notice that feature numbers 1 and 22 had no users. The goal is to avoid an arms race on features that forces you to create a commodity product that nobody wants and on which you can't make money. Understanding what features are used and valued by customers is part of a conjoint analysis to look at trade-offs between features and price.

The ethnographic input suggested that either the company should design two different products (one for nurses, the other for physicians), or find a way to make it easier for both audiences to find and use exactly the features they want (such as having a simpler front panel display). The company opted for the latter approach. Designers then had to come up with a design that made it obvious and simple for nurses to use the four features they needed, but still accommodate the wider range of features used by doctors. The result was a single product with a simple set of four visual control knobs for the high-use features used by nurses (most people still prefer a control knob instead of a digital input), with a door that hid all the complex features in a digital format (similar to some TV remotes). The product was far more successful than its competitors, who fought back with even more features and continued to build complex front panels on their products that did not address the frustrations of their largest user population.

Designed experiments and conjoint analysis can help you innovate both in the design of your products or services *and* in the processes and systems used to create those offerings. The results are impressive. Capital One's designed experiments, for example, let them determine what combination of features will succeed in a given market segment, which means they can go to the mass markets with a proven product. ITT Industries has applied DOE to every facet of their manufacturing, engineering, and test processes. For example, applying DOE to their night-vision goggles has improved the yield and allowed their Roanoke division to earn positive economic profit in a capital-intensive industry, a feat no competitor has matched (they've also delighted the Army and Marine Corps with their performance).

The much broader lesson from these examples is that you need expertise with a broad range of VOC methods if you want to be able to deliver differentiated products and services at prices that will keep you profitable, growing, and competitive. Our suggestion is that most of your effort should be "up close and personal," built around ethnography, brainstorming, prototyping, conducting Innovation Blitzes, etc. Questionnaires, surveys, and focus groups will simply not create a breakthrough insight, and in fact may be misleading. The value of these latter techniques lies more in suggesting new directions to evaluate rather than in providing design insight. Hossein Eslambolchi, Chief Technology Officer of AT&T, commented at the November 2004 Fortune Innovation conference:

> In the past our belief was, "If a product ain't broke, it doesn't have enough features yet."

Beauty is in the eye of the beholder, and the value of an offering can best be found by ethnographic observation of customers, and enhanced by experiences such as the Innovation Blitz—not by having an engineer reading competitive specifications, not by creating fancy new technology, and not by relying on judgment based on past experience (unless these insights are first tested by prototypes and customer observations).

Increasing Trust in Your VOC

We've seen a number of executive teams decide *against* investing in a disruptive innovation or ignore the results from a design team because they didn't understand or didn't believe the customer data.

There are specific steps you can take to increase confidence in your VOC systems—in effect, expand your corporate comfort zone and make it safer to take actions you might once have thought risky:

- **Build cross-functional teams**—You want to have employees with different viewpoints and from different levels (frontline to executive) in the company observing and talking to customers as part of your ethnographic studies. When these employees get back to the office, they can compare notes and interpretations. The same advice applies to gathering and analyzing all of your customer data. Only by using staff from different backgrounds and with different biases will you come up with a collective best interpretation that most closely reflects customer needs.

- **Include nontraditional skill sets on teams** (appropriate to the design challenge)—Look to people outside of traditional engineering or product and service design for your teams. Involve people from sales, marketing, human resources, and/or other areas, who can help you understand and interpret the "human factors" relevant to your product or service. (As an aside, not all of these people need to work on the team full-time. They may be advisors, or perhaps can be included in an intensive Innovation Blitz session.)

- **Regularly update managers/executives on what the data are showing**—Frequent feedback loops with the Chief Innovation

Officer and executive sponsors are just as important as frequent feedback loops with customers. As noted previously, that doesn't mean the leaders in your company have to become experts, but they should be involved regularly in the evolution of the thinking that drives the innovation. If they are left behind, they will mistrust VOC data or the concept it drives, and may opt for a solution consistent with their experience rather than with the data.

Conclusion

We've used the term Heart of the Customer throughout this book to denote a depth of customer understanding that goes beyond what most companies settle for—which often amounts to a quick survey here or there and involving customers only at the end of the design process ("What do you think about this new service we've just finished?"). Perhaps we should be using the term "Heart of Innovation" because that's what it really is. If you don't have a deep understanding of customer needs, don't involve customers throughout the design process, and don't ensure that your executives are willing to go with what the data show, at best you'll end up with me-too offerings that delight no one (including your shareholders).

Endnotes

22 Anthony Curtis is a Senior Consultant with George Group Consulting. He spent six years in various management positions in retail, then moved into Six Sigma implementation where he became a certified Master Black Belt. He has a particular interest in Voice of the Customer techniques, and is an expert in curriculum development, training, coaching, and mentoring for Lean Six Sigma application in services. In addition to his retail experience, Tony has consulted in the governmental, advertising, and pharmaceutical industries.

23 We've discussed DOE in our previous books (*Lean Six Sigma* and *Lean Six Sigma for Service,* both from McGraw-Hill), and conjoint analysis in *Conquering Complexity in Your Business*. There are also a lot of other resources on these topics. We highly recommend that you look into these disciplines.

24 Stefan Thomke, *R&D Comes to Services: Bank of America's Pathbreaking Experiments* (HBR OnPoint Enhanced Edition), April 2003, Product Number 3246.

SPOTLIGHT ON

Creating an Idea-Rich Environment

If you study companies known for being innovation hotbeds, you'll find that one of their biggest strengths is the ability to create a work environment where ideas are constantly percolating to the surface. Some of the ideas are generated in focused settings, like working on a project or trying to solve a particular challenge. But the main sense you get is that coming up with new ideas is a way of life. (To be Fast, you need to limit the number of *active* projects in development, but still want a good stockpile of *potential* projects that you can draw on according to your capability and market demands.) The result is an atmosphere charged with creativity, where new connections and insights are made every day.

Here are three suggestions for creating a workplace where ideas and creativity are generated as reliably as overnight delivery from FedEx.

1. Raise awareness of innovation opportunities

It is important to expand the potential sources of innovation beyond your official designers to encompass the whole company. We suggest that a significant percentage of all employees receive familiarization training in the Three Dimensions of Innovation and other Fast Innovation principles. Have them read excerpts from this book plus a description of the company's goals and direction. Include the topic in your basic employee training. Have staff take a course on innovation. Ask your managers to lead a discussion about the Three Dimensions at staff meetings. You may want to develop a simple innovation certification quiz to verify what employees have learned. While development of new products or services *may* be the sole purview of your developers, designers, or engineers, any shrewd observer may find opportunities for market definition or process/business model innovations. People who receive this training will "self select" as innovators. Ask people who have been through this training in to participate in the Idea Forum (*see* below) and Innovation Blitzes.

2. Create an Idea Forum

One of the keys to making innovation every employee's business is to provide a forum where everyone has an opportunity to become involved. An Idea Forum event is one way to make this goal a reality. An Idea Forum is a two- to three-day event where selected employees, customers, and suppliers come together to share ideas around a central theme. The theme changes each time, so participation will change as well, and ideally every employee will eventually have the opportunity to participate in one. Experience has shown that Idea Forums work best when they...

a) **Are highly focused**, designed around a central question or theme. The challenge is coming up with questions that are broad enough to allow diverse reactions but targeted enough to contribute to a business need of the company. Examples include:

- Where are competitors beating us badly?

- What blockbuster ideas do you have that could generate big sales?

- What's the most exciting development in [XYZ] field?

- What ideas in your area do you think could be re-used in other products/services in the company?

- What things have really delighted your customers?

- What do you see on the horizon that could threaten our business in 2 years? 5 years? 10 years?

b) **Limit participation to people selected based on criteria established specifically for each Idea Forum** (i.e., it is not an open invitation to just anyone). One way to do this is to post a preliminary description of the purpose for the event (the business case) on your intranet and then invite anyone who thinks they could contribute to submit a request for participation. The Chief Innovation Officer and his/her staff evaluate the requests and selects those who best fit the purpose. (The key here is that while, over time, lots of different people will get a chance to participate, each individual Idea Forum is attended by a selected, diverse group of people who have knowledge relevant to a specific business need.)

c) **Start with a sharing session.** The purpose and structure of Idea Forums vary, but generally you'll want to start off with a sharing session.

   – If you have a smaller group (fewer than 20 or 25 people), do this by having each person present to the rest of the group, one at a time. Inject creativity into the session by requiring people to create clay models, skits, or some physical symbol of their message.

   – If you have a larger group (more than 25 people), consider using a "poster session" approach like that used at many conferences. Everyone has to come with a prepared storyboard showing charts, graphs, photos, etc., that illustrate their key points. Half of the group stands by their storyboards responding to the questions of the other half who are milling around; halfway through the session, the roles reverse (the presenters become wanderers and vice versa).

d) **Follow up with focused brainstorming and processing sessions.** After the sharing sessions, divide participants into mini design teams and lead them in focused brainstorming sessions. (What did they learn? What inspiration did they have around the stated purpose of the event?) Work through the ideas they've heard that seem most promising for the company. End the event with teams presenting their ideas to each other.

e) **End by presenting a summary of innovative ideas to the Chief Innovation Officer.** The goal of the Idea Forum is to come up with ideas that have practical value to the company and that can be developed through specific development projects, an Innovation Blitz, or further investigation. Be sure to highlight ideas you think could disrupt the market, as those will be the most valuable to your company in the long run.

Using an intranet to support knowledge development

Intranets are commonly used to help people accomplish everyday work, so why not devote a portion of your intranet to support innovation? The possibilities are endless for using an intranet to advance knowledge. You can have open forums devoted to an issue where anyone in the company can post any information they think is relevant. You could have a moderator pose a "question of the week" and invite responses. You could sponsor reading groups and post reviews of books or journal articles, or post summaries of highlights from your Idea Forums.

Recognize, however, that doing an innovation website well takes time and attention, just as any other effort inside your company. You'll get the most from the effort if you focus the site on issues or capabilities that your company regards as critical to its future.

CHAPTER 10

Fast and Flexible

The New Corporate Mantra for Design Work

You'll sometimes hear people say, "If only we could nail down the performance specs at the outset and stick with them, we would have a faster and more effective process." Companies that do nail down the specs up front always hear a lot of valid grumbling about all the changes demanded by marketing after the design is well advanced. These changes, while causing time delay and cost overruns, may save the innovation from oblivion!

The nail-it-down-early approach (an "early freeze") has the appearance of logic, and would also appear to obey the Law of Lead Time: the fewer changes in features and specs along the way, the fewer tasks-in-process, and the shorter the development time. The problem with this approach is that **we want to deliver a delighter, not a dud**... and we want to do it fast.

Unfortunately, nailing down all specs and performance requirements at the outset will increase the odds of delivering a dud, delivering very late, or both! Going for an early freeze means predicting *exactly* how successful your innovation teams will be at delivering creativity, breakthroughs, and a pre-defined level of performance, neither better nor worse. If they unexpectedly come up with the possibility of something better than spec, they have no authority or incentive to spend extra energy in exploration. If they run into unexpected trouble with a given performance parameter, they must doggedly slug it out and very possibly delay the whole program.

So yes, a nail-it-down approach appears to obey the Law of Lead Time by reducing the number of tasks in a project to a single list of features. But it flouts the Law of Innovation Variation in that it does not accommodate tasks that take longer than estimated nor relax a difficult or impossible performance parameter until serious damage has been done to the time buffers or the schedule. Knowing that every project has tasks that run into time trouble, nailing it down almost guarantees me-too offerings because it effectively strangles creative energy upon which differentiation and innovation depend. Worse, it can cause long delays while a team struggles with the impossible. In fact, picking a single list of specs is a prime reason for the high variation in task times and lack of innovative products.

Fortunately for most companies, this ideal of a single list of performance specs is a dream never fully executed to its nightmarish conclusion. A project may start with nailed-down specs, but marketing or production or sales intervenes with a great new idea that requires a change in the design, and interdepartmental warfare often results—and the project is delayed, with a virtual guarantee of missing the time-to-market target and incurring huge cost overruns. Innovators are a passionate lot, and they may stand up for a better solution even if they get batted down. In truth, the problem isn't with the people—it is with the process. While this warfare occasionally ends up transforming me-too designs into highly differentiated offerings, it does nothing to proactively foster that result, and it takes longer and generates higher cost.

What's the solution? Here's an example:

> *A producer of microprocessors found that trying to nail down specs at the start of a project blocked their development team from exploiting creative, differentiated options that arose later in the project (sometimes as the result of a rapidly changing marketplace). And since product marketing and design worked in silos, communication between them was almost non-existent. Product marketing would provide nailed-down specs early in the project, only to pry the nails out two or three months later and put them in another spot. As a result, design teams could not get motivated to really drive the design because they knew the requirements would likely get pulled out from under them.*

*Two solutions changed the innovation delivery immeasurably
in this company. New management drove the teams to hold
weekly cross-functional meetings that lasted nearly all day
and included the right players from design, marketing, sales,
research and production. Everyone was on the same page and
able to understand the need to react and change when either
marketing got new data or when designers made a breakthrough, creating new possibilities.*

*The second solution was dividing the specs into three basic
categories: (1) non-negotiable "must haves," (2) minimum
performance or feature specs (more is better but must meet
the minimum), and (3) desired features and design elements
whose requirements could fluctuate depending on the current
state of research and testing (with customer feedback). As a
result of these changes, the company launched its most competitive, successful product in its history.*

Flexible Performance Targets: How to be creative without sacrificing lead time

You may know that Fred Brooks led one of the first big commercial software development projects, IBM's System 360. After many years of
success and failure, he came to the conclusion that:

*It is impossible for customers to specify completely, precisely
and correctly the exact requirement of a product before having
tried some version of the product they are specifying.*

Microsoft came to a similar conclusion, as we quoted in Part I of this
book:[25]

*The spec should always be incomplete, and you always, as a
developer, want it to be incomplete. We've seen in IBM the
horrors of writing directly to a spec, because **nobody is that
smart!***

These examples set the foundation for understanding why **Flexible Performance Target Designing** is a key component of Fast Innovation. (Toyota calls it "Set Based Design" because they explore a set of possible targets, i.e., more than one performance level.)[26] By planning for the need to pursue multiple performance targets, you allow for the unexpected upside of people's creativity, while still delivering highly differentiated offerings to the market in half the time of the competition. The fact is that the very process of development will tell you what performance you can meet with surprising ease and what is unexpectedly difficult. This knowledge arises from experience and investigation; rarely can it be predicted before the project begins. Hence the futility of nailing down the specs at that point.

The Fast Innovation approach is to delay the freeze on key design features as long the schedule will permit. This allows teams to *create new information* during development by eliminating the uncertainty about how to deliver performance specs on time and within market targets. (*See* sidebar, next page.)

Designing to Flexible Performance Targets

A major problem in completely specifying a product is that the marketing people generally want more features than are feasible to develop within a tight schedule. Let's say you launch a design team with a single solution in mind that you're confident will delight customers, but it turns out to be difficult or impossible to develop *on time*. Or maybe the agreed-on single solution has a me-too performance—you can get it to the market on time, but it will likely underperform expectations.

Flexible Performance Target Design seeks to achieve the best possible design that meets the maximum number of customer delighters within the required time-to-market deadlines. In other words, it pushes design teams to delight if possible but to make schedule in any case. To explain exactly how Flexible Performance Target Designing is different, we first need to review traditional design approaches.

What is Information?

The need to allow specifications to emerge during a development project is an outgrowth of Information Theory. Here is how Craig Wynett, the general manager of future growth initiatives at Procter & Gamble, puts it:

*At P&G, we think of creativity not as a mysterious gift of the talented few but as the everyday task of making **nonobvious** connections*

Non-obvious is another way of saying "surprise." Thus the amount of information in a statement has something to do with the probability of the event. Here's a quick example: Assume it's August in Dallas: How much information is contained in these two statements?:

"It's hot and humid"   vs.   "It's cold and snowing"

We expect it to be hot in Dallas in August, so there is very little surprise, hence very little information, in the first statement. But to say that it is snowing is entirely unexpected, very surprising, and conveys a lot of information. Exploring multiple options opens you up to surprise, and there's a greater chance of generating useful information, as shown in Figure 10-01 (its derivation is described in Appendix 3).

Figure 10-01: Information theory

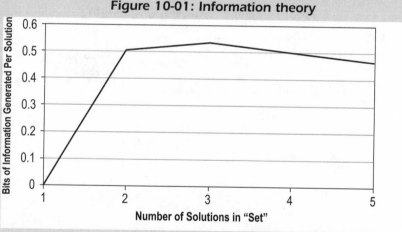

If you specify one performance level, nothing has been learned in the development process. But if you just try two performance levels, you are generating information near the maximum and will in fact learn more—of course with additional development cost and time, the investment may well let you identify a delighter that will propel the project to market success.

Traditional design approaches

In traditional design, teams develop all the features based on the original solution or written specification and *then* seek feedback from customers and others. This is sometimes called serial design (*see* Figure 10-02).

Figure 10-02: Traditional Serial Design

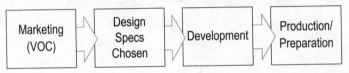

An improvement on this model is called concurrent design (Figure 10-03), which inserts formal feedback reviews by *downstream* teams throughout the process, which may result in modifications. This is certainly better than the traditional approach of getting feedback late in the process. But concurrent development is effectively inwardly focused: it seeks to solve manufacturability or quality problems and generally does not involve customer input.

Figure 10-03: Concurrent Engineering

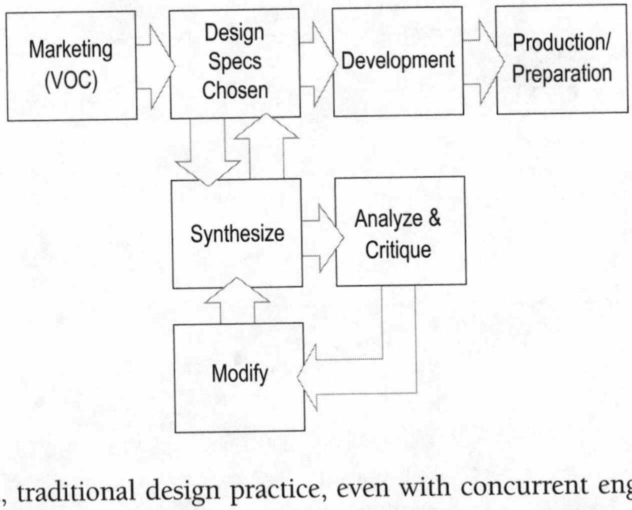

In short, traditional design practice, even with concurrent engineering, consciously tries to pick an overall solution and specification as early as possible then reworks that solution until it meets design objectives and internal demands. This design approach keeps iterating on one solution out of many potential solutions.

The flexible approach

In contrast, Flexible Performance Target Design delays the convergence on a single solution in the belief that the creativity of innovators (faced with the challenge of delighting customers) will surpass expectations. It employs the more rapid feedback regimen of concurrent design but gives customers more options to react to through alternative "customer delighter" and "satisfier" solutions. Considering several possible solutions from the start increases the possibility that the team will find the best possible solution (highly differentiated with lowest cost and shortest development time). It can't do worse than traditional "fixed spec"

Principles of Flexible Performance Target Design

1) **Understand the intended need; provide outlines of specifications.** Program managers and engineers should start with ethnographic inputs and then add more details as the development effort evolves, because they know it is unrealistic to freeze the features and their details too early. Some readers may see the similarity with Systems Engineering.

2) **Allow specifications to emerge or evolve with time.** The spec *emerges* based on the vision, the outline, and performance of the innovators. All this flies in the face of conventional product development logic, stated or unstated. It's impossible to tie down all specs at the start of a project. You are simultaneously asking too much *and* too little. You are either specifying an offering that is impossible to develop within schedule and that likely has differentiation that nobody wants, or one that will result in a me-too offering.

3) **Early freeze re-used design elements; delay the freeze for critical differentiators.** All specifications ultimately must be frozen for a release to take place. But as you may recall, having a high degree of re-use is a critical element in Fast Innovation. Presuming you've adopted that advice, you can shorten overall design time by freezing the re-used elements early in a project, thereby allowing you to devote more time, energy, and flexibility to the critical features that will provide differentiation. The longer you can explore alternatives (consistent with schedule), the more likely it is that you'll uncover a new combination or design that will delight customers.

design (though that would be a sad commentary on the creativity of your innovators!). And best case, you'll find new feature combinations or design elements that maximize customer delight at low cost.

How Flexible Performance Target Design works

A team starts by gathering detailed Heart of the Customer data so they have a deep understanding of customer needs. They can invoke an **early freeze** for re-used components, and for new design elements that are transparent to the customer (features that customers either don't notice and/or don't care about because they don't affect performance).

All other design features—those that likely will contribute most to differentiation—are subject to a **delayed final freeze**, reached after the team…

- Uses the customer data to identify likely customer reactions to different levels of performance. (These levels are often tagged with labels like "satisfiers" or "delighters.")

- Assigns different team members or subgroups to come up with solutions targeted at the various performance levels.

- Has the subgroups present mock-ups, prototypes, etc., on all performance alternatives to customers. For products, this means developing physical prototypes the customers can play with; in services, develop a role-play where customer can experience the service and provide feedback. (Remember the principle of Rapid Prototyping discussed on p. 65.)

- Processes this customer input, better informed now of what they can develop within the required schedule, and thus closer to having a firm definition of the ultimate offering than was possible at the outset. Depending on the outcome of the feedback session, the team may want to play with additional prototypes or role plays, and do one or more cycles of customer feedback before finalizing the design.

The timing of the freeze is flexible, with reviews starting somewhere around the half-way point to completion (usually judged by estimating the median time needed for similar tasks, and using half that value). At that midpoint, developers and managers need to assess progress towards customer delighters, and decide whether to invoke the final freeze (*see* sidebar) even if the delighter level of performance hasn't been attained yet, or to continue exploration. The assessment should be based on:

- how much additional development time it will take to create the delighter vs. the satisfier

- the value the customers place on delighters vs. satisfiers

- whether some features can be deleted or delayed (added to later revisions)

- the difference between the cost of development and the cost of the offering (i.e., if investing more in development will lead to an offering that is priced above the market, it's time to freeze)

- how much total remaining buffer time the project has[27]

You may need to use a performance weighting process (next page) to help you make the best trade-off decision.

The challenge of the Final Freeze

During the final freeze stage, development teams are faced with competing priorities. On the one hand, developers may be working on two or three targets that contribute to different levels of performance and customer satisfaction—ranging from a high-risk delighter to a low-risk me-too that meets minimal satisfaction levels. On the other hand are Voice of the Business issues such as cost, lead time-to-market, and the technical risks of that product or service. Remember: time-to-market targets are critical because of the early entrant advantage (see p. 19).

Making the right choice at this point requires that you have a good handle on your Voice of Customer data *and* on your business/market needs so you make the best trade-off decisions. Remember, to meet schedule you may have to settle for a "customer satisfier" at the first launch. But the knowledge gained by failing to develop the "customer delighter" should be carefully archived, as it may become more feasible to apply to the next release when commoditization is about to ensue, or to some other project.

The Performance Weighting Process

Let us take the example of developing the final freeze for an engine design that needs to address a range of competing and contradictory performance parameters. If, for example, power is much more important than fuel consumption to the customer, then you will be inclined to design the more powerful engine. But if designing a high-power engine will take a long time, and result in a high product cost and late arrival to the market, then the Voice of the Business (VOB) will resist that solution.

The field of decision theory can offer some insights to this type of dilemma. It encompasses both complicated and simple techniques; we favor a simpler approach using the Analytic Hierarchy Process (AHP), first developed at the RAND Corporation,[28] and the Pugh Matrix[29] (both methods introduced earlier as part of the DfLSS toolset).

The AHP relies on paired comparisons in which each option is compared with every other option based on both VOC and VOB criteria. This approach has the advantage of allowing an estimation of *how much* more (on a scale of 1 to 10) one alternative is preferred over another, as opposed to just stating that one is better. (For the mathphiles, information theory tells us we can input $\log_2 10 = 3.3$ bits of information with AHP vs. just 1 bit of information for a simple paired-comparison. See Appendix 3.) Further, AHP can work with a circular conundrum or what economists call "utility reversals":

I prefer apples to oranges, and oranges to bananas,

but I prefer bananas to apples.

Once the AHP comparisons are performed, the outcome is input to a Pugh Matrix, where you can evaluate the relative benefits or penalties of each option and get a final, weighted analysis. Here is an example of how the process works:

Suppose you were a car manufacturer that determined its target customer class considers power, fuel consumption, and reliability as key performance parameters. You list these criteria in the first three columns and rows of an AHP matrix (*see* Figure 10-04). Why list in both columns and rows? Because it makes it easier to do the comparisons.

Figure 10-04: Analytic Hierarchy Process

Score summary

Engine Features	Power	Fuel Consumption	Reliability	Product Cost	Lead Time to Develop	Technical Risk	Sum of Normalized Ratings	Relative Score	Weighting
Power	1.00	5.00	0.14	0.14	0.11	5.00	0.98	16.4%	3
Fuel Consumption	0.20	1.00	0.14	0.14	5.00	0.14	0.39	6.6%	1
Reliability	7.00	7.00	1.00	7.00	0.14	0.14	1.16	19.3%	3
Product Cost	7.00	7.00	0.14	1.00	7.00	0.20	1.09	18.13%	3
Lead Time to Develop	9.00	0.20	7.00	0.14	1.00	0.33	0.95	15.8%	3
Technical Risk	0.20	7.00	7.00	5.00	3.00	1.00	1.42	23.7%	4

Cell 1,2 is the inverse of Cell 2,1 (1/5 = 0.2)

Reliability is very strongly more important than product cost

Cell 2,1 shows that power is strongly more important than fuel consumption

In this table, each cell is asking the question, "how does the item listed in the column compare to the item listed in the row?" For example, cell 2,1—second column, first row—asks "how important is fuel consumption compared to power?" The number "5" in that cell means fuel consumption is "strongly more important" than power. (For symmetry, there is a corresponding cell 1,2—first column, second row—that asks the reciprocal question: "how important is power compared to fuel consumption?" The numerical value of 0.2 is the inverse of the number in cell 2,1.) The weighting scores are assigned based on the Relative Scores, with 1 being least important and 4 being most important (in this case).

In this example, the VOC requirements are listed in the first three columns and rows; the next three list VOB concerns (cost, lead time to develop, and technical risk). The numbers here show that product cost and lead time to develop will be adversely affected by high power. (Another note for mathphiles: the weighting shown in the last column is the result of matrix[30] algebra.)

This AHP process allowed the company to identify customer and business priorities. The next step was completing a Pugh Matrix (Figure 10-05) that shows how the company evaluated four technical solutions for meeting the key customer needs. For example, the first option, a small engine with electronically actuated valves (such as Honda uses)...

- Yields the same power as the baseline engine (S = same) with excellent fuel consumption (++)

- Is slightly more reliable (+)

- Involves higher product cost (–) and more technical risk (–)

- Can be developed in the same amount of time as the baseline reference (S)

Figure 10-05: Pugh Matrix

Concepts

Customer and Business Requirements	Small Engine with Electronic Variably Actuated Valves	Small Engine with Infinitely Variable Transmission	Alternate Fuel Normal Sized Engine with 4 Spd Lock-Up Transmission	Petroleum Powered Engine with 4-Spd Lock-Up Transmission	Importance Rating
Power	S	S	+	B	3
Fuel Consumption	++	+	S	B	1
Reliability	+	–	+	B	3
Product Cost	–	S	S	B	3
Lead Time to Develop	S	S	S	B	3
Technical Risk	–	S	S	B	4
Total	1	0	2	0	
Weighted Total	**-2**	**-2**	**6**	**0**	

B = baseline (all options compared relative to this standard)
S = same   + = better   ++ = much better   – = worse   – – = much worse

The team then multiplies the importance rating derived from AHP by the concept value. (S gets a 0, ++ is given a +2, the – gets a –1, etc.) The sums are added up to obtain a weighted total. Here, the alternative fuel engine with a lockup transmission is the design selected (it gets a weighted total of +6). This option provides the power and reliability the customer wants, yet reflects the VOB in fast lead time to development and low product cost based on innovation progress to date.

Because there are only three VOC needs and three VOB performance parameters in conflict in this example, the solution seems obvious (especially after the fact). But in a real design with dozens of performance features and scores of technical solutions, the right design approach is seldom as intuitive. In those cases, this weighting process for evaluating competing parameters really helps develop a final design.

Note that a heavy weighting of schedule lead time and probability of execution will tilt the conclusion toward a solution with fewer items or a lower performance level, at least in version 1 of the offering. But remember that options that don't make it in version 1.0 can always be incorporated in later releases.

Toyota: A case study in flexible designing

As cost and lead time data show, Toyota is a world leader in product development, propelling their growth as the only company in their market to double revenue in the last decade. They refer to Flexible Performance Target Design as set-based design (*see* Figure 10-06, next page), and give it a great deal of credit for their high performance.

Toyota is renowned for having a chief developer who is totally responsible for all aspects of a product. The chief is usually the best developer on the project and makes all the technical decisions. But remarkably, the people who help the chief developer don't report directly to him or her. Rather, the chief's role is largely to teach and coach others. He or she monitors the project status by continually reviewing prototypes and analyses (as opposed to doing an after-the-fact review of completed tasks).

Figure 10-06: Flexible Target Design
(aka Set-Based Concurrent Engineering)

Cost to Develop

By exploring multiple targets (different sets of specifications) simultaneously, a team can often come up with solutions that weren't originally anticipated. If time and/or cost prevent them from providing all of the customer delighters (like Target C in this case), they may still be able to deliver more than if they had stuck with a safe target (like Target A) within the required deadline and cost ceiling.

The Toyota system has been described as **responsibility-based** rather than **task-based:** The chief developer sets the schedule for system-level events, such as body design, related tooling, dies, and drive train. All subsystem workgroups know this schedule and drive to those dates. If a specific highly differentiated feature is not ready on time, they have a backup option on hand (probably based on re-use of an existing element) that can be substituted. Even the solution ideas in the set that "failed" are not wasted; they are added to the solution archive because they may be useful in future designs as a breakthrough (and at the least can help prevent future failure).

This approach is consistent with Toyota's Knowledge Rule:

> *Nature and markets make the rules. We profit by learning them.*

It's a principle shared by many others:

> *My motto is, "Always make new mistakes." There's no shame in making a mistake. But then learn from it and don't make*

the same one again. Everything I've learned, I've learned by making mistakes.

Esther Dyson, chairman of EDventure Holdings and
author of Release 2. 0: A Design for Living in the Digital Age

---

Balancing multiple targets with lead time demands

Using a Flexible Performance Target approach is like launching one-and-a-half projects instead of one. Requiring designers to consider several solutions, some of which are challenging, adds to the number of tasks they have to perform—which, as we know through the Laws of Lead Time and Innovation Variation, will *slow down* time-to-market unless you either add resources above usual levels or reduce the total number of projects in process.

You may, in fact, want to cut back on the number of active projects, but in truth the impact of designing to multiple targets isn't as bad as it sounds at first. Why? Recall that another key ingredient in achieving Fast Innovation is striving for greater levels of re-use. Doing so will dramatically reduce both task time and variation of the majority of the project—and leave your teams with *more time* to devote to exploring design alternatives around key differentiators.

Conclusion

The purpose of this chapter was to help you achieve two goals embodied in this book: First, to make the innovation process so fast that you get to the market before customer tastes or needs have changed. Second, to recognize that at the outset of development you *can't know* which features on the VOC list will be easy to develop, which will be hard, and which will be impossible.

Nailing down all the specs at the outset of development guarantees a me-too offering, a late launch with cost overruns, or both. It also prevents creativity, presumes that your developers will NOT learn anything interesting from customers during development that will change their minds, and may demand an impossible performance level.

In contrast, Flexible Performance Target Design starts with an outline of performance and customer delighters so specifications can be continuously updated throughout the design process. A developer will typically consider at least two alternative targets (usually a satisfier and a delighter). Through a highly iterative process with customers, specs don't reach the final freeze until about half the median time to completion, after which the team converges on an optimal solution.

Endnotes

25 Michael A. Cusumano and Richard W. Selby, *Microsoft Secrets: How the World's Most Powerful Software Company Creates Technology, Shapes Markets, and Manages People* (New York: Free Press, 1998), pp. 208-219.

26 A.Ward, J.K.Liker, J.J.Cristiano, and D.K.Sobek II, "The Second Toyota Paradox: How Delaying Decisions Can Make Better Cars Faster," *Sloan Management Review* (Spring, 1995), pp. 43-61.

27 A full discussion of buffers is in Appendix 2.

28 By Thomas Saaty (on loan to RAND from Wharton), *Decision Making for Leaders: The Analytic Hierarchy Process for Decisions in a Complex World* (Pittsburgh, PA: RWS Publications, 1999/2000 Edition).

29 Stuart Pugh, Scottish Professor of Engineering, Univ of Strathclyde, first presented the Pugh Matrix at the International Design Engineering Conference in Rome, 1981. *See* also his book, *Total Design: Integrated Methods for Successful Product Engineering* (New York: Addison-Wesley, 1991).

30 Saaty, *op. cit.* (*see* note 28).

CHAPTER 11

Institutionalizing Re-use

In Part I, we introduced the 80-80-80 Rule: if you achieve 80% re-use on your designs, you'll be able to operate most design staff at 80% utilization (higher than the 65% utilization cap required for from-scratch design work) and will also be able to reduce delays in your design process by 80%. Obviously, re-use plays a key role in achieving the dramatic cuts in lead-time-to-market seen under Fast Innovation. If you think that 80% re-use does not apply to your business, then set a lower goal. Appendix 1 will let you estimate how much benefit you will derive. But whatever your goal, get started! And remember, the power of re-use is limited only by your imagination and your ego strength in overcoming the naysayers!

Though re-use sounds simple—"Do we have an existing business process, material, component, service offering, etc., that would serve for the new product or service?"—the subtleties are easy to overlook. And as pointed out in Part I, you're likely to encounter resistance to re-use because designers and innovators often view their jobs as creating something *new*—new knowledge, new technologies, new designs. We'll address all these issues in this chapter, taking a quick look at the basic definition of re-use, then exploring some ways to apply re-use thinking that are not obvious (but may be highly profitable), and ending with a discussion of how to institutionalize re-use in your company.

The Many Faces of Re-use

As we discussed in Chapter 6, the basic premise of re-use is exactly what it sounds like: re-using something that already exists in your department, your corporation, or somewhere on the planet. That "something" can be anything: an idea, a technology, a business process, a piece of software, a channel, a module, a component. Re-use speeds up the design process and generates a return on existing intellectual capital that you or someone else already paid for.

For many of us, it's easiest to think of re-use in terms of physical products, such as having a standard chassis for several different models of cars, or a standard wiring diagram for different computer models. It's also evident in some service applications, such as "individualized" training that is really 80% or 90% standard modules plus a few customized examples.

In fact, re-use applies to any kind of product or service, tangible or intangible, and even to the other dimensions of innovation. Here are some examples showing just how widely re-use can be applied.

Re-use and Innovation by Analogy

Diamonds have natural flaws: facets, cleavages or cracks. Attempting to cut a diamond with a chisel is an art that in fact introduces more flaws. An entirely different approach to cutting diamonds was developed by applying 2,000 pounds of gas pressure, allowing the pressure to stabilize inside the diamond, then suddenly releasing the external pressure, which causes the diamond to cleave along its natural flaws. This process yields the largest possible flawless diamonds.

Now comes the fun part. Walnut producers want to extract a whole walnut meat so they can command higher prices. Anyone who has ever cracked a walnut knows this is a difficult task. How to do it—and do it through mass production at very low labor cost? Rather than start from scratch, walnut producers re-used the concept long used in the diamond industry. Apply lots of pressure, suddenly release the pressure, and off flies the shell, yielding a whole meat!

The same method has been used to remove seeds from bell peppers, remove sunflower hearts from the seed cover, remove the rust from metal, make powdered sugar, clean filters, and on and on. All these applications use a sudden pressure drop and all require engineering effort in order to determine the best system and operating conditions to apply the method. Splitting diamonds requires 2,000 atmospheres of pressure, while processing peppers requires only 5. Shelling cedar nuts uses high-pressure water, whereas shelling sunflower seeds uses air.

You could, of course, start searching the patent literature yourself if you have a particular technological challenge to solve. But there's a much faster solution available to us today: Clearly state your case on a website like InnoCentive (p. 99) that is frequented by innovators and offer a financial reward for its solution. Someone in the world has probably already worked on a similar if not identical problem.

Re-use vs. unique innovation

Creative thinking and internal development are still an essential part of the innovation process because there will always be some research and development issues that simply cannot be solved by either internal or external sources of re-use. Unique innovations that only you can supply allow you to control a part of your customer's value chain which, in turn, may be a springboard for further innovation and growth.

Re-use and Best Practices

If we broaden our definition to include re-use of knowledge, then re-use has actually been applied in businesses for many years under the rubric of best practices. An important client of ours has electronic manufacturing divisions around the world using wave solder machines to connect components on printed circuit boards. All the machines are the same, and the printed circuit boards highly similar. However, every machine originally had different settings for solder temperature, flux height, chain speed, etc.—which meant each one had a very different quality yield of solder defects.

So long as every division worked in splendid isolation, this situation worked very well. But an effort to establish corporate-wide best practices exposed the inconsistencies. The company had to establish the means for continuous interaction among the divisions to develop the optimal settings for each type of product. Rather than have each division try to solve these technical problems separately, each could profit by the experience and insight of all. The result was a dramatic and consistent increase in yield, and the creation of a "recipe" for new sites, with feedback to engineering on design rules.

Thanks in large part to Lean Six Sigma and its predecessors, this form of re-use is now quite common within businesses. The lesson for innovators is to not restrict their search for re-use potential to the parts and components of products or services, but to best-practice procedures they could adapt to their design, development, and delivery systems.

Re-use and Channels

Recently, Dell decided to enter the consumer electronics business. Critics cautioned that consumer electronics is a tough business and Dell really only knows PCs. But Dell sees it differently. And if you look carefully, this appears to be a careful strategy of re-use.

In a recent interview in *Fortune* (March 7, 2005) Dell CEO Kevin Rollins says: "Consumer electronics is a lousy category—boom boxes, television, VCRs—it's been terrible." But Rollins has a different take on Dell's entry into televisions. "Ah, but it's flat screens, a transition technology with a new profit pool, and we leverage off our existing business." Dell is essentially capitalizing on the re-use of two big elements in its arsenal:

1) Its supply chain. Dell sells more flat-screen PC monitors than any company in the world, giving it a tremendous advantage on the side of product supply

2) Its very powerful channel and consumer customer bas

It is too early to see the financial results of this strategy for Dell, but this appears to be a tailor-made approach to the Religion of Re-use to innovate in a new market segment.

Re-use and Intangible Products

Software development is a rapidly growing component of development cost and time in many products, and re-use is a vital component of success. After all, if you have a piece of code that compiles and works and can be re-used, the fact that it may contain more lines of code than required for a specific application is no longer of any importance given the advances in microprocessor, memory, and data bus speeds.

You might think that the benefit of re-use is so obvious that all companies would already employ it. But not true. We have never assessed a company that did not have gigantic opportunities related to institutionalizing the Religion of Re-use:

> *At one point, for example, Microsoft managers determined they had 14 different collections of text-processing code in their products; they also had several versions of code that did math calculations, graphing and charting, help functions, and other tasks.*
>
> *Microsoft Secrets, p. 395*

Late delivery and the need to improve quality led to the creation of Microsoft's Interoperability Committee in 1993. Specific tools such as DLL[31] and OLE have been created to facilitate the re-use of code, including individual components that different applications can utilize.

> *Microsoft re-uses a significant amount of code (over 50 percent) within a series of versions for a particular product, such as from version 1.0 to 2.0 and across the PC and Macintosh platforms.*

Note that re-use within Microsoft is driven by the CEO!

> *There's only one piece of charting code in the whole company. But there's a lot of pieces of text-processing code. I can explain how we got there, and why it's not as stupid as it might seem. But if we'd been super clever about architecting the requirements and the framework, we could have avoided a lot of inefficiency there.*
>
> *Bill Gates*

Bill Gates shouldn't beat himself up about not being super clever! The platform is part of an evolutionary process... you just can't know which future innovation or feature is going to drive revenue through the roof.

Microsoft groups are now learning how to share more of what they build; nevertheless, even Gates acknowledged that projects still do not re-use as much code as they could, and in our view that will continue to cause variation in delivering beyond beta test. (As a rule of thumb for software developers, if you must rewrite more than 25% of the lines of source code, you are probably better off starting from scratch... but that still gives you a lot of opportunity.)

Open Innovation: Re-using ideas you didn't invent

Re-use in the broadest sense means exploiting knowledge from any source—inside or outside your company—that helps you increase revenue growth and ROIC. That includes products and services that others have developed.

Looking outside yourself is called Open Innovation, a topic we've mentioned many times. The main thrust of the argument is that companies pay the price for Closed Innovation—when, like Bell Labs and Lucent, they rely solely on their own internal resources to invent new knowledge. This can be viewed as essentially a *zero re-use* of all external developments.

In contrast, Cisco's pursuit of "complete solutions" (whatever their networking customers needed or wanted) from any source, anywhere, has been the genesis of all its new products. As an example, when Cisco started losing orders to upstart Crescendo for an intelligent "best alternative route" router product, Cisco purchased the $10 million revenue company for $97 million. How's that for dilution! Cisco thus engages in *100% re-use* of external innovations to the extent that they are part of the complete customer solution.

Re-use Resistance (and How to Overcome It)

Given that re-use has such a positive impact on the speed and cost of innovation, you might wonder why it is the least-used and least-appreciated of all innovation processes. We've touched on some of the reasons why re-use is easily accepted, and now want to summarize the arguments against re-use and how to counteract them.

Argument #1: Developing re-usable designs is too expensive

The cost of developing a "component" (hardware, block of code, service modules) that you know you want to re-use for multiple purposes is often two to three times more than developing a one-off component. And if the original developer is going to use the design only once, with benefits accruing to other organizations or projects, re-use may be stymied and the company as a whole may suffer from local suboptimization.

As shown by the Xerox example in Chapter 6, business unit managers will be reluctant to make such an investment—they'd rather be the people re-using the design than developing it (that way they get the benefit without the cost).

Solutions

You can address this concerns on two levels:

- The Chief Innovation Officer's budget should be used to fund the upfront work of establishing re-use standards. That way, the cost does not hurt the budgets of individual P&L managers.

- Be as collaborative and cross-functional as feasible when establishing the standards to make sure that *everyone* benefits.

This may sound overly generous, but there is no sense in jeopardizing something as important as re-use with complex sharing agreements which simply institutionalize the silo mentality.

For example, at International Power Machines, a typical unit cost about $25,000 and it cost about $75,000 to build the first platform design that could be applied across initially seven different power ratings. When IPM later replicated that design, the development and manufacturing unit cost eventually fell by about 20%, principally in direct labor and overhead cost. So the break-even point on the investment was:

$$\text{Break-Even Point}_{\text{ReUse}} = \frac{\text{Investment}}{\text{Payback/Unit}} = \frac{3 \text{ Units of Cost of Goods Sold}}{0.2 \text{ Units of Cost of Goods Sold/Unit}} = 15 \text{ Units}$$

Since IPM delivered about a dozen units per month, the payback was less than two months. But if they only produced 1 unit per month, it would have taken an Accounting IRR 15 months to hit break-even, and using discounted cash flow, more than 20 months depending on discount rate. If they made the investment under those conditions, the most benefit would have accrued to the developer or department who re-used the component (not the original developer).

Also, if a technology is fast moving, the design could well be nearly obsolete before you reached the payback point. Therefore, re-use needs to be embraced by as wide a constituency as possible in the business to look for commonalities that will move the break-even point (per operation) back to that of being a sure winner. If this is achieved, and the competition does not or cannot match you, re-use becomes the trump card!

Tracz[32] and others observe that the break-even point is just three uses of a common design in their software products, and a report on software development from IEEE[33] reports on a case where re-use reduced the time-to-market by 23% per year for six years, a compounded reduction of 79%. These are some of the case studies that will encourage the resolve of managers to attain supremacy through the Religion of Re-use.

Argument #2: "I'm a creator, not a re-user"

In addition to the organizational impediments to applying re-use, designers used to relying on their creativity are naturally reluctant to accept it. This problem of innovators refusing to implement re-use is not a new one, and was recognized by Dr. Simon Ramo,[34] one of the founders and chairman of TRW during the development of the ICBM (Inter Continental Ballistic Missile) Program in the 1950s, who said:

> *Scientists and engineers have high professional pride... which tends to bring with it a preference for attacking each task in an individual, personal way, starting from scratch rather than making use of the results of others.*

Thus there is a strong personal penchant to reinvent the wheel, a penchant that can be overcome only by making innovators aware of the power of re-use and coaching them in its application.

Solutions

All of your innovation staff need to be trained in understanding the benefits of re-use and the 80-80-80 rule. Once they get over their initial reluctance, many creative staff come to embrace re-use because it gets them away from mundane design work and gives them more time to work on the demands of providing true differentiation.

Other Ways to Facilitate Re-use

Having policies for funding the upfront work at the corporate level and having a strong leader (the Chief Innovation Officer) strongly championing re-use are both great starts, but you need to make sure re-use is pushed down to your operating divisions as well. Here are some additional tips:

1. **Build an awareness, create engagement and ultimately fire a passion around the idea of creating a new service or product only when it absolutely drives new value for the customer and eliminates all complexity that fails to add value.** You need the organization to live and breathe the mantra around conquering complexity. This case can be initially built by completing a re-use diagnostic to understand the current level of re-use and the value of re-use to your organization.

2. **Establish productivity measures** of innovation that focus on the time-to-market (lead time) and the number of designs per year (productivity)—both of which should dramatically improve as re-use gets established. (In contrast, measures of how many designs or modules were internally developed rewards *effort* rather than *outcome*.)

3. **Establish a metric of design "goodness"** that measures the % of a new product/service that consists of re-used elements. This should be part of the merit review process of each innovator. You can get a baseline by measuring the percentage of re-use on all your current designs.

4. **Establish a searchable database:** To successfully implement re-use, everyone involved in design and development work in your company needs to knows what you already have in stock, so to speak. Since

most companies now have intranets, it should be relatively easy to develop a searchable database that lists all the parts, documents, components, elements, modules, etc., of your products and services. The goal is to make it easier for anyone in your company to discover if you already have something that meets a specific need, not capture detailed designs of entire products or service modules. This process has been facilitated by technologies such as Xerox's web-based *DocuShare*,[35] which enables everyone, regardless of skill or location, to dynamically collaborate, store, access and share content via standard web tools and desktop applications. For example, Dow Chemical has loaded 5 million pages of molecular structures, etc., onto this system. However, the system is also used by small and medium-sized companies.

We suggest writing short descriptions (25 words or less) of every reusable design that include predefined keywords for individual components or technologies. For example, a training company would list individual modules separately (brainstorming, data collecting) not entire courses ("team leader training"). If you list only the complete product, system, or service, it will be too difficult for other people to tell if an individual unit matches their needs.

5. **Establish policies/processes around "external" re-use:** If you follow our advice to search the planet (not just your company) for solutions to your design challenges, you'll need to define policies and processes for people to follow. When is it OK to look outside? When is it not? Do you need your own InnoCentive-type website? Who will set up and manage it? Is there funding for rewards? How much? And so on.

Conclusion

For most companies, the purpose for driving re-use is just what Steve McConnell said, as we quoted in in Chapter 6:

> *Re-use can produce greater schedule and effort savings than any other rapid-development practice.*

But even though the benefits of re-use are easily demonstrated (*see* the IPM example on p. 117), organizations will not automatically evolve from the chaos of individual project efforts to a common re-use methodology. Like any system, you need to expend corporate energy to eliminate disconnected random efforts, as demonstrated by the Microsoft and Xerox examples and the corrective action both firms took.

The benefits and challenges of re-use are why we strongly advocate that the Chief Innovation Officer (or the equivalent) be responsible for institutionalizing and nurturing re-use *across the corporation* and for exploiting the Open Innovation model (re-using others' ideas). The enormous benefits of marching toward an 80% re-use goal and attaining an 80% compression of schedule while reducing development cost conveys enormous competitive advantage.

Endnotes

31 Standardization Tools such as DLL do require customers to keep all applications upgraded to the latest release, thus keep their DLL libraries up to date.

32 Will Tracz, *Confessions of a Used Program Salesman* (New York: Addison Wesley 1995).

33 IEEE Software, Sept 1994.

34 Simon Ramo, *The Management of Innovative Technological Corporations* (New York: John Wiley & Sons, Inc., 1980), p. 198.

35 Xerox describes DocuShare as follows: "Affordable Web-based document and content management application lets businesses of every size rapidly deploy a world-class Enterprise Content Management (ECM) solution to help reduce costs, optimize information flow, and reduce risk."

Part II Conclusion

Our goal in writing this book is to give you a starting point to create an entire business that can do what few have ever done: sustainably grow revenue and shareholder returns at above-average rates for decades. Part II has begun to build the prescription, providing you with key elements of the foundation for turning your company into a Fast Innovator:

- Having engaged executives with the knowledge necessary to champion the changes that Fast Innovation demands

- Changing management practices to eliminate barriers to Fast Innovation within business units

- Appointing a Chief Innovation Officer to oversee your innovation efforts and take on the role of championing disruptive opportunities in particular (because, unlike sustaining innovations, they seldom flourish with business units)

- Establishing methods for monitoring and controlling complexity and its costs to balance the equation of shareholder value versus offering proliferation

- Investing a lot more (typically twice as much) than you do now to discover and use knowledge about customer needs

- Adopting a "fast and flexible" development mantra

- Institutionalizing the Religion of Re-use

If your purview is closer to the project or portfolio level, read on. Part III will provide you with the rest of the prescription—the key methods for driving Fast Innovation at the project level.

PART III

Deploying Fast Innovation Projects

Introduction to Part III

Fast Innovation principles infiltrate all aspects of innovation project launch and execution:

- Selecting the right projects (*see* Chapter 12)

- Setting the right goals and targets for the project and allowing creativity within the right bounds

- Providing executive sponsorship, especially for disruptive innovation, which by definition will require significant incubation and support to survive the status quo

- Adopting new methods for resource management that account for what we now know through the Laws of Lead Time and Innovation Variation (*see* Chapter 13)

- Speeding up development using the Innovation Blitz approach (*see* Spotlight p. 277)

- Incorporating the Laws of Lead Time and Innovation Variation into the review gates in a development system (Chapter 14)

- Taking every opportunity to inject creativity into design work (Chapter 15)

CHAPTER 12

Project Screening and Selection

A good managerial record (measured by economic returns) is more a function of which boat you get into rather than how effectively you row... If you find yourself on a chronically leaking boat, energy devoted to changing boats is likely to be more productive than energy devoted to patching leaks.

Warren Buffet, Berkshire-Hathaway Annual Report, 1985

As unlikely at it seems, Buffet's pithy and profound wisdom applies to project selection. As we saw in Chapter 5 on Open Innovation, Bell Labs/Lucent fed projects into the innovation process that were *not congruent with their market needs*, yet they virtually *never* killed any of the projects. Yes, they created a lot of notable scientific knowledge (which led to six Nobel prizes in physics and most of the inventions up to the past ten years), but little of it benefited the company or its shareholders.

Feeding high-value projects *into* the innovation development process and killing those that have exhibited little value potential *during* the development process is just as important as anything we do *during* the process to quickly deliver differentiated offerings or business models to the market. In comparing companies that do very well at innovation with those that don't, it's clear that the former excel at two things: what they feed into the development process (identifying the best potential ideas and rigorously screening those they decide to work on), *and* monitoring projects during development so they can identify and quickly kill any that appear unlikely to meet market needs. This control over and purging of the project portfolio is crucial to maintaining the speed of the process based on the Law of Lead Time. This chapter covers some of the secrets to making sure the projects you select represent the highest potential value to your company; later chapters will address how to filter out projects that appear unlikely to live up to expectations.

Identifying Opportunities

Innovation project opportunities can emerge from numerous sources, including Idea Forums, Open Innovation contact with experts from around the world, ethnography and other Voice of Customer studies, spinoffs from other projects, competitive analysis studies, direct and unsolicited customer feedback, and internal suggestion systems. Some companies also sponsor formal creativity brainstorming sessions to generate ideas around a specific need or opportunity. Most important, make sure your company is capturing the ideas that represent the maximum value potential by:

- Leveraging ethnographic or other direct customer observation and input.

- Putting cross-functional groups of people together to ensure cross-pollination of ideas.

- Maximizing team creativity (*see* Chapter 15).

- Using *all* the inputs to guide the high-level strategic direction of your company.

- Making sure the process deliberately seeks out disruptive innovation opportunities. Ideas for sustaining innovations come more easily because they build on something that already exists. Yet, as we showed in Chapter 2, disruptive innovations will likely have greater potential to generate above-average shareholder returns. You need to take advantage of opportunities to improve or expand on existing offerings and business models, but make sure that you're also looking at opportunities that will take you out of your comfort zone.

The process you use to achieve these goals must be structured to ensure that idea generation itself is a sustainable process in which ideas are routinely created then systematically captured and evaluated—and not just a one-off, haphazard event.

Managing Sustaining vs. Disruptive Evaluation Processes

The relative ease of exploiting sustaining innovation opportunities continues through the screening phase because these opportunities can usually be evaluated in terms of their impact on existing metrics: expanded sales through existing channels, improved efficiency of an existing process or business model, impact on Net Present Value, and so on. It's also relatively easy to evaluate the cost side of the sustaining equation because, by definition, sustaining innovations use technologies, methods, materials, etc., that already exist.

For those reasons, sustaining innovation opportunities should be managed within the incumbent business unit structure; the leaders of those units should spearhead the process for filtering, screening, and selecting which to pursue. For example, who would know the most about the video rental company's retail business unit? Clearly its business unit leadership team. They would know more about their customers than corporate leaders, and would bring better insights to the decision about what kinds of sustaining innovations could drive the next level of business growth.

Selecting disruptive innovation opportunities, in contrast, requires a very different process, one controlled at the corporate level that uses different metrics. Why? By nature, disruptive ideas are not well developed when they enter the innovation pipeline because of considerable unknowns around what the final outcome will look like, the potential market size, the technology, the cost, the schedule, the ultimate benefit, and probably even the strategic fit. Initially there will also be a lot of volatility and uncertainty around the ultimate value creation, though those issues will become clearer at each subsequent step of development. In fact, some in your organization may be afraid that a successful disruptive innovation will disrupt your market and competition, and perhaps disrupt the company itself. Consequently, if disruptive innovations are submitted to the same tests as sustaining innovations, business will almost always choose the familiar—the sustaining innovation.

Similarly, a business unit leader trying to drive the tactical success of the operating unit is not going to want to disrupt his or her own business. To use our previous example, would you expect the VP of store operations at a video rental company to develop and support the idea of delivering videos over the internet? What if he or she succeeds? While internet-assisted delivery may create significant economic value for the company, it may have dire consequences for existing retail business.

The differences in how disruptive innovations vs. sustaining innovations are perceived is why you need two mechanisms for evaluating and selecting potential projects: Allow existing business units to select and manage sustaining innovations, but use a Chief Innovation Officer (as described in Chapter 8) as an internal venture capitalist who will use sufficient rigor to address disruptive opportunities. As discussed previously, the Chief Innovation Officer plays the role of the portfolio manager for disruptive opportunities, working with the executive team to decide which opportunities to fund (consistent with strategy), the level of available funding, the probability of driving the disruptive innovation to its next milestone, and whether continued investment is warranted (*see* Real Options Theory, p. 188). As appropriate, the Chief Innovation Officer should also partner with outside venture capitalists so that the company will have a seat at the table on potentially promising disruptive innovations. These relationships are also valuable for gaining an outside perspective on the value of a potential disruptive innovation, for perhaps sharing some of the investment risk, and for deciding which disruptive ideas may be able to stand on their own.

In most cases, the disruptive portfolio will comprise a number of subportfolios representing disruptive projects or opportunities at different stages of development—and hence representing different levels of risk and different types of "bets" (per Real Options Theory) about what it will take to move them to the next development stage. (All the opportunities in the "idea" stage subportfolio represent low-risk, low-investment bets for moving to the business-case stage; opportunities that have moved into the final freeze stage subportfolio likely represent much greater investment bets to reach final prototype prior to handing off the design to manufacturing or production.)

Disruptive innovation opportunities should be evaluated both within and across subportfolios with a heavy emphasis on the go/no-go decision. Evaluation should weight the ultimate anticipated value (benefit and the volatility of that benefit) against the size of the bet required to get to the next stage (in terms of cost, time, and probability of success). It should also address key risk and upside factors such as competitors' ability to copy the innovation quickly, how close the idea is to your existing businesses (products/services, markets, customer base), and the potential to create a service-level breakpoint through operational/ business model innovation.

Screening Ideas at the Business Unit Level

The business unit leadership team should compile all innovation ideas and screen them to eliminate the real dogs and keep anything with potential (winnowing down the list of opportunities so that later analysis is more practical). Typically, the screening proceeds in several stages, as described below.

Screen #1: Rough "go/no-go" filter

Be sure to KEEP ideas that have a clear strategic fit with your current offering portfolio, business models, etc., plus any ideas for sustaining innovations that you think could be taken to market quickly enough to confer a disruptive advantage.

You may want to involve the Chief Innovation Officer, or even funnel decisions up to the corporate level for the following kinds of opportunities:

- Any ideas that look like they will endow you with a disruptive advantage in the market (even if you think the expertise needed to deliver on the idea doesn't currently exist within your company—remember, you'll be working from an Open Innovation foundation). These need corporate attention because they may require special funding.

253

- Ideas that have no adjacent strategic fit for your business unit from a brand, customer, channel, or core competency perspective (i.e., disruptive opportunities). While business units should avoid sustaining innovation opportunities that have NO adjacency to current offerings, you want to be careful. Too many firms rule out the opportunity to disrupt because they want to innovate only in areas that have full adjacency (same customers, channels, and core competencies). The best and most disruptive opportunities will often be those that have some adjacency to your current business.

  - One good example we have seen recently is Pfizer's development of the SudaCare product line. SudaCare is adjacent to Pfizer's SudaFed medication line in terms of product/channels but the comparisons end there. SudaCare was envisioned not as a medicinal product line but as non-medicinal comfort-care product that would make you feel better during a cold. The SudaFed team could easily have said that development of the line was outside their world because it did not fit perfectly, but instead took advantage of the adjacencies that did exist and have begun to build an exciting new brand.

- Sustaining innovation ideas that require technologies you think no one on the planet has invented yet. These are better to send up to be considered in the disruptive sense.

- Ideas whose horizons are simply too far out to meet your strategic business needs (these may be something that the Chief Innovation Officer could collaborate with academics to address).

Screen #2: Composite scores on attractiveness and effort

Any sustaining ideas that survive the first screen (and haven't been channeled upward to the Chief Innovation Officer) need to go through a second screen where they are scored on two additional criteria: innovation attractiveness and effort. Innovation attractiveness means determining the potential benefit of each innovation project opportunity; effort means estimating what kind of investment (people, time, money) will be needed to achieve the benefit. Begin the process by answering questions such as those shown in Table 12-A.

Table 12-A: Project Selection Rating

INNOVATION ATTRACTIVENESS	EFFORT REQUIRED
General questions **(For all types of innovation)**	**General questions** **(For all types of innovation)**
Is there compelling "Heart of the Customer" input supporting the need for this project?	What level of effort by how many people will it take to achieve the goals?
What is the value creation opportunity?	What is the estimated time-to-market (products/services) or time-to-completion (market definition or business model innovations)?
Is this a strategic fit? Are we the best firm to take this on or is a competitor better qualified?	
Will accomplishing this project generate a disruptive advantage in offerings, delivery systems, or business model?	Will this effort require a substantial capital investment?
When will this innovation project be cash positive?	What risks need to be considered?
Product/service questions	**Product/service questions**
Do the markets affected have high growth potential?	Is the market currently dominated by other large competitors (i.e., how much would you have to invest to steal market share)?
What is the market segment attractiveness level (market profitability and growth)?	If the market is of sufficient size, what expansions or distribution system enhancements will be required?
How does this product or service compare with competing offerings? Is there a clear, compelling difference?	Does our company have access to the needed marketing/sales/distribution channels? If not, what would it take to establish them?
What economic profit can be generated by this new product?	What is the cycle time required to bring this product/service to market?
What are the advantages to the customer?	How many resources will be required to bring this product/service to market?
	Are there any cost savings to our company as a result of bringing this product/service to market?
Business Model questions	**Market Definition questions** Is the new market a direct adjacency to our existing products, services, and capabilities?
Is there an opportunity to create a "service level breakpoint"?	**Business Model questions**
Does the innovation require process improvement only or new technology?	Does the new business model require brand new technology/capability or can we leverage existing capabilities?
	Does the new business model depend on breakthrough improvement in existing processes or does it require brand new process/capability?

For the purpose of this screen, it's not essential that you have hard data on each of these questions. Rather than simply answering the questions yes/no, it works best to score each project on a standard scale that you develop internally (such as defining five levels each for effort and potential). That way everyone will know what it means if Project A scores a 3 on market potential but a 1 on effort required, while Project B scores a 4 on potential and a 2 on effort.

This rating analysis will give you a composite score on both criteria for each project. Then plot all the scores on a grid like that shown in Figure 12-01 and compare the opportunities to each other. What is most important is to compare the *relative* value and *relative* effort of each potential project. You are only trying to pick the best opportunities, not to define the exact benefit or effort for any given idea at this point.

Figure 12-01: Project Rating Grid

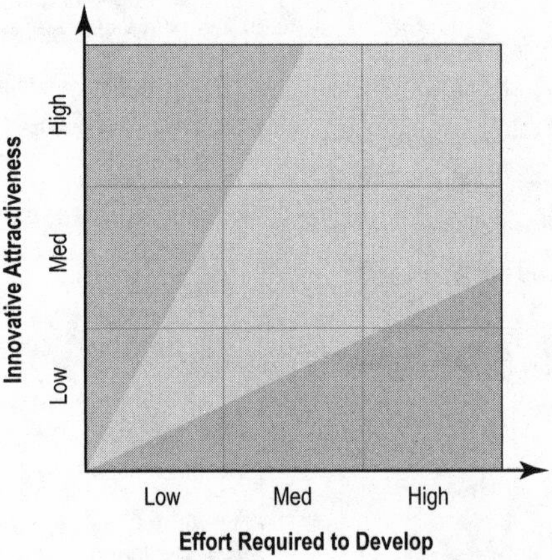

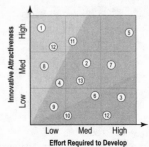

Where the projects fall on the grid can help point the way towards the next step, as shown in Figure 12-02a and 02b.

Figure 12-02a: Project Selection

How projects fall the grid...

continued on next page

Figure 12-02b: Project Selection

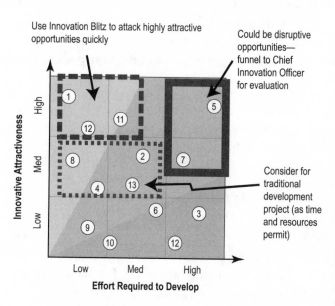

Use Innovation Blitz to attack highly attractive opportunities quickly

Could be disruptive opportunities— funnel to Chief Innovation Officer for evaluation

Consider for traditional development project (as time and resources permit)

... Guides decisions about how to react.

For example, anything that is highly attractive should be addressed immediately; those that are relatively easy to moderate with an Innovation Blitz.

Ideas that look like they require a lot of effort should be communicated to the Chief Innovation Officer because they may represent a disruptive opportunity and/or require connections (through Open Innovation) to get the needed knowledge.

Ideas that are moderately attractive can be channeled through the traditional development pipeline. As for ideas with low attractiveness—why waste the resources? Even if they require "low effort," you'll be clogging your project queue (remember, increasing projects-in-process will delay ALL projects) for little benefit.

Screen #3: Business case development and project selection

The business unit leadership also has the responsibility to see that more detailed business cases are developed for any projects that fall onto desirable portions of the screening grid. Again, projects that are clearly disruptive in nature (high effort, high risk) but have high potential should be funneled to the Chief Innovation Officer for evaluation.

The questions at this stage are the same as those for the second screening (*see* Table 12-A, p. 255), only this time around you need to get more rigorous in your answers and ultimately build a Net Present Value model. For example, just exactly how much value creation could you expect? What data do you have or can you get related to time-to-market opportunity?

Once you have the business cases prepared, you may want to use a decision matrix or other formal decision-making process to compare the projects and select the best ones for implementation.

Let's take a historical example of a sustaining innovation that really looked good. As we mentioned in Part I, the first mammoth application of integrated circuits was the Minuteman Missile. The next market beyond initial military and computer applications was industrial settings, where potential customers (Square D, Allen-Bradley, Cutler-Hammer, etc.) indicated that that circuits would need to have a higher noise margin. When Amelco introduced High Threshold Logic (HTL), it was touted in the press as the "wave of the future." However, engineers at Texas Instruments, one of the leading producers of integrated circuits at the time, hated the HTL solution. They felt that a higher noise margin would cause the power dissipation to be too high for complex circuits, and that they could solve the noise problem more elegantly with lower impedance circuits. In the language of the Analytic Hierarchy Process (*see* p. 228), at TI the Voice of the Business was strongly negative for HTL technology.

However, given that HTL was the wave of the future, the Texas Instruments' then-VP of Marketing, Dick Hanschen, went to the next screening step by asking how much value could be created. He asked each salesman to report how much HTL business they could book in the next 18 months based on current prototype efforts. The response was underwhelming, and he commented: "HTL is evidently a growing market with no demand." So this sustaining innovation flunked the second screen, the value creation test. As it later turned out HTL did fail in the market, and TI's engineers did come up with a more elegant solution that appealed to customers.

Hold Off on That Launch!

Just because a project has made it through the early filters doesn't mean you should immediately launch it into development. All projects will need to go through a FastGate check (p. 287) to determine their likely impact on lead time and utilization. However, if management feels the project has an extremely high potential, consider going directly into an Innovation Blitz (p. 277) as long as that will not jeopardize other high-priority projects. The FastGate check asks you to make decisions about the impact on resources, so we'll explore that topic first (in the next chapter) before going into details about the FastGate itself.

CHAPTER 13

Increasing Innovation Capacity Without Adding Resources

Do you recall the single most important barrier to innovation that CEOs articulated in the Preface? Time and cost overruns! Do you remember what came in second? Competing development priorities! Our intent in this chapter is to explain why so many companies struggle with competing priorities and to articulate for the first time a detailed approach that, if followed with discipline, will allow you to solve this problem once and for all.

The issues boils down to this question: How would you like to improve your innovation process to accomplish the following results *without adding any new resources?*

- Increase throughput in new offerings by 40% per year

- Reduce schedule slips by 50%

- Reduce time-to-market by 40%

Think of the financial impact these kinds of gains would have for your company in terms of revenue growth, margin growth, and most important, shareholder value growth. Recall the impact of fast vs. slow innovation (Figure 13-01):

Figure 13-01: Fast vs. Slow Innovation

When most companies realize that a project may miss its market window—and therefore eat away at the early entrant benefit—their first reaction is to simply pour more resources into the project. Unfortunately, this strategy actually works against Fast Innovation.

For example, when co-author Mike George was the CEO of International Power Machines, he encountered a familiar situation: trying to develop a new product with unknown and unknowable future problems. Not surprisingly, the biggest variation was linked to portions of the design that required *completely new* technology solutions using faster power switching devices.[1] Development times that were planned to reach what's called the independent test stage within 1 to 2 months dragged out to 10 or 12 months, thanks to quality problems unknown to the supplier.

With that long a development cycle, the original team eventually ran out of gas and IPM had to throw all of its best resources at the problem. But the result wasn't what they were looking for. After a couple of months of despair, IPM realized that by adding resources late in the program, they had actually *slowed down the process*. Why? Because the original team, forced now to spend time bringing the new people up to speed, were distracted from their value-add work. The original team members were so far ahead of the newcomers in terms of time invested and knowledge gained, that the new team members were unable to add enough productivity to offset this task interruption. Unfortunately, by that time IPM had no choice other than to finish what it had started… it was a matter of satisfying key customers. Ultimately, IPM realized that if it had staffed this task adequately at the front end, they likely would have been only two months late rather than nearly a year late.

Why didn't IPM put more resources on at the beginning? Two reasons:

- First of all, they were pursuing two major projects at once, which divided their team. (Adhering to the Law of Lead Time would have helped here had they known about it at the time.)

- Second, they were too concerned with targeted cost and had never calculated the cost of being late to market. One of IPM's major markets for this fast switching technology was IBM mainframes. By the time IPM hit production, they were a year behind schedule, and by this time IBM had decided to offer a motor generator set that effectively killed off the market. So IPM lost at least half of the operating profit potential and return on investment because they missed the first year of a two-year selling cycle, and might have forestalled IBM's move or at least blunted its effect!

Both of these case studies confirm another of **Brooks' Law**:

Adding manpower to a late project makes it later.[2]

When a project is in trouble, managers intuitively think that doubling the number of developers will split the load and cut the time in half. However, that strategy fails to account for several issues:

1) An exponential increase in the complexity and communication cost associated with coordinating and then merging the work of multiple designers. Hence the second of Brooks' Laws: "The delays due to communications rise as the square of the number of people on the team." So doubling the number of developers will increase communications delay by a factor of four (we call this the N^2 effect). This is why small teams of people devoted full-time to a design project (skunk works) are most effective; larger teams where members work only part-time on the project fall victim to the N^2 problem. Recall also the *Law of Two Pizzas*, the *Law of World Class*, and the *Law of Gilligan's Island* on p. 121.

2) Innovators are not fungible resources; they are not just so many man-months that anyone can replace. Rather, most Critical Resources have unique capabilities. Adding new people to a project cannot help unless you have a formalized cross-training initiative so that replacements can competently fill the expert's shoes (for at least a portion of their work). This is so important that Fred Brooks titled his famous book *The Mythical Man-Month*.

A lot of companies have made major capital investments in making the innovation process more productive. A better approach to resource management starts with getting a handle on how much time your innovators really innovate, then using that information to better inform decisions about utilization and investment.

Gathering the Necessary Data

The Law of Lead Time shows that the average completion rate is a large determinant of lead time. Average completion rate, in turn, is hindered by a lot of non-value-add time, such as process inefficiencies, meetings, budget reviews, scheduling reviews, etc. To understand where you need improvement, you first need to know how much non-value-add time (and therefore cost) is in your design process—and how much of that non-value-add time results from assigning developers to several projects at once. The answers are a mystery to most organizations.

> *"Holmes, this is indeed a mystery," I remarked. "What do you imagine that it means?"*
>
> *"I have no data yet, Watson! It is a capital mistake to theorize before one has data. Insensibly one begins to twist facts to suit theories, instead of theories to suit facts!"*
>
> Sherlock Holmes, A Scandal in Bohemia[3]

To achieve the goals of Fast Innovation and conquer innovation resource management, you need data on how your innovators spend their time. Though data has a long history of being used to control and improve manufacturing processes (due to the pioneering work of Taylor's time studies, Gilbreath's motion study, and Deming's Quality work), little has been done to study time use in development work. Here are some suggestions for how to start.

Step 1: Categorize your developers' activities

The first step is categorizing each activity by *task* rather than by *venue*. (For example, a meeting is a venue; it can be either value-add or non-value-add depending on whether it supports or enables design work). Dr. John Evers (formerly of TI and now with Raytheon) found the categories in Table B useful; he was operating in a product development arena, but most of the categories are applicable to most kinds of innovation work.

Table 13-A: Categorizing Design/Development Tasks

Analysis Categories and Descriptions
Design Work: Includes work by an individual or IPTs in developing, creating, considering, revising, testing and validating a design or design model
Design Support: Includes work to obtain specifications, requirements, support information, data sheets, preparatory work to allow creating the design model, research, internal design reviews, and generating/reviewing/releasing internal drawing/documents
Rework: Includes ALL design work and design support activities resulting from flowed-down or allocated requirement changes, TBD requirement clarifications, missing/adding requirements, bad information (e.g., wrong interface definition)
Program Contractual Obligations: Includes work to generate/review/release Data Items and any other work that is contractually specified but not under design work or support or rework.
Program/Process Support: Includes work to support program reviews, preparing and/or giving presentations, budget support, schedule support, planning, communication efforts, status reports, miscellaneous program-required paperwork (e.g., clearance requests), metrics collection/reporting, other scientific/technical reports not required by contract.
Overhead: Training, general meetings, inter- and intra-site travel, team building, miscellaneous overhead codes.
Interruptions: Phone calls, conversations (people stopping by to chat, etc.), MSGs, e-mail.
Work Stop: Time bank, lunch, breaks
© 1994-1996 Texas Instruments Incorporated

This table shows how Texas Instruments defined the categories of work for their development teams.

Step 2: Gather time data

There are many ways to do this. You can create worksheets (paper or electronic) that list all the categories, with spaces for developers to track how much time they spend on each over a period of several weeks. John Evers' group came up with a very clever means of tracking data, in particular the interruptions experienced by the developers. They encoded the work categories and interruption categories into bar codes printed on a piece of paper which was permanently fixed on each developer's desk (Figure 13-02).

The developers then just needed to scan a wand over the right code (Figure 13-03, next page). You can enter the data directly into a computer worksheet, but the paper and wand are visible reminders and a psychological barrier to interruptions.

**Figure 13-02:
Bar Codes for Tracking
Work**

Employee (In/out)   Error

Design Work   Documentation

Information   Rework

Interruption   Administration

Status Reports   Overhead

Contract Obligation   Workstop

Copyright © 1994 - 1996
Texas Instruments Incorporated

Evers comments:

> *Having the physical item and bar scan sheet right in their eye view also turned out to make it easier for them to remember to do it. It was quick and painless for them to do. Many of the engineers wanted to keep the barcode reader, as they found the visible device reduced the interruptions they faced—just the act of picking up the barcode reader caused potential intruders to leave the engineer alone to their work.*

Even before the data collection was complete, this process had an immediate effect: If someone came up to the desk of an innovator and said, "Hi, I have a question for you," the innovator would say, "Just a moment, I have to wand-in my interruption code." Most interrupters would then say, "Never mind, it's not that important!" The data showed how much non-value-add time was being consumed, and that a typical developer *changed activities 15 times per day!* This constant shifting of focus hinders creativity and innovation. We've seen data for cases where interruptions took up more time than core design work!

Figure 13-03: Tracking interruptions

Push and hold down the button... Smooth scan... Hear the beep.

Perform scan when:
  Starting Shift (scan employee barcode)
  Each Time Change Activity (scan categories barcode)
  Ending Shift (scan employee barcode)

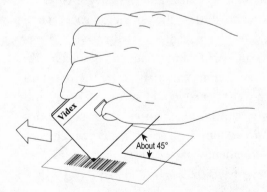

Bottom line: it doesn't matter *how* you get the data. Just *get it* because it will really inform management action! Collect data for the shortest period of time that is sufficient to catch all changes in categories twice (for TI, that was 10 days). If that doesn't sound like enough data, consider that it takes just one quick glance to tell if there's a traffic jam on a freeway. Jim Patell, the Herbert Hoover Professor of Public and

Private Management at the Stanford Graduate School of Business, quips that one of the facts of queues is that: "Everybody gets to share everybody else's experience."

Once you have gathered this data, the opportunities for innovation process improvement will almost certainly jump out at you. You are very likely to find large chunks of time that are consumed by non-value-added activities, which if eliminated will instantly give you more innovation capacity.

Optimizing Utilization: A case study

With better data on how our innovators spend their time, we are in a better position to understand how much time they have available for innovation and therefore what level of utilization is most appropriate. Before we get into detailing the methods for optimizing utilization, let's first look at a real-life example shared with us by Emery Powell, a new product development director within a division of the Semiconductor Group at Texas Instruments that builds digital signal processing chips, analog chips, etc. So far, they have been able to fend off formidable competition from the likes of Intel.

Emery has been a leader in the development and application of the Fast Innovation process. His goal for much of his career has been to:

- Understand capacity constraints, multi-tasking, and its impact on development throughput and cycle time

- Apply the Laws of Lead Time and Innovation Variation to find throughput constraints (bottlenecks) for the Critical Resource, identify and prioritize Critical Resources, and balance resource capacity versus demand to minimize lead time

- Allocate dedicated and pooled resources, based on project priorities, to hundreds of projects per year

- Deal with the above across geographical, world time zone, and cultural boundaries

TI first incorporated these principles into its version of new product development (NPD) in the 1990s and continues to look for opportunities to leverage these principles for faster innovation. Figure 3-06 (p. 63) depicted part of the results from one study that TI conducted. The full results are in Figure 13-04, which compares actual data from two different situations:

- Multi-tasking: The traditional NPD approach in which development staff were assigned to at least two projects simultaneously (top pie chart)

- Single-tasking: An alternative where developers were assigned to only one project at a time (lower pie chart).

Figure 13-04: Time Use in Single- vs. Multi-tasked Innovators

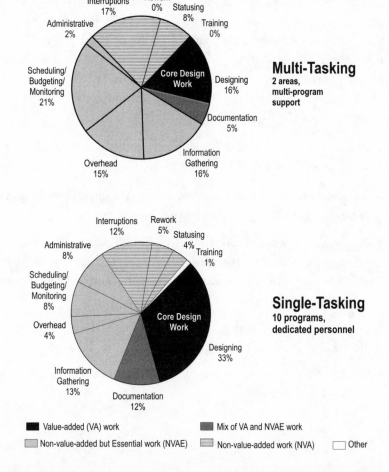

As you can see, the amount of work that was totally or partially value-add—which they defined as including core design work and documentation—more than doubled (from 21% for multi-taskers to more than 45% for the single-taskers). Here, an engineer dedicated to one project spent about 33% of the time in actual design work, a number that fell to 16% for engineers who were multi-tasked.

Emery reports that this approach to increasing resource capacity has been a major factor in the improvement of TI's product development execution in each business applying the principles. Examples of one-year improvements include:

- Design iterations were reduced by 25%

- Throughput in products per year increased by 40%

- Schedule slips dropped by 50%

- Time-to-market was reduced by 40%

The use of data to drive planning decisions resulted in other benefits:

- Data now takes precedence over opinion, experience, or guessing

- Less fighting between marketing and resource owners over when to start a new development project

- New projects started only when resource capacity will be available

- Resource demand versus capacity can now be planned 18 to 24 months in advance

- Designers who finish a project are available to help someone else or do research until there is capacity to assemble a full product development team

- Management pays more attention to front end of development

- Greater resource stability, less multi-tasking, less fire-fighting, less overtime

Obeying the Laws of Lead Time and Innovation Variation, and single-tasking Critical Resources allows you to double your progress towards the fundamental goals of Fast Innovation (quick time-to-market, more differentiation, more innovation). For example, multi-tasked resources spend only 16% of their time on actual design, compared to 33% for dedicated resources. In addition, many of the non-value-add tasks can be reduced.

The lesson? An important change in management policy from focusing on individual efficiency (keeping designers busy) to focusing on lead time while boosting individual output. This effectively doubled the capacity of critical bottleneck resources. Rather than spending a lot of money on tools to increase productivity, first consider the no-cost option of changing your management policies (as we'll discuss below). Then you can invest in tools that will increase the developers' efficiency during the time they work on value-added activities.

But the loss of time is not the only reason why multi-tasking works against innovation, as we'll discuss next.

Improve the 21% or the 79%?

Until now, companies that wanted to increase innovation productivity often looked to expensive new design tools or programs. But since the developers were still multi-tasked, that's the equivalent of trying to improve the effectiveness of the 21% spent on value-add work, rather than attacking the 79% spent on non-value-added work on the upper graph of Figure 13-04.

Eliminating multi-tasking will get rid of a big chunk of the 79%: by single-tasking Critical Resources, you are guaranteed to double their core design work (from 16% to 33% in the example we're using)—a very dramatic improvement made with very little cost! You'll need to collect data on your own process, but we assure you the opportunity is significant and well worth the effort.

Also, you might also have noted that in Figure 13-04, "scheduling and monitoring" was a much bigger piece of the pie than the value-add work. This kind of work will also diminish when you go to a single-tasking model.

Multi-Tasking Harms Creativity

Multi-tasking, frequent interruptions, and changing tasks all work against creativity. The mathematician Stan Ulam, creator of the famous *Monte Carlo* method, illuminates the creative process:

> *My facility to solve difficult math problems is due to the ability to hold that problem in my mind uninterrupted for many hours at a time.*[4]

Clearly you can't hold a problem in your mind uninterrupted if you have to change activities 15 times a day (as the TI innovators did)!

Two decades of research on innovation and creativity by Theresa Amabile[5] of Harvard provides some counterintuitive but relevant insights into this issue. Amabile studied 22 development teams in seven industries. Over 75,000 specific responses were received to 9,000 daily questionnaires. Measurements included degree of multi-tasking, time pressure, evidence of creative thinking, etc. She found that **high pressure with multi-tasking leads to low creativity**: an innovator who must multi-task may be 45% less creative per hour of value-add time than a person dedicated and immersed in a problem without interruption. (Other key findings are summarized in the sidebar.)

Figure 13-04 (p. 268) showed that an innovator devoted to a single task applies 33% of his or her time to "core design work," compared to only 16% for innovators who have to multi-task. If we apply the 45% loss in

---

Theresa Amabile's innovation insights

In addition to the effect of multi-tasking described in the text, Amabile's research led to the following conclusions:

- **Creativity is reduced if unrealistic goals are imposed** (such as forcing developers to accept schedules that they know are not attainable)

- **Abrupt scheduling changes hurt creativity**

- **High pressure may cause a 45% loss of creativity:** the 45% reduction in creativity is consistent with Amabile's data but is not presented as an established fact at this time

---

creativity to the 16% of the time spent on design work, the multi-tasking innovator will be creative just 9% of the time. If true, it means that a single-tasking person is approximately four times as creative as a multi-tasker. And since differentiation is strongly driven by creativity, and offering success is strongly driven by differentiation (Figure 2-02), the company that single-tasks will have a huge advantage over those that multi-task, in both differentiation and the number of projects completed per year. This is why you must be adamant about focusing attention upstream on the requirements that Critical Resources have identified, so that they can be single-tasked on that work.

Attacking the Causes of Multi-tasking

Why do projects take too long? Most development project leaders try their best to estimate project lead time using project management tools. But since these tools do not employ the Laws of Lead Time and Innovation Variation, they fail to take into account the effects of delays caused by other projects getting in the way. Ignoring project workloads and variation time makes it impossible to estimate project lead time. In addition, because business leaders are always under pressure to innovate more and to achieve faster growth, the typical business leader will take actions that inadvertently add to delays...

- Dictate a shorter schedule deadline for the project to create a sense of urgency

- Add more projects into the pipeline in the hopes that at least something will come out

- Initially understaff a project, which results in a longer average completion rate (via the Law of Lead Time), and hence longer lead times to market, and eventually an exponential increase in lead time as resource utilization rises to near 100%

- Add additional resources to a late project in an attempt to speed it up, which only makes the project even later, according to one of Brooks' Law (as we just discussed above)

The combination of overly optimistic schedules and these four common management actions make it virtually impossible to implement an innovation according to the original schedule. You might as well drop a ball and expect the Law of Gravity to reverse itself so that the ball falls up.

Given this discussion, it seems apparent that new innovation projects are often under-resourced. The seemingly obvious solution is to add more resources to a project at the beginning to ensure on-time completion. Unfortunately, if you are like most business leaders, you don't have extra innovation team resources sitting around waiting for a project. The good news: Adding extra resources may not require hiring more people and incurring extra cost. Because most companies are not deploying their innovation teams effectively, there is an enormous productivity opportunity available. If you are able to take advantage of even a fraction of this productivity opportunity, the need for hiring extra resources will immediately evaporate. How do we know? Let's return to the data on how innovators spend their time (*see* Figure 13-04).

Figure 13-04 {Repeated}

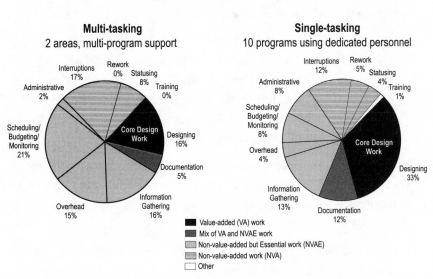

An initial study of the data showed that most of TI's design team members were assigned to more than one project (multi-tasked), and spent only 16% of their time on core design work. In contrast, innovators who were dedicated to one project (single-tasked) spent 33% of their time on core design work. Further, by single-tasking, non-value-add costs were reduced by a net of 25%, without attacking issues like inter-ruptions (12% of time spent). You can now understand why the seventh consequence of the Law of Variation (p. 59) was to eliminate multi-tasking for the Critical Resources. But how do you do this, and why does multi-tasking occur in the first place?

The three biggest causes of multi-tasking and the Fast Innovation solutions are:

1) **Shortages**: The most common reason that multi-tasking occurs is that an innovator is assigned to the highest-priority project, and then eventually gets stopped by a shortage: he or she needs a piece of test equipment, a test report from another organization, material from a supplier, and so on. While waiting for that gap to be filled, the inno-vator begins work on a lower-priority project so he or she is not completely unproductive. Then the shortage is filled and the innova-tor changes back to the first project. This switching back and forth between projects requires a lot of mental setup time that causes lost productivity and lower creativity.

   Solution: Have the Critical Resources inform all upstream activities what they are going to need and by when, which will help set common priorities. This costs virtually nothing and the resulting single-tasking will double the average completion rate and halve the lead time of the Critical Resource! This is one quick solution to the problem of under-resourced projects.

2) **Changes in management priorities**: An irate customer who demands something quickly can cause a huge chain reaction that has enormous consequences, including late time-to-market and all that that means financially.

   Solution: We're not saying that changes in priorities can be prevented, but at least if you understand the costs, you can make sound decisions and/or find ways to mitigate the impact. For example, if a given innovator can finish his or her current task in a few days, then that may be the best solution to the problem. Remember, if you can keep innovators single-tasked, you will likely double their productivity anyway.

3) **Aggressive program managers:** One way you get promoted is to be successful, and that is best accomplished by getting the best people to work on your project—by whatever means. Successful program managers want to see progress on their projects, and win no points by waiting, hence they unwittingly contribute to lateness by trying to force multi-tasking.

> *Solution*: All program managers should be educated about the principles of Fast Innovation, and particularly the huge productivity costs of multi-tasking and the impact (per Little's Law) on lead time when too many projects are crammed into the pipeline all at once. Most will comprehend the issue, but senior management still needs to enforce the single-tasking policy on Critical Resources.

Conclusion

Most of us have lived through situations where we give management our best estimate of how long it will take to complete a project, only to have them cut it in half ("Eighteen months is too long! Do it in nine!"). If, by some miracle, the project was completed that quickly, there was usually a high cost involved. And in many cases, the project simply couldn't meet the shorter deadlines.

Why does management often arbitrarily set development lead times? Because they are under intense pressure to grow revenue and shareholder value through innovation and do not know the Law of Lead Time or its implications. What the Law of Lead Time enforces is choices:

> *Given the current load on development, if you want to add or accelerate a project, you must either reduce the number of projects-in-process or add resources at the outset.*

For example, if there were a true market need to get a project done in 9 months rather than the estimated 18 months, the company's best options would be to:

- Abandon the project since they couldn't make the market window

- Postpone or cancel other projects (reducing the number of projects-in-process which, per Little's Law, will improve the average completion rate)

- Add *expert* resource capacity from the project start (remember Brooks' rule about adding unskilled resources—it will more likely slow you down)

The company could also expect gains through application of re-use and Design for Lean Six Sigma techniques as we discussed in Part II.

It is essential to right-size development processes from the start and plan appropriate buffer times or resources, especially where cutting-edge development is ongoing. Staff your projects with world-class talent and work to retain that talent. Failing to follow these prescriptions is all summed up in the old saw:

> *"Anybody dumb enough to get behind is not smart enough to catch up."*

Endnotes

1 For those who want a specific example: the company originally used Silicon Controlled Rectifiers (SCR) to convert DC to AC power. As part of the MOS revolution, power transistors that could switch a hundred times faster became available. Initial prototypes worked perfectly, but over time (months) a small number of mysterious failures occurred which could damage our reputation. The failures were not a quality but an application problem never before seen by the manufacturer. It took nearly a year to diagnose the problem because some of the team were in "denial" which delayed staffing the problem with adequate technical resources.

2 Fred Brooks, a manager of IBM's large development efforts.

3 Arthur Conan Doyle, *The Annotated Sherlock Holmes* (New York: Clarkson N. Potter, 1967), p. 349.

4 S.M. [Stanislaw M.] Ulam, *The Adventures of a Mathematician* (Berkeley, CA: University of California Press, 1991).

5 Theresa Amabile, Constance N. Hadley, Steven J. Kramer, *Creativity Under the Gun* (HBR OnPoint Enhanced Edition), August 2002, HBR Product No. 1571.

SPOTLIGHT ON

The
Innovation Blitz

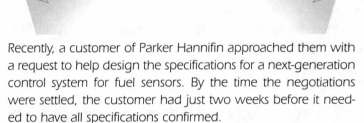

Recently, a customer of Parker Hannifin approached them with a request to help design the specifications for a next-generation control system for fuel sensors. By the time the negotiations were settled, the customer had just two weeks before it needed to have all specifications confirmed.

Normally, the complete design process would take nine months. But Parker had been experimenting with an entirely new approach to design and development, which we have referred to as the Innovation Blitz: sequestering hand-picked, cross-functional teams with the customer and supplier for a week and putting them through a carefully structured design process. So they pulled together a team made up of the customer and a number of developers, and led by expert facilitator Pete Buca.

The result? In just four days, this team completed 80% of the specifications for desired features and design work, including drawings of a few patentable components. Most of the detailed work had to be executed by competent developers, but it was a winning product that nobody, neither the customer nor Parker (nor even the competition!) could have conceived of before the Blitz. This project laid the groundwork that allowed Parker to not only define a new market but also to establish and maintain leadership differentiation in a new technology.

The chief engineer, initially the biggest doubter of the Blitz approach, became its biggest advocate by the end of the week. The customer was ecstatic because the Blitz led to solutions and capabilities he had not known existed, and developers were happy to find a problem to fit the solution they'd already developed.

This Innovation Blitz was so successful that Pete Buca ran 10 more of them over the next year, leading to innovations that are projected to generate $260 million in differentiated offerings in a highly competitive market—a great example of Fast Innovation in action.

The next chapter will discuss a variety of ways to speed up more traditional innovation processes, but with results like those Pete shared with us, it should come as no surprise that we view the Innovation Blitz as one of the best speed weapons available to innovators today. In fact, we're convinced that developing expertise in the Blitz can become a disruptive advantage for your company.

Traditional vs. Blitz Model: Trench warfare vs. a lightning attack?

The Innovation Blitz that we have described is quite different from the way potential innovations are generated in most companies. In a traditional approach, all the stages are drawn out and there are a lot of delays (specifications are sent back and forth between design groups or between a company and its customers) and a lot of opportunities to get it wrong (working in isolation, the supplier company often has to guess what its customer wants).

The Innovation Blitz gives the best information to all three parties (customers, suppliers, and innovators) and derives the best solution in just four days! From the perspective of the Law of Lead Time, the Innovation Blitz involves much more information flow in both directions—with speed measured with a watch, not a calendar! Thus the lead time to get the best answer for the customer on one project-in-process is at least 20 times faster. In addition, a Blitz approach...

- Eliminates major design iterations caused by *concept errors* that arise from a lack of interaction with the customer and with internal thought leaders.

- Avoids the problem of having specifications change during the development cycle (a lot more can change in a year-long project than in a four-day project).

- Exploits perhaps the most overlooked and undervalued attribute of swift innovation: **focus**. Time and again, in a number of different settings, successful innovators will tell you that innovation requires an initial concentrated effort (preferably with a small but talented cross-functional team).

- Develops a high-energy environment with direct customer participation.

In short, the Innovation Blitz is a means of creating growth, competitive advantage and higher margins.

Using the Blitz Approach

The Parker Hannifin story that Pete Buca shared with us shows a perfect use for the Innovation Blitz:

- The problem was narrowly defined: to meet the customer's specifications for a new technology surrounding detection of fuel levels (a major challenge for the facilitator is to maintain this narrow focus throughout the Blitz).

- The Blitz team consisted of the main target customer plus diverse marketing and development staff and suppliers.

- By working together in the Innovation Blitz, the customer learned about capabilities they didn't know the manufacturer had, and the manufacturer's developers got immediate feedback on general concepts that they could later refine.

- The event was structured to ensure genuine valuable output by the end of the week.

- There was a strong facilitator who had both excellent people skills and enough subject matter knowledge to be able to evaluate the progress. Finding (or creating) people capable of, and passionate about, facilitating Innovation Blitzes can itself be a critical limiter unless you have a formal training process.

If you decide to conduct an Innovation Blitz, consider these factors:

- Carefully select the purpose: likely a specific customer (a hungry lead user) with a particular need that is congruent with a high-priority target for your business.

- Conduct adequate prework so that the session can be most effective. Business and strategic objectives should be clear. Advanced Voice of the Customer results must be available to the team.

- Plan how and where you will isolate people from their normal environments (and all the distractions therein).

Leading the Innovation Blitz process

Leading Innovation Blitzes effectively requires extraordinarily strong facilitation skills, knowledge of the Fast Innovation process, and an understanding of best practices for product/service development. The ideal candidate:

- Is an excellent facilitator and communicator, especially in inquiry skills. Research on group dynamics and interaction has consistently shown that there is much more individual knowledge in a team than is traditionally brought to bear in a group discussion.

- Has a broad understanding of innovation trends across multiple industries, insatiably reads about and studies innovation and creativity techniques, and is always looking for insights and techniques to shamelessly steal from others (a truly Open Innovation mindset).

- Understands emerging best practices for product/service development, and has design experience.

- Is knowledgeable about innovation trends in the industry, is able to identify and screen innovation opportunities, and perceives competitive threats. The facilitator can lead the team towards the optimal result.

- Is a leader in your business, interested in being a major force for innovation in your company, and in taking the lead in establishing methods for turning a division or business unit into an idea incubator.

These are skills that can be taught, and, when supplemented with coaching, can result in the internal capability to generate innovations.

- Create a cross-functional team composed of different specialties; whenever possible and appropriate include one or two customers and supplier representatives (optimal team size is 7 to 12 people)

- Plan the Blitz so you can deliver a design by the end of Day 4 (see Figure SP5-01).

Figure SP5-01: The Innovation Blitz Process

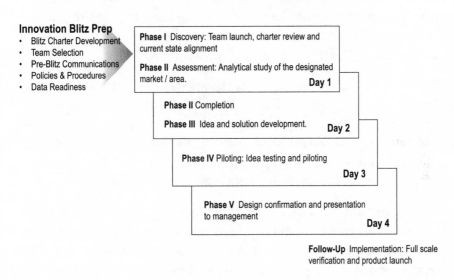

Innovation Blitz Prep
- Blitz Charter Development
- Team Selection
- Pre-Blitz Communications
- Policies & Procedures
- Data Readiness

Phase I Discovery: Team launch, charter review and current state alignment

Phase II Assessment: Analytical study of the designated market / area. **Day 1**

Phase II Completion

Phase III Idea and solution development. **Day 2**

Phase IV Piloting: Idea testing and piloting **Day 3**

Phase V Design confirmation and presentation to management **Day 4**

Follow-Up Implementation: Full scale verification and product launch

The hardest part, says Pete Buca of Parker Hannifin, is applying the people skills needed to lead the first two days of a Blitz session.

> *"I've seen it so often that it's now a predictable pattern," says Pete. "People come to the first day of the Blitz grumbling about having to be there. By the end of the second day they're ready to walk out the door, frustrated at what they see as a lack of anything tangible to show for their efforts. Every single time, one or more people from the team will take me aside that second night and express their complaints."*

But Pete doesn't panic because he knows something the team doesn't know:

> *"Sometime late on the second day or early on the third day there is always, always, a breakthrough," he says. "The team*

> *gets an incredible amount of work done before the end of the fourth day."*

We have conducted dozens of similar Blitz events with very similar outcomes.

We realize that it won't be practical for companies to completely switch over to a Blitz approach for all projects right away. Instead, we suggest that you experiment with the Blitz on a few focused, high-priority efforts. Not only will this contribute to meeting your growth targets, but it will also give you experience developing innovation skill sets.

The goal is to prove to doubting Thomases and customers that the Innovation Blitz is win-win. Nothing builds enthusiasm for a new methodology like early results. While success may require a few attempts, the goal should be to make the Innovation Blitz part of your corporate culture and the engine for the sustained creation of customer-valued differentiation and competitive advantage.

Pete would also like to see a day when attendance at a Blitz becomes mandatory for managers. "Just imagine how powerful it would be to tell managers that all of your company's key products or services for the coming year were going to be defined and designed during four-day Blitz sessions," Pete told us. "I think that would motivate them to clear their calendars during those time periods, and make for even greater engagement in innovation by the company leadership."

Creating customer demand for the Blitz

Encourage customers to participate in an Innovation Blitz. We highly recommend that once you've mastered this technique, you use your experience as a tool in your marketing arsenal—to demonstrate your company's collaborative, customer-centric approach to joint innovation, geared toward meeting market requirements.

If customers refuse to participate in an Innovation Blitz, they are effectively cutting you off from really understanding what they want, and cutting themselves off from getting the best input from you (and likely better solutions to their needs than they thought possible). And you get cut off from the highest margins and growth!

CHAPTER 14

The FastGate Method

How to Control Innovation Lead Time

Many attempts have been made in the past to reduce the lead time of innovation. Most notable have been the Stage/Gate (*see*, for example, Cooper)[6] and the equivalent Phase/Gate (McGrath) approaches. The concept of both was to divide the development process into a small number of stages (typically five) with "gates" between them where management reviews what the team has done and makes a go/no-go decision. (*See* Figure 14-01.)

Figure 14-01: Typical Stage/Gate Process

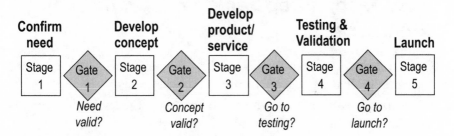

This flowchart shows typical stages of a product development process. Most companies will have at least four checkpoints (gates) during the process and sometimes more (adding "subgate" checks during development, for example).

This Stage/Gate approach was a great step forward as it forced a systematic evaluation of a project's merits: fit with strategy, technical and/or logistical feasibility, potential for conveying competitive advantage, etc. And because not all projects will get the go-ahead and then pass through subsequent gates, this approach has the potential to achieve a Fast Innovation goal: reducing the number of projects-in-process and therefore reducing lead time (assuming no new projects are added).

However, the original Stage/Gate process never asks questions that we know are essential to meeting time-to-market targets:

- How many projects are in process?

- How many tasks does each innovator work on?

- What is the average completion rate?

- What are the Critical Resources? What is the percent utilization?

- What is the current lead time through development?

- How will the lead time of existing projects be affected by adding another project?

Clearly, without this knowledge, you cannot predict the lead time of the development of any project. At a minimum, therefore, the innovation version of a Stage/Gate process must include data that will help us answer the questions about completion time.

FastGate, Feedback and Critical Resources

Chapter 3 discussed that the biggest determinant of overall innovation lead time is what happens with the Critical Resources—the individual innovators or work groups who insert the longest delay in the project lead times. Here is where that principle comes to life.

In his book *Critical Chain*, Goldratt suggested that new projects should be released into the development process at a rate no greater than the average completion rate for the Critical Resources. Thus if a project requires the use of a particular Critical Resource, and that Critical Resource completes one project per month, that should be the launch rate for new projects requiring that Critical Resource.

On average this approach is correct, but does not use the Law of Lead Time, and hence does not predict lead times nor suggest a set of tools to reduce the lead time to a level demanded by the market. And as we all know, *actual* completion rate of the Critical Resource varies widely from the *average* completion rate. The more direct trigger for launching a project is to first determine whether the Critical Resource *has actually completed* a project, then install a feedback loop (refreshed daily or weekly by email) that keeps business unit managers and/or the Chief Innovation Officer informed about the number of tasks-in-process and cumulative task time for all Critical Resources.

If the Critical Resource is working on an easy project and completes the work ahead of schedule, the company could launch a new project into the process earlier. If the Critical Resource is working a project more difficult than average, the company would know to delay the launch of the next project (or risk increasing the queue).

This approach compensates for our unavoidable ignorance of the *actual rate* of project completion by the Critical Resource. Today, unit managers or project leaders don't discover a project is late until the team comes together for a meeting or holds a scheduled review—*very slow* forms of feedback. This feedback at the project management level is shown as the upper line in the Figure 14-02.

Figure 14-02: Benefits of Monitoring Tasks-in-Process

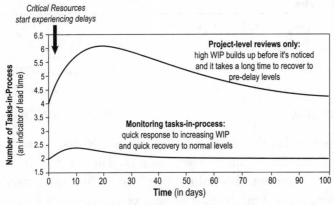

In traditional project management, a lot of work- or tasks-in-process can build up as the result of delays or variation. The effect of those delays lasts for a long time. The Fast Innovation approach is to moni-. tor tasks-in-process, which gives a quicker alert, faster response (up to five times faster), and faster recovery.

However, a feedback signal on tasks-in-process is a forward indicator of potential lead time problems, triggering management to take early action ranging from stopping any additional releases to offloading tasks to cross-trained individuals (*see* the lower line of Figure 14-02). You will note that the lead time settles down to within 10% of the starting value in about one-fifth the time of project management. In practice, that means a task between two gates that gets bunched up provides an immediate signal that something is wrong in the process.

In short, feedback data must drive the decision to release a project. Based on the actual completion of a task, we must load Critical Resources to no more than 65% of capacity, and establish feedback loops given the uncertainty, both good and bad, about the time it takes for the innovation tasks and our knowledge about that time.

Adding knowledge of impact on lead time and on Critical Resources produces the next evolution of the phase/gate approach, known as the **FastGate**. One example of a decision point in a FastGate system is shown in Table 14-A.

Table 14-A: FastGate™ Example

Gate between building a business case and development

Metrics	Data
# of projects in Development	57
Avg Completion Rate	4.3/Month
Current Lead time	13.2 Months
Lead time Plan	12 Months
DECISION	**DELAY LAUNCH!**

You will notice that the decision in this case was to delay launching the project into the development stage, based on data and the Law of Lead Time. If management determines that current priorities *require* the launch, then other projects must be removed or more resources added. The FastGate process therefore provides a control mechanism on innovation lead time. If you want to cut lead time by 50%, one of the quickest ways to achieve that goal is to stop releasing new projects into the process until the average number of active projects has fallen by 50%.

This principle can be applied at the project level, as in the example above, or at the task level, for example, to gauge the workload of a designer whose capacity is a constraint. In fact, we also recommend installing subgates within development so that you know if and when a critical design milestone is missed. Now that you've seen the big picture, let's take a closer look at the FastGate method.

The FastGate Method for Innovation Project Management

We've made the point many times that any project management system needs to account for the impact on lead time and resource utilization of any new project that enters the pipeline. The discussion above adds a new twist: we have to pay particular attention to what's happening with our Critical Resources.

This knowledge has led to the evolution of **FastGate™** reviews (*see* Figure 14-03) for key decision points in the Stage/Gate process. Presuming a project meets all the other gate criteria (related to VOC, business case, etc.), a FastGate decision point means you release that project into the next development stage IF AND ONLY IF it will not increase lead time beyond the market-driven goal (usually that means that the project will not add delays when it reaches a Critical Resource). If for some reason the project *must* proceed to the next phase, then you have to either de-prioritize another project that has already passed the gate or add resources effectively to support the greater work load.

Figure 14-03: FastGate Approach

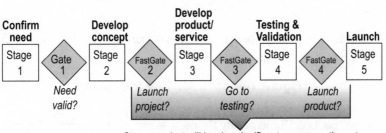

Once a project will involve significant resources, the gates
must include a check on utilization and # of projects-in-process

A FastGate review ensures that a project is released into the next stage of development only when data shows that lead time and utilization of Critical Resources in the next stage will not be pushed beyond plan.

Making the initial adjustments

Before you decide whether to launch *new* projects, you'll first have to adjust your current project pipeline. Here's how that process should go.

STEP 1: Determine current operational status

a) Determine the number of projects-in-process at every development stage.

b) Compute a queue time (the average time that a task sits around waiting to be worked on) for every activity in the innovation process.

c) Identify Critical Resources: Identify the innovation activity with the longest queue time for each project. There may be a different Critical Resource for each project.

d) Determine % utilization for all Critical Resources and verify they are loaded at no more than 65% capacity and are single-tasked. Assign a cross-trained backup.

e) Identify the longest route of dependent steps (using a critical path method). This will determine overall lead time.

f) Identify the market-defined delivery target.

g) Calculate the average completion rate across all projects.

h Use Little's Law (below) to determine overall lead time of the development process.

i) Install feedback loops between points suspected of containing Critical Resources and measure tasks-in-process at appropriate intervals.

Figure 14-04: Little's Law (repeated)

$$\text{Average Lead Time of Any Process} = \frac{\text{Number of Things-in-Process}}{\text{Average Completion Rate}}$$

STEP 2: *Adjust work systems and workloads*

a) Make immediate adjustments to Critical Resource utilization to meet time-to-market targets. If a Critical Resource is approaching a 50% time overrun, you must evaluate:
  - How much buffer is in the project schedule (see Appendix 2). If slack exists, you may be able to carry on without change, but should assign cross-trained personnel if a queue is building.
  - The technical capacity of individuals to solve the problems: If they can't cut it, you will have to bring in additional resources, realizing that this will in fact slow down the process.

b) De-prioritize projects if a specific task is 50% over planned time. You run the risk of alienating important customers or abandoning a strategically important market, but sometimes that is the only rational course to enable the company to grow where it can forge a competitive advantage. (*See* story of Intel's decision to drop the memory business, Chapter 2.)

c) Install a time buffer for each project (to get the buffer, add together all the median task times along the critical path, then divide in half).
  - Keep the Critical Resources informed of the amount of buffer consumed for each of their projects
  - Give priority to the project with least amount of buffer remaining, assuming it remains high priority for completion
  - Continue using time buffers and a daily buffer monitor so that the buffer time for each project is visible and becomes the global metric of development

d) Cap planned utilization for Critical Resources at 65%; for others at 80%.

If market-defined deadlines appear to be in jeopardy, remember that there is enormous value in being among the first to the market in most businesses (*see* p. 19). If you are not among the first three to market, you may not even earn back the development investment. That should justify a reasonable investment in additional upfront resources, if necessary.

Ongoing Use of FastGate Reviews

After you've made the initial adjustments, *every gate in your system should be converted into a FastGate check.* That means adding considerations about lead time and utilization *on top of* all the other things you check in a particular gate. The gate after an exploration stage, for example, would include determining whether the concept is still valid, verifying if there seemed to be a viable disruptive opportunity, etc., PLUS checking on what the impact would be on lead time and utilization if the project moved into development.

FastGate Check: Evaluate the impact on Average Lead Time and on Critical Resources

1) Review the data on your current projects-in-process, average completion rate, lead-time-to-market, and % utilization.

2) Determine whether moving the project under consideration into the next phase would cause the lead time to extend beyond plan. If so, DO NOT release the project unless...

   – You are willing to shut down some other active project to make room for the new project. This SHOULD happen if the new project has a higher value-creating potential than an active project.

   – You are willing to live with longer lead times (all projects will go slower). This SHOULD happen if you think this project is higher priority than meeting previous release-to-market targets.

3) Determine the effect on Critical Resources

   – Compute the lead time impact of the proposed project on all of your Critical Resource innovators. Compute lead time as the number of projects lined up behind an activity—"in queue"—divided by the average completion rate *plus* the time to complete the projects currently in process. The number of projects in queue can be determined by observation.

   – Sort the results in descending order of lead time.

- In general, do not launch a project until the required Critical Resource has completed a project, or else the queue and lead time will grow. If this review shows that the lead time of existing projects will not be compromised, the project can be released to development.

Tracking Project Performance

Effective use of the FastGate method requires that you have good data on hand about planned and actual project performance. Just as the Chief Innovation Officer needs to track compiled statistics across all innovation efforts for the corporation, business unit leaders should track the progress of individual sustaining innovation projects. The goal is to focus on that minimum set of metrics that determine the success of your process. Common examples include:

- Process: Development process cost, lead time, number of iterations, % utilization, re-use

- Output: Quality (customer satisfaction), value created by the innovation

- Program: Variance of budget, schedule, target cost, and customer satisfaction

- Financial: % of revenue/profit from new innovations, % of business case achieved

Note that each constituency is measuring cost, lead time, and quality from a perspective that is meaningful to how it increases creation of shareholder value.

Other criteria for evaluating project success will depend on what exactly is being innovated. An example from a construction equipment manufacturer is shown in Figure 14-05 (next page).

Figure 14-05: Sample metrics

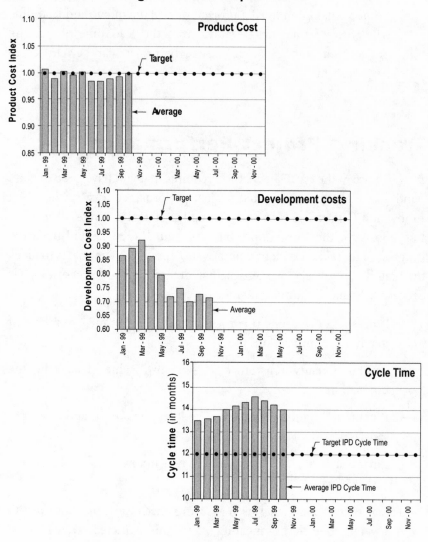

A product development dashboard from a construction equipment manufacturer is shown above. They struggled with hitting the product's cost and weight targets—the new machines were perpetually over-weight and over-budget. Fixing these issues late in the design cycle led to increased product development cycle times. They included a design stability metric to track quality issues from pilot audits. To increase the visibility of adherence to the gate review checklists, they tracked the % of deliverables met at each gate review. This dashboard linked a higher-level corporate dashboard with specific revenue-timing objectives.

An important metric to help avoid cost overruns

The risk of unpleasant cost overruns can be greatly reduced by proactively utilizing a target-costing approach on each project. The central premise of target costing is that the market sets the price, the business establishes its

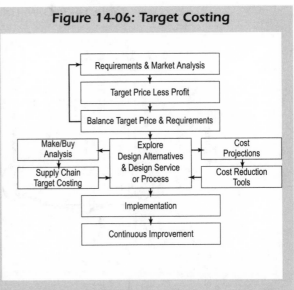

Figure 14-06: Target Costing

market objectives, and the remainder is the project's target cost. The overall target cost is then subdivided into its major elements (for example, material cost, manufacturing, transportation, and packaging) and these cost targets are attacked over the development life cycle with an Innovation Blitz that includes suppliers and customers.

Oregon Productivity Matrix

Another project tracking approach is represented by the Oregon Productivity Matrix. It is similar to the better-known Balanced Scorecard but has the advantage that it rolls up total weighted performance metrics into a *single metric* according to the process shown in Figure 14-07.

Figure 14-07: Elements of an Oregon Productivity Matrix

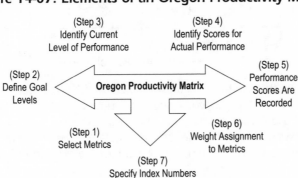

Table 14-B: OPM Data

2003 Priorities	CUST SAT			PEOPLE			PROCESS			FINANCIALS			Score
	OTD	Score-card	Market Share	EM	Retention	IDP	Time to Market	Design Passes	% Re-Use	R&D Costs	Econ Profit	Revenue	
	%	Index	%	Index	%	%	Months	No.	No.	Index	%	$M	
Current Results	93.2	350	31	2.3	91.2	100	17.5	2.5	78.0	15.7	5	975.0	
Upper Limit	97.8	1000	45	10	95.5	100	12	1.2	85.0	10.0	12	1000.0	10
	96.9	900	35	9	94.5	98	13	1.4	84.0	11.0	10	990.0	9
	96.1	800	35	8	93.5	96	14	1.6	83.0	12.0	8	980.0	8
	95.2	700	30	7	92.5	94	15	1.8	82.0	13.0	6	970.0	7
	94.2	600	25	6	92.0	92	16	2.0	81.0	14.0	4	960.0	6
	93.6	500	20	5	91.5	90	17	2.2	80.0	15.0	2	950.0	5
	93.0	400	15	4	91.0	88	18	2.4	79.0	16.0	0	940.0	4
	92.0	300	10	3	90.5	86	19	2.6	78.0	17.0	-2	930.0	3
	91.0	200	5	2	90.0	84	20	2.8	59.0	18.0	-4	920.0	2
Lower Limit	90.0	100	2	1	89.5	82	21	3.0	56.0	19.0	-6	910.0	1
SCORE	4	3	7	2	4	10	5	3	3	4	6	7	
WEIGHT	11	7	14	5	10	3	12	4	4	3	8	19	
VALUE	44	21	98	10	40	30	60	12	12	12	48	133	= 520

Scoring System

Add all the Values to generate ──────> Composite Score

This OPM shows three metrics in each of four categories (= 12 metrics). Near the top you'll see the "current results" for this time period. The center of the chart shows the scoring system. Follow the arrows to track how one score is calculated. The scores are multiplied by the weights, then the total values are summed to give an overall score of 520.

The OPM may seem complicated at first because of all the numbers that go into it. But once the system is up and running and a standard scoring system is in place, the decision makers can focus on the single overall score (520 in this example).

We would recommend that the weighting be related to the estimated shareholder value attributed to the metric. Chapter 1 suggested a means of estimating the value of time-to-market. Chapter 11 discussed reducing the cost of development and lead time by applying the Religion of Re-use. The value of retaining Critical Resources can similarly be estimated based on the impact that turnover would have on time-to-market. It should be pointed out that no single set of metrics is appropriate for or can satisfy the perspective of each constituency/stakeholder in the innovation process.

Conclusion

Try as you might, you cannot break the Laws of Lead Time and Innovation Variation any more than you can break the Law of Gravity! This chapter provided a framework to take control of the speed of your innovation process from beginning to end. We purposefully went into a lot of detail because this process directly attacks the two biggest barriers to growth that CEOs identified in the survey described in the Preface: 60% of CEOs believe time and cost overruns are a critical roadblock to successful innovation, and 53% believe competing development priorities are a critical roadblock.

The FastGate method helps overcome both of those hurdles. The key is to modify your stage/gate checks to include information on workloads and completion rates of Critical Resources. But before you even get to that point, you need to answer the following questions:

- Do you understand who the Critical Resources are in your innovation process? What utilization levels are you planning for them? For other team members?

- Have you calculated average lead time for your current innovation projects using Little's Law?

- Have you used market data to determine a time-to-market target for each project?

Invest the time now in gathering good data that will help you answer those questions and you'll be well on your way to controlling innovation lead time.

Endnotes

6 Robert G. Cooper, *Product Leadership: Creating and Launching Superior New Products* (New York: Perseus Books Group/HarperCollins Publishers, 2000), and Michael E. McGrath, *Setting the PACE in Product Development, A Guide to Product and Cycle-time Excellence* (Burlington, MA: Elsevier Science (Butterworth-Heinemann, 1996). These books were written before the Laws of Lead Time and Utilization were applied to innovation.

CHAPTER 15

Creating Innovation Incubators

How to Catalyze Creativity on Your Teams

With Pete Buca[7]

In our many years of helping companies improve performance, we have learned that team engagement is at least equally important (and likely more so) than the technical tools. Our research on team dynamics led us to develop a science-based approach to driving powerful teams, taught to teams in a week-long workshop.[8] During this workshop, each participant is asked to read background information, then answer a set of questions. The participants are then divided into teams, which are each asked to work together to come up with a collective set of answers to the same questions. No matter what the setting—and we've compiled the results from this exercise run in hundreds of different companies, different sectors, different types of teams, different languages and cultures—the outcome is always the same:

1) The best score that individuals achieve is usually around 30% correct

2) The best score that the teams achieve is around 40% (indicating that the best teams are able to garner some synergy over the best individual on the team)

3) Most important, if you look at all the answers given by people on a team and ask "Did ANYONE get this question right?" it turns out that 95% to 100% of the time *at least one person* on the team had the right answer

The obvious challenge for these teams (and their managers) is: "You had the knowledge within your team to score 100% correct. Why didn't you?"

As shown by our research, part of the answer to that question is that the people with the right answers don't always advocate for their ideas or are not listened to when they do. To explain this phenomenon, we started collecting data on another exercise performed in this workshop where teams are asked to come up with one strength and one area for improvement for each team member (as well as plans for how the team will help each person improve in that area). What we found is that relatively few people will advocate too much (about 30% to 40%) while the majority (60% to 70%) advocate too little—that is, they are more passive.

The lessons we've taken away from this pattern are profound. We've learned that teams and their companies are smarter than they think they are. If they can tap into the knowledge and creativity of *everyone* on the team, they will come up with right answers a lot more often than they do now.

The data also shows why having a strong innovation project leader is absolutely essential for innovation teams. The leader must have good inquiry skills to draw out the best from the team, must be successful at encouraging those who advocate too little, and must fly aircover for them against those who tend to dominate. In an environment where teams have to push the boundaries to look for disruptive opportunities, it's likely that a lot of the ideas will get laughed at!

This chapter provides proven guidance for project leaders on how to increase participation and creativity on teams. It covers techniques we know work in practice, not just in theory. It looks at a wide range of factors—from size and composition of teams, to time pressure, and team dynamics—that all affect whether your teams will deliver ho-hum outputs or will become true incubators of innovation.

Constructing effective teams

There is a large body of knowledge about constructing teams that generate high levels of creativity and work effectively.

In our previous books, for example, we've discussed the work of Dr. Meredith Belbin of Cambridge University (described in his book *Team Roles at Work*). Belbin's contributions were in identifying a number of **preferred roles** that people automatically adopt when on a team, and in providing guidance on how to proactively shape team composition to make sure the right balance of roles is represented on all teams.

There are many other issues about what it takes to build creative teams—such as emphasizing learning and inquiry skills—the details of which are beyond the scope of this book. The point is that there is a science to teamwork just as there is science behind resource management and project selection. We encourage you to research the literature so you can set your teams up for success.

Becoming a Catalyst for Creativity

There are two phases in a team's development work when creative efforts benefit from strong facilitation by a **creativity catalyst** (someone whose role is to spark the thinking in other people):

1) **Before the snap:** If you've ever experienced the creative process, you know firsthand that progress is made only after you reach the snap (or "aha" as some people describe it), when diverse ideas and half-formed thoughts merge into coherent insight. On the downside, there's no way to predict with any certainty when or where that snap will occur. On the upside, there are many techniques for helping people reach a state where the aha is more likely. Think of it as trying to deliberately create conditions where an exciting accident will occur!

2) **While evaluating and refining solutions:** If we were inventors instead of innovators, we might be happy just reaching the aha. But since we all work for businesses, we need to push through the rest of the development process, looking for ways to convert brilliant insights into usable products, services, technologies, or processes. Creativity is needed in these stages just as much as when coming up with the idea

in the first place. This is a place where many idea-rich companies fail to deliver. Recall from Part I that the primary concerns of CEOs surveyed are related to the actual delivery of innovations, not to a dearth of initial good ideas.

The following techniques can help in both of these situations.

1. Immerse team members in customer knowledge and other background

Studies of creativity have confirmed that people reach the aha stage only after they spend time wallowing in as much information about the issue or challenge as they can take in. (Most people call this **immersion**.) A catalyst's role here is to:

- Make sure immersion time is built into development planning

- Help teams identify all the areas of knowledge they need to explore; point them towards internal and external resources; provide access to customers, etc.

- Create forums for sharing ideas within a team (with the rise of intranets, this isn't the challenge it used to be—most companies create electronic billboards where any team member can post relevant information such as customer or process data, journal articles, notes from conversations with experts, and so on)

2. Make the problem difficult and specific

Creativity research has shown that people accomplish more when they have a goal that is both **difficult** (perceived by them as challenging, beyond their current skill or knowledge level) and **specific**. You or the other creativity catalysts in your company must make sure that each team is given a specific definition for a problem that no one in your company knows how to solve.

Facilitating all stages of the creative process

In the past two decades a lot of research has gone into creativity. Studies in disciplines as diverse as cognitive psychology, entrepreneurial business, engineering, architecture, and the basic sciences (to name just a few) have confirmed that innovators pass through different stages prior to and after the creative breakthrough. Though the models in each discipline vary by name and details, they all describe a progression with at least four phases:

1 **Immersion or preparation:** Learning about and defining the problem, challenge or need. The term "immersion" reflects both a state of intense focus, when people's mental concentration is entirely consumed by what they are learning, and the sense that the person is literally surrounded by information about the problem or issue.

2 **Incubation:** A period of reflection, when ideas develop. The incubation period is the least predictable in terms of time; it can come as people begin immersion in the issue or after months of pondering the problem.

3 **Insight or illumination:** We call this the "snap" because that's how people have described the sensation (which matches our own experience). Your brain is shifting thoughts around and suddenly there is a snap where the jigsaw pieces fall into place and you see connections you never saw before. **Once you've snapped, you can never go back to seeing the situation the same as you did before.**

4 **Evaluation or verification:** Creative insight sets off a flurry of activity where the innovator tests out the idea to see if it works in reality. If not (and that happens often!), the innovator either goes back to immersion and incubation, or performs additional work to investigate what it would take to make the idea work.

Some models separate preparation from immersion; others add an "elaboration" step after evaluation. But the overall pattern is consistent. Most of the techniques described in this chapter can be used in several stages. Brainstorming can help people identify what they've learned through immersion, help extract insights, or identify ways to test an idea; creativity and critical thinking skills are similarly multipurpose.

3. Push the boundaries in brainstorming

The best way to get a good idea is to get a lot of ideas.

Linus Pauling, Nobel Prize–winning chemist

Brainstorming sessions perform a critical role in collaborative creativity, often providing the sparks that lead to innovation. When using brainstorming as part of a development process, the typical rules apply—only more so!

- Record *every* idea.
  - *Especially* welcome those that seem dumb or infeasible
  - Don't allow any judgment or evaluation during the brainstorm; no self-censorship
  - Don't worry if the idea seems tangential to the problem or customer needs

- Make sure everyone in the room has an equal chance to participate (to help ensure equal participation, have people write down ideas first, do a round robin when sharing ideas, etc.).

- Piggyback as much as possible—encourage people to build off ideas suggested by others.

- Push past the initial lull: There is always a rush of ideas during the first few minutes of a brainstorming session. That's when people are drawing on what is most familiar to them, i.e., the safe ideas. Do NOT let the session stop there. It's usually when people get their second or third wind that the truly innovative ideas emerge.

Critical: Separate idea generation from evaluation

In any early development work, and particularly during a brainstorming session, is it critical that people do not evaluate ideas as they are being generated. This is harder to do than it sounds. How often have you sat in a meeting and thought (or even said aloud), "That's a stupid idea," in reaction to someone else's suggestion? This sentiment is captured in the famed Disney practice of allowing only "Yes, and… " comments to a story idea (no "Yes, buts" allowed).

If you're working with a group new to innovation brainstorms, do whatever you can to get participants out of their comfort zones. Seed the process by prepping a few participants with outrageous ideas they can raise during the sessions. And remember, this is one activity where quantity is better than quality (because we don't know what quality is yet). There are a lot of advanced brainstorming techniques that can help generate creative thinking as well.

4. Help (or even force) people to think in new ways

As we've pointed out several times in this book, innovation is *not* about creating new information (that's the realm of invention). Rather, innovators are usually looking at information that's available to everyone. What's different is that they see the information in new ways. Your role as a catalyst is clear: you want to do everything you can to help people make new connections, take new perspectives. Here are five of the most effective techniques:

a. Have as diverse a team as possible

When we say diverse, we mean it in every possible sense of the word: gender, age, background, education/training, ethnicity, natural strengths, birthplace, knowledge about the problem/challenge, areas of expertise, and on and on. You may think that some of these factors are superfluous to business innovation or just "nice to have," but trust us when we say they aren't. As much as anything else, a team's success will be determined by their ability to develop new perspectives on an issue—and the more different team members are, the greater the chances of seeing things in a new way. Since we can't predict ahead of time what will make the difference, what will spark the light bulb or an aha moment, the best we can do is do everything in our power to bring new perspectives *into* the team.

Chapter contributor Pete Buca, for example, often pulls together product development teams that have a mix of:

- Disciplines (he looks for a mix of marketing, sales, manufacturing, accounting, design, etc.).

- Technology specialists (one or two would work).

- Customers and suppliers (whenever possible)—as Pete told us, "Our innovation teams have told me that it is often the first time they've met the customer face-to-face." The approach has proven exceedingly successful for both sides: customers learn about capabilities that Parker has that they were unaware of, and Parker developers see the full context of customer needs.

- Users (where applicable).

- Backgrounds (frontline experience vs. academic training vs. research, for example).

There are no limits on what you should do to increase diversity. For example, you may be thinking that because design teams are, by definition, designing something (a product, service, business system), that participants should all be expert at whatever is being designed. That's rarely the case. Often you'll get better results if you include people who do NOT know your capabilities that well, including:

- Customers, who will know their needs intimately but not your capabilities

- Naive users or contributors

- Employees from work areas peripheral to the problem (if designing products or services, that might mean including someone from finance, accounting, or human resources; if revamping financial systems, that might mean including someone from purchasing, manufacturing, or customer service)

The way in which these outsiders help a team is probably self-evident: they come in with no preconceived notions about what's possible or impossible. So they're going to ask questions that will push the thinking of the experts: "Why couldn't we do this... ?" or "Wouldn't it be possible to... ?" or "I think there's a new way to look at this."

b. Keep creativity "toy boxes"

Physical items can be used in multiple ways to help spark creativity. A creativity catalyst will often compile...

1) **A box of small toys that can be handed out during the team meeting.** Such toys are there purely for the kinesthetic experience: Truth is, many people can think and speak more clearly if their hands are busy. So you just need something they can manipulate.

2) **A box of items that serve as metaphors or symbols of the challenge or goal.** Have each team talk about the problem in non-business terms. Trying to design a fuel sensor that can work in any orientation? Take a gyroscope out of the box. Trying to design a hospital that makes people feel like they're in a hotel? Take one of those miniature shampoo bottles out of the box.

3) **A box of eclectic parts, components, materials, odds-and-ends, junk:** The best example of this is IDEO's "Tech Box," a collection of "interesting things that might some day be useful." All of the designers contributed their private collections of gadgets and anything else they had held on to. As Tom Kelley writes in *The Art of Innovation*, "The Tech Box became our corporate spark plug. Need inspiration for a project or thorny design issue? Grab something from the box to toss on the table and spark new ideas."

These boxes come in handy throughout the design process, helping to spark new ideas in early brainstorming sessions and to speed up prototype development.

c. Get people thinking with the right sides of their brains

Being able to see and even touch something real can evoke much stronger reactions than simply describing an idea in words or even symbols. Require your teams to sketch or draw their ideas, and/or to produce models or prototypes of their concepts.

d. Teach creative thinking skills

French symbolist poet Arthur Rimbaud argued for the "systematic derangement of the senses" in order to create poetry and visual art. While derangement may be too severe a word for our purposes, the notion that we have to break out of traditional thinking patterns is certainly applicable. You want to teach people to look at innovation challenges as puzzles they need to examine from many viewpoints.

Just one example is using the **Time Travel** challenge: Innovation is all about creating the future, but far too often people get stuck in the here and now, in how things work today. An important role for the creativity catalyst is helping them project into the future. Ask your teams to leave their current space and imagine they are in a world that exists after the problem is solved. Have them answer questions such as...

- What does the world look like?

- How do people behave?

- What has changed in customers' lives now that the problem is solved?

- What does the new product look and feel like? (or What does it feel like to experience this new service?)

- What took place that enabled this new world to come into being?

e. Teach critical thinking skills

One goal of creativity work is to look beyond self-imposed boundaries, the preconditions that people have set in their minds about what is or isn't possible. A creativity catalyst needs to...

- **Ask people to put their assumptions into words.** This may take some digging—our assumptions become so ingrained that we aren't even aware of them. For example, people may have preset notions about costs, materials, delivery modes, customer needs, and so on. You need to get all these out on the table so they can be evaluated. (Is this really true? How do we know? What would it take to change that assumption?)

- Require that people support their statements with facts, data, or documentation: If someone says, "Customers would like that idea," you need to challenge them: How do they know? Where's the data to support that statement? It is critical that this requirement be placed on all team members—don't let long-term employees, experts, or even managers get away with making statements that are based solely on opinion.

5. Look at the whole value stream; keep their minds open to all steps

No matter what type of innovation a team is working on, the impact will ripple to many parts of your organization. Whether it affects a product, service, or process, a new design will change everything from purchasing to finance, order entry to production, delivery to customer service. One way to help people think creatively is to make sure the entire value stream is reflected in their deliberations:

- Have them physically walk through any relevant processes (material procurement, order entry, production, assembly, delivery, etc.)

- Make sure they have a full understanding of the customer experience, either by having customer reps on the team or by using ethnographic techniques (p. 41) to see it firsthand

- Have representatives from different parts of the organization participate in brainstorming and knowledge-sharing sessions

6. Allow space for thinking/ruminating

One of the most precious commodities in the creative process is time, but not in the usual business sense where effectiveness and efficiency are prime. Here, precious time means:

- *Silent* thinking time in brainstorming sessions

- Time allotted between or even in the middle of development steps where the only charge is to "go think about what you've learned"

- Time when team members are forced to get up and go for a walk or do some other physical activity (don't let that be optional—people will simply go back to their desks or start answering voicemails; the purpose is to get their bodies moving)

Conclusion

Bringing people together and generating high levels of creativity and energy is the lifeblood of innovation. We've only been able to scratch the surface in this chapter on how to make it happen. The most important conclusions we hope you take away are:

- Powerful synergistic teams do not have to be infrequent, unexpected, but pleasant occurrences. There is a science behind driving productive, highly creative teams.

- Creativity is essential throughout the innovation process, not just on the fuzzy front end of innovation. By applying the techniques described in this chapter, you can greatly enhance the flow of good ideas and creativity, and do it sustainably.

Endnotes

7 Pete Buca is currently the Vice President of Technology and Innovation, Fluid Connectors Group, at Parker Hannifin Corporation based in Cleveland, Ohio. Pete has 25 years of experience in all aspects of design and manufacture of jet engine fuel injection products for GE, RR, UTC/PWA, and Honeywell. His career has involved key responsibilities in manufacturing engineering, quality, R&D, and innovation and technology management. His focus for the past several years has been on creating growth through innovative product development in aerospace and other markets. He is an expert facilitator of innovation.

8 The workshop was originally developed by Max Isaac and colleagues at 3Circle Partners.

Recap of Part III

At the project level, Fast Innovation is a matter of both merging new priorities into existing project management systems and adopting some new practices. For example:

- The selection process for sustaining innovations is reasonably straightforward (because they involve existing offerings or processes), but you need to create a parallel system for identifying and evaluating disruptive opportunities, which by virtue of their disruptive nature will seldom be a strategic fit with existing business unit priorities or capabilities.

- You'll need to collect data on how much time your innovators really spend on innovation in order to make decisions about how many projects can be active at any given time and what level of utilization is most appropriate. Chances are this data will be startling and illuminating. It will also identify opportunities for process improvement that will frequently free up the capacity you need.

- Most companies already use some type of Stage/Gate system for checking projects at strategic points during development. Few companies use the Stage/Gate system to rigorously control the number of projects in each phase. This system becomes a FastGate model when management must evaluate the impact on resource utilization and lead time before allowing a project through each gate into the next phase of development. And fast feedback loops at the task level give you early warning signals not available from project management.

- The best way to jumpstart any innovation project is to use the Innovation Blitz approach, where the team (including customers and suppliers, as appropriate) is brought together for a four- or five-day session where they work ONLY on the innovation opportunity. By focusing all these resources on a single question or issue at the same time, and establishing immediate feedback cycles, you can often accomplish in days what would normally take months.

- You need to raise the bar on creativity, exposing teams to a much greater diversity of inputs. This includes both team makeup (drawing people from a variety of backgrounds, specialties, ethnicities, and so) and the activities you put them through (ethnographic studies, market research, prototyping, etc.).

These tactics all rely on an open mindset to new models. This book has presented some of the most powerful practices available today for accelerating innovation processes, but we fully expect knowledge in this area to continue evolving. In fact, we continue our own drive to develop even better methods. So the best advice we can give is to keep learning: about customers, from the marketplace, from each other, about innovation practices, and about how to make Fast Innovation work for you to drive sustainable, long-term, profitable growth.

APPENDIX 1

The Impact of Task Variation and Utilization on Lead Time

To understand the impact of variation in task times, let's first look at a case with no variation. Assume a project designer:

- Performs design tasks for every project (A, B, C,...) *exactly* 5 days

- Receives a new project exactly every 5.25 days (the engineer is about 95% utilized)

In this scenario, what is the delay between projects—or, in the words of Lean, how many tasks are in queue? The answer: none. The designer works on one design task at a time, completes that design task in 5 days, then gets the next project two hours after that first task is done. There is no waiting involved, no queue time before the designer begins working the project.

Now let's inject a little realism into the scenario, changing the "exactly" figures above to "on average":

- The designer can complete a project *on average* in 5 days, but has a standard deviation[i] of 2.5 days. That means 68% of the tasks take between 2.5 days and 7.5 days (in math-speak, we're assuming for the moment that the distribution of task times is Gaussian).

- New projects/tasks arrive on average every 5.25 days with a standard deviation of 2.6 days

Given this scenario, how many jobs will be in queue on average? Well, sometimes the projects will arrive every 2.6 days and the designer will be completing jobs every 7.5 days. The fast-arriving projects will bunch up in queue at the designer. On the other hand, sometimes projects that the designer can complete in 2.5 days will arrive every 7.5 days—meaning any work entering the queue gets worked on immediately and the designer sits around for 5 days (unproductively) waiting for the next task to arrive.

It looks like, on average, there will be more than zero jobs in queue due to variation. *But how many?* The short answer is that it depends on the *amount* of variation.

How much variation is there in innovation tasks?

Here are some data that may surprise you:

> *In a recent product, some features were so large that individuals worked on them (one per feature) for an entire year, although this is unusual. Most features consume about three person-weeks—that is, one person working for three weeks. The smallest features may take just three days or so.*
>
> *Microsoft Secrets, p. 236*

This seems to be a lot of variation, and it sure doesn't look like the familiar Gaussian we used in our first example. But one data point does not an average make.

Few companies have consistently measured variation in task times. One of the largest data sets comes from the development of the software for the Space Shuttle, consisting of hundreds of projects culminating in the production of 25 million source lines of code (SLOC). Approximately 17 million SLOC were developed by IBM Federal Systems. The data showed that the variation in task time around the mean for all "from-scratch" development projects followed the distribution[ii] below (Figure App1-01). This distribution is knows as the Rayleigh Distribution, and has a coefficient of variation of 0.52 for both arrivals and task times.[iii] You will note that the Rayleigh distribution has a long tail on it, and this means that some innovation projects will have exceptionally long task times, like the Microsoft project referenced above. (As an aside, we have more data on software development than on hardware and service design, but have found consistent results across many applications.)

Figure App1-01: Variation in From-Scratch Task Times

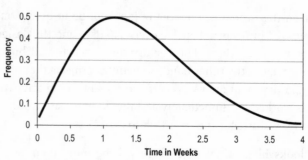

Typical variation in task times follows what's called a Rayleigh Distribution. There is about a 50% variation in task time around the mean—a figure that most people agree with at a gut level. The reason we make the caveat *from scratch* is that there are very practical ways to make huge reductions in both the mean time and the variation of design tasks (see sidebar).

The Coefficient of Variation

Since our goal is to quantify the number of tasks in queue, we need a way to quantify the amount of variation in a process.

This is a math problem that has a fairly simple equation thanks to the study of Queuing theory. The subject got started when Napoleon asked the mathematician Poisson how many cannons he would have to send to get 100 cannons to a battle with a probability of 80%, which resulted in the Poisson Distribution. The problem we posed of "how many" items get bunched up was not solvediv until the 1930s by Polaczek and Khintchine, and we refer to it, for the purposes of this book, as the Law of Innovation Variation.

Before we give you the full equation, let's focus first on the issue of quantifying variation. Think of it this way: a variation of ±1 hour on an average has a very different impact depending on whether the mean task time is 100 hours or 10

Reducing time and variation in design tasks

Some of the variation in task time has to do with the difficulty of the challenge, a difficulty we can't always predict and have relatively little control over. However, much of the variation is caused by factors we *can* control, such as premature release (causing additional starts/stops), changing specifications (causing rework, minimally, or sparking entirely new tasks), lack of support from procurement, etc. These are many of the same problems that caused us to multi-task (Chapter 13).

Simply stopping those practices is one way to reduce mean task time and variation. Another tactic is to avoid those situations entirely by enforcing re-use, as discussed at length in Chapter 11. Re-using something that already exists can...

- Reduce the mean task time: cutting some task time to near zero (if the pre-existing thing can be used as-is) or at least dramatically reducing it
- Reduce the kind of design struggles that create the long tail (high variation) on the Rayleigh Distribution

Initially, these kinds of gains will be obscured by the high levels of variation in all the other design tasks. (That is, don't expect a lot of reduction in the mean task times or variation when you first start pushing re-use.) The gains will become more noticeable—start to have a significant impact on mean design time and variation—as your re-use program matures.

hours. So what we want to do is look at **relative variation**, which means dividing the hours of spread that contain one standard deviation of variation by the average hours. We call this ratio the **Coefficient of Variation, C.**

In the original scenario we laid out above, the appropriate figures are:

$$C_{Arrivals} = \frac{2.625}{5.25} = 0.5 \qquad C_{Task\ Time} = \frac{2.5}{5} = 0.5$$

From the actual software design data we have, the figures are:

$$C_{Task\ Time\ From\ Scratch} = 0.52 \qquad C_{Task\ Time\ Re\text{-}use} \leq 0.2$$

Note that the actual coefficient for from-scratch design was only slightly higher than that used in our practice scenario (0.52 vs. 0.50). More importantly, note that the coefficient drops radically (often to less than 0.2) when the designers were able to re-use existing code—more on re-use later.

The Law of Innovation Variation

If you read Chapter 3 you know that there are three factors that affect design task time:

- The mean time

- Percent utilization of resources

- The number of available cross-trained resources

For the purposes of our discussion here, we're going to ignore the cross-training issue (but we'll get back to it soon). Using the data from the scenario we laid out above, what we see is that...

From-Scratch Design at 95% Utilization

$$\text{Avg. \# of projects-in-queue} = \left(\frac{\rho^2}{1-\rho}\right)\left(\frac{C^2_{arrivals} + C^2_{task\ times}}{2}\right)$$

the $C_{arrivals}$ will be the same as the previous activity, which we will also assume is a from-scratch activity and hence has a Rayleigh Distribution with $C = 0.52$ and with an ρ (utilization) = 95% or 0.95. That gives us:

$$\text{Avg. \# of projects-in-queue} = \left(\frac{0.95^2}{1-0.95}\right)\left(\frac{0.52^2 + 0.52^2}{2}\right) = \left(\frac{0.9}{0.05}\right)(0.27) = 4.9$$

Using the Law of Lead Time:

$$\text{Avg. queue time} = \frac{\text{\# of projects-in-queue}}{\text{Avg completion rate}} = \frac{4.9 \text{ projects}}{1 \text{ project/ } 5 \text{ days}} = 24.7 \text{ days}$$

$$\text{Avg. total lead time of the activity} = \text{queue time} + \text{processing time/unit}$$
$$= 24.7 \text{ days} + 5 \text{ days} = 29.7 \text{ days}$$

Let's compare the lead time of this level of task time variation to the first case, when there was no variation (*see* Figure App1-02, next page). You will note that with no variation there is no queue time until the innovator reaches capacity, at which point new tasks start to stack up.

Figure App1-02: Impact of Variation on Lead Time

At 95% utilization, the design time for a task that on average will take about 5 days jumps to 30 days.

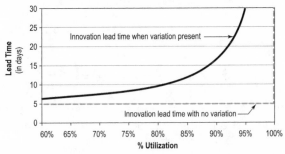

Adding nearly 25 days of queue time to 5 days of value-add design time at a given developer's desk will have a major impact on overall project lead time. When you think about this happening for *all* the developers, it becomes obvious why program managers today—who are not trained in these equations—have a such a hard time predicting project lead times with any accuracy. In fact most program management approaches try to just add up the value-add times down the critical path with some "fudge factors" to predict lead time. Your own first-hand experience probably confirms that this approach invariably leads to an underestimation of actual design time.

How can program managers today justify long queue times to management without some form of analysis to back them up? As the graph of the Law of Innovation Variation shows, the queue time is a very sensitive function of the percent utilization of the innovator. We call it a Law for the same reason as Little's Law (what we call the Law of Lead Time) is a Law: it works *regardless* of the distribution of arrivals and task times. The arrivals can be exponential and the task times Rayleigh, Gaussian, or any other[v] and it still works! If you don't use the Laws of Lead Time and Innovation Variation, and you load up the developers to 95% capacity, you are always going to be "surprised" by schedule slippages. If you do use the Laws of Lead Time and Innovation Variation, you can predict and prevent schedule slippages!

Now let's assume that you followed the Seven Imperatives of the Law of Innovation Variation (p. 59), and loaded the from-scratch innovators up at 65% of capacity. What would be the queue time?

From-Scratch Design at 65% Utilization

Note that the curve on Figure App1-02 really takes off after about 65% utilization. That means if we constrain from-scratch innovation tasks to designers allocated at 65% utilization or less, we should be able to dramatically reduce lead time. Does that work? Here are the figures:

From Scratch Design at 65% Utilization

$$\text{Avg. \# of projects-in-queue} = \left(\frac{\rho^2}{1-\rho}\right)\left(\frac{C^2_{\text{arrivals}} + C^2_{\text{task times}}}{2}\right)$$

the C_{arrivals} will be the same as the previous activity, which we will also assume is a from-scratch activity and hence has a Rayleigh Distribution with C = 0.52 and with an ρ (utilization) = 65% or 0.65. That gives us:

$$\text{Avg. \# of projects-in-queue} = \left(\frac{0.65^2}{1-0.65}\right)\left(\frac{0.52^2 + 0.52^2}{2}\right) = \left(\frac{0.42}{0.35}\right)(0.27) = 0.32$$

Using the Law of Lead Time:

As $$\text{Avg. queue time} = \frac{\text{\# of projects-in-queue}}{\text{Avg completion rate}} = \frac{0.32 \text{ projects}}{1 \text{ project/ 5 days}} = 1.6 \text{ days}$$

$$\text{Avg. total lead time of the activity} = \text{queue time} + \text{processing time/unit}$$
$$= 1.6 \text{ days} + 5 \text{ days} = 6.6 \text{ days}$$

you can see the total lead time has been reduced from 29.7 days to 6.6 days, a dramatic improvement in time-to-market when you multiply these numbers by let's say 10 innovators down the Critical path, its 66 days vs. 297 days! Having to limit designers to 65% utilization may sound like a completely cost-inefficient process, but we'll show you how to mitigate that in a moment.

Re-use Design at 85% Utilization

If you adopt the Religion of Re-use, the Coefficient of Variation will likely drop to something near 0.2:

Re-use Design at 85% Utilization

$$\text{Avg. \# of projects-in-queue} = \left(\frac{\rho^2}{1-\rho}\right)\left(\frac{C^2_{arrivals} + C^2_{task\ times}}{2}\right)$$

Because the tasks are now relying on re-use, the C figures drop down to 0.2 (vs C = 0.52 for from-scratch work). With a ρ (utilization) = 85% or 0.85, that gives us:

$$\text{Avg. \# of projects-in-queue} = \left(\frac{0.85^2}{1-0.85}\right)\left(\frac{0.2^2 + 0.2^2}{2}\right) = \left(\frac{0.72}{0.15}\right)(0.04) = 0.19$$

Using the Law of Lead Time:

$$\text{Avg. queue time} = \frac{\text{\# of projects-in-queue}}{\text{Avg completion rate}} = \frac{0.19\ projects}{1\ project/\ 5\ days} = 1\ days$$

$$\text{Avg. total lead time of the activity} = \text{queue time} + \text{processing time/unit}$$
$$= 1\ days + 5\ days = 6\ days$$

This means an innovator can be loaded up with Re-use tasks to an 85% utilization percentage, and still only waste a day in queue time! Because the queue time is so small compared to value-add time, the overall lead time *is* approaching the sum of value-add times down the critical path!

The 80-80-80 Rule

Now let's put it all together: Let's assume that we apply re-use to 80% of the innovators while the remaining 20% are working from-scratch. What is the overall utilization?

$$\text{Average Utilization} = \frac{(20)(0.65) + (80)(.85)}{100} = \frac{13 + 68}{100} = 81\%$$

What is the average lead time with 80% of the activities at 6 days and 20% at 6.6 days?

$$\text{Average Lead Time} = \frac{(20)(6.6) + (80)(6)}{100} = \frac{132 + 480}{100} = 6.1\ days/innovator$$

This compares to 29.7 days if there is no re-use and you load all innovators to 95% utilization:

$$\text{Percent Lead Time Reduction} = \frac{29.7 - 6.1}{29.7} = 80\%$$

This is the foundation of the 80-80-80 rule (Figure App1-03): *If an innovation consists of 80% Re-use, then Lead Time can be cut by 80% at 80% average utilization*

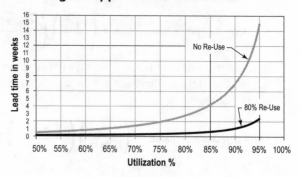

Figure App1-03: 80-80-80 Rule

Even if you cannot drive re-use to 80%, you can use this type of analysis to estimate the savings at other values. The smaller mean values of task time will reduce overall utilization% and has the same overall effect as the 80-80-80 Rule. You can even have a re-use innovator supplying work to a from-scratch innovator, which will result in a variation term like $(0.52^2 + 0.2^2)$, etc., or vice versa, although this is a small effect. The point is that the Law of Innovation Variation gives you the power to understand and control your process to a desired lead time, as Alexander Pope tells us:

> *Nature and Nature's laws lay hid in night*
> *God said "Let Newton be!"*
> *And all was light.*

And the same can be said for Polaczek and Khintchine! Now in innovation tasks, you also have to be prepared for that task that turns out to be impossible to perform. For this reason we recommend the use of feedback loops to monitor tasks-in-process and exits in real time, which is discussed in Appendix 2.

Queue Time Reductions Through Cross-Training

As discussed in Chapter 3, one of the best ways to react to the unknown is to develop flexibility in resource planning via cross-training. The resultant *reduction* in lead time is just as staggering as was the *increase* in lead time due to variation!

You *know* that there is going to be unpredictable variation in task times, especially in cutting-edge innovation. That means your specialist developers will certainly, sooner or later, run into a task that bogs them down (this may make them a Critical Resource, as defined previously). If this specialist has critical or unique skills, you can avoid the consequences of this variation by training one or more backups who can handle some of the less-challenging projects (in addition to their primary job). This will allow the specialist to be dedicated to the critical task, increasing productivity and hopefully keeping the task off the critical path.

Figure App1-04: Impact of Cross-Training

This leads to the final version of the Law of Innovation Variation:

$$\text{Number of Tasks-in-Queue} = \left(\frac{1}{N+1} \right) \left(\frac{\rho^2}{1-\rho} \right) \left(\frac{c_A^2 + c_T^2}{2} \right)$$

Where N = the number of cross-trained resources

Summary

- Innovation tasks have high variation which results in long lead times when scheduling from-scratch innovators at more than 65% capacity

- There are tactics for reducing both the mean task time and variation in design work: Religion of Re-use, Open Innovation and cross-training

- To the extent that we cannot avoid variation, we must provide schedule time buffers (*see* Appendix 2)

Endnotes

[i] To read more about computing the standard deviation consult *Lean Six Sigma Toolbook*, by George, Price, et al.

[ii] The distribution known as the Rayleigh Distribution and posited by Peter Norden to apply to R&D efforts as early as the 1960s, and later to innovation specifically (*see* L.H. Putnam and R.W. Wolverton, "Quantitative Management - Software Cost Estimating," a tutorial given at the IEEE Computer Society First International Computer Software & Applications Conference, Chicago, Nov. 8-11, 1977, IEEE Catalog No. EHO 129-7). It has since been confirmed in many projects including IBM Federal Systems development of 17 million Source Lines of Code for the Space Shuttle, *see* Rone, K Y 1990, Proceedings of the Fifteenth Annual Software Engineering Workshop(Greenbelt MD, Nov 28-29) and many other sources. A later reference with the same distribution in other innovation applications is Putman,L.H. and Ware Myers, *Measures for Excellence,*1992.

[iii] Rayleigh Distribution Coefficient of Variation: The mean, variance of the Rayleigh Probability distribution are:

$$P(r) = \frac{re^{-r^2/2s^2}}{s^2} \qquad \mu = s\sqrt{\frac{\pi}{2}} \qquad \sigma = \frac{4-\pi}{2}s^2$$

Therefore the Coefficient of Variation is:

$$C_v = \frac{\sigma}{\mu} = \frac{\sqrt{\frac{4-\pi}{2}s^2}}{s\sqrt{\frac{\pi}{2}}} = \frac{0.65s}{1.253s} = 0.52$$

[v] Known as the Kingman or Pollaczek-Khintchine equation. *See* Randolph Hall, *Queuing Methods for Services and Manufacturing* (Englewood Cliffs, NJ: Prentice Hall, 1991), p. 151 (figure 5.64). Note:in this equation Hall assumes exponential arrivals hence $C_A=1$ which is a special case of our equation. In our application we assume that $C_A= 0.52$ since the arrivals distribution equals the departure distribution of upstream innovators which is Rayleigh.

APPENDIX 2

Time Buffers
and Feedback Systems

Even without having actual data on design cycle time, no prudent or experienced designer is going to estimate a task time equal to what they perceive as the usual or actual task duration. For our discussion here, let's label that "usual" task time as the "median"—meaning the chance of being late was 50% (half of all projects are above the median, half below). So the estimates any developer (or you) would give, even by gut feeling, will likely be much longer.

In fact, asked how much time a project will take, most developers will guess at a time that equates to an 80% probability of finishing on time (*see* Figure App2-01). If this is a *from-scratch* design, this means that they will guess about twice the median time; they are, in essence, adding their own **time buffer** to their estimate, as labeled on the figure.

Figure App2-01: Task Time Estimates

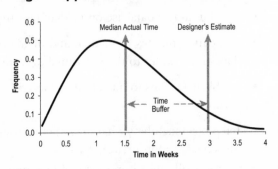

The effect of time buffers is to build room for variation into a project schedule. But if we go with gut feelings, half the projects will get completed before the median time—yet are scheduled to last up to *twice* the median time. What happens to that extra time? How can we take advantage of early finishers to accelerate overall lead time? The issue boils down to two questions:

1) How big should time buffers be?

2) Should the buffers be built into the schedule at the project level (covering *all* developers) or at the task level (targeted at specific developers)?

The answers to both are related:

1) Individual developers or teams should be given about half of their estimated buffer

2) The rest of the buffer should go into a common pool for the project as a whole

So if the median time is 10 days, and the developer or team estimates 20 days, assign them 15 days with the other 5 days going into the buffer pool for the project.

Any errors in these estimates will be caught by a feedback control system described below. The purpose of the estimates is to determine if a given innovator or department is likely to be a Critical Resource, so that we know where to install feedback loops. If the critical path schedule cannot allow this amount of delay time, you should increase the team effort *at the outset* (to avoid the impact of Brooks' Law,[vi] "Adding manpower to a late project makes it later").

Developing a buffer plan: Where and how big?

- Allocate Critical Resources at about 65% (per the Law of Innovation Variation, this means they should have few delays caused by variation)
- Start building a database on median task times
- Compare estimates to median and divide the buffer as prescribed above (half of the buffer to the individual or team, half to the project pool)
- Establish a means to track buffers for Critical Resources and the project as a whole
- Tell project members what the buffer metrics are for each project, each day (or week, as appropriate)
  - With all innovators aware of how much buffer remains on each project, they will be better focused on their task and less susceptible to distractions (others asking them to help with non-priority projects, etc.)
  - If you can, establish a system for innovators to track the use of their time (like the bar code tracking system discussed in Chapter 13)
- Monitor progress against the metrics and adjust accordingly
  - If upstream tasks chew up time from the buffer, adjust priorities for those steps or adjust priorities/resources in later steps to compensate
  - Time saved by tasks completed early (under time budget) gets added into the overall project buffer as a cushion for those that take longer than planned.
  - If design team members believe they can add customer delighters if

> allowed to work beyond the local buffer, they can ask for time from the project buffer
> - Projects that become time challenged will rise to the top of your priority list so you can adjust resources as necessary

This approach will lead to smaller individual buffers for individual team members and give them tighter completion dates to work against. In addition, use of a buffer metric focuses innovators on finishing the task and getting on to the next project. There will less "polishing of the cannonball" as is generally the case when projects are completed ahead of the median time. Overall, the pluses will tend to cancel out the minuses and you'll end up with a tighter distribution of lead times (meaning more predictability in project duration).[vii]

Closed Feedback Control of Tasks-in-Process

So far we have been relying on the innovator to make an intelligent guess as to the 80% probability point of the amount of time each task will take. This is a subjective measure, based on history, but could be in error. It is the nature of innovation tasks to have unforeseen good and bad luck, or unforeseen opportunities that could become delighters among the flexible target performance levels. This variation is portrayed by the Rayleigh Distribution.

We therefore need some form of feedback control so if we are stuck we don't add more projects at the wrong place and extend the lead time beyond the commitment to marketing. Every process will have at least one person or group that is the **Critical Resource**—the workstation with the largest number of tasks or task time queued up behind it and thereby inserting the longest lead time in the project on the critical path. However, we may not know for sure where the Critical Resource lies because it can vary by project and task. By automatically monitoring the number of tasks and total task time between a few points in the process we form a "closed feedback loop," reporting on a daily or weekly basis any sudden increase in task time at the *task level* for potential management action. This may disclose an unpredicted Critical Resource. Closed feedback about task time and queues is a **forward predictor**, in stark contrast to the much slower feedback at the *project level* that gets reported at meetings, which is dependent on human initiative and insight. Figure App2-03 compares the response of task versus project feedback systems.

Figure App2-03: Feedback Cycle Time

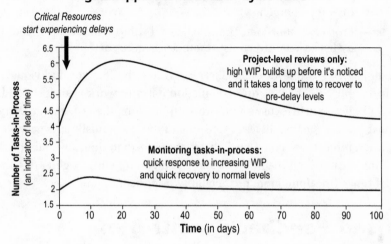

We have proposed cross-training personnel who are outside the Critical Resource in the less challenging tasks that the Critical Resource must service. This resource will be assigned the largest buffer if the innovators have made the right estimates of task times. Since these estimates are faulty, we need to track the number of projects-in-process at all potentially Critical Resources (typically less than 25% of the total) as well as the completion rate over the last month or longer time period.

A simple yet less-precise rule is to not launch the next project that requires work at the Critical Resource until the current project is completed. If that number is increasing beyond plan, you must:

- Quit launching projects that add load to this Critical Resource
- Investigate the causes of delay
  - Look at data on time usage
  - Determine if the resource is dedicated or has drifted to multitasking
  - Determine if the Critical Resource needs top priority for upstream resources
- Institute corrective actions:
  - Cross-train personnel and make sure they are allocated appropriately
  - Dedicate resourcing and upstream priorities
  - Decide to chew up more of the common buffer and re-start launches

Goldratt discussed this issue in *Critical Chain,* and correctly suggests that projects be launched at the completion rate of the Critical Resource. However, it's hard to know that rate accurately due to the Rayleigh Distribution. We therefore suggest that creating a feedback control system in which we monitor the queue time in front of the Critical Resource will compensate for any uncertainty in task time estimates or actual performance.

People who are familiar with Lean will recognize the parallel with the Kanban control in the Pull system, which in its simplest form is box with a maximum capacity to hold work-in-process. Once the top has been reached, all workstations that supply this box must shut down. We have effectively assigned a maximum queue time using the Law of Lead Time. Innovation processes that have not defined either the Critical Resource or the maximum buffer time have virtually no control over lead time of the projects.

Endnotes

[vi] Not applicable to distributions where the coefficient of variation is not defined. (e.g. Cauchy).

[vii] Brooks, *Mythical Man-Month*, p. 198.

[viii] This is an example of the Central Limit Theorem. Even though the individual distribution of task times vary widely, when you add samples from several distributions you approach a Gaussian distribution even though the underlying distribution is Rayleigh. The idea of the common buffer is espoused by Goldratt in *Critical Chain*. However, he does not directly employ the Laws of Lead Time or Variation and hence does not provide a numerical prediction of lead time vs. capacity utilization. Nevertheless, his insight was a significant step.

APPENDIX 3

Innovation and Information Creation

One sidebar in Chapter 10 posed the question of how much information there is in the statement that it is hot in Dallas on the 4th of July. Very little. But if you were told there was four feet of snow on the ground, you would conclude that the surprise factor has something to do with the amount of information.

Crude ideas around the "quantity of information" were transformed into a mathematical theory of information that resulted in some utterly unexpected and spectacular results.[ix] The foundation of the theory is being able to put a number on the amount of information.

Let's take a coin flip as an example. Clearly the probability that the coin lands on heads is 50%, and the same for tails. Then the amount of information needed to define the outcome of a coin flip is:[x]

Information = information if heads + information if tails

P_H = probability of heads P_T = probability of tails

Information = $-(P_H \log_2 P_H + P_T \log_2 P_T)$

Information = $-[0.5(-1) + 0.5(-1)] = +1$ bit

By comparison, think for a moment about traditional product development practice where a team is assigned to seek out only *one* level of performance per spec parameter and that they *must* make it work. So they don't even get the "surprise" seeing either a head or a tail. They're assigned a head and have to produce a head. That means the probability is 1, and the information gained from development is zero:

Information = $(1)\log_2(1) = (1)(0) = 0$

In plain English: if you tie down your specifications and work until you meet that spec, you lose all chance of creating new knowledge which could lead to a highly differentiated offering.

Information theory explains why so many innovative offerings turn out to be me-too or moderately advantaged—because the company has not allowed for new learning.

How do you allow new knowledge to emerge? Part of the solution is to give your innovators only a *vision statement* and *a basic outline* of specification at first. That will give them the freedom and incentive to explore alternatives. They may surprise you and completely outperform your expectations.

The optimal situation is to have innovators investigate at least two (and perhaps more) sets of solutions: an option that just satisfies basic customer requirements and has a high probability of success, plus an option that includes at least one "delighter" that could contribute to a highly differentiated offering, even if its odds of success are only 50/50.

How many possible solutions should we have in a set for a spec that could be a high differentiator? The answer is up to the innovator, but the amount of information per number of possible solutions in the set peaks at 3, per Figure App3-01.[xi,xii]

Figure App3-01: Information in Alternative Solutions

The figure tells us to let our innovators surprise us; it may be good, it may be bad, it will most likely be a mixture—but it is the best of all possible worlds and has a much better chance of creating a differentiated offering.

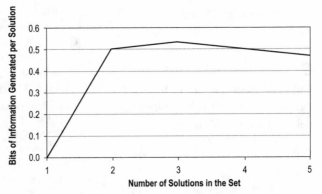

Endnotes

[ix] Product Development Forum (www.npd-solutions.com/glossary.html)

[x] People always thought that if you transmitted a radio message in the presence of a lightning storm that some of the information would be lost. One of the astounding results of Information Theory is that you *can* transmit the message absolutely error free! This set off the search for new codes that are now used in CDs and DVDs, etc.

[xi] If you are a little rusty on logarithms, remember that the $\log_2 0.5$ (logarithm to base 2 of 0.5) means, what number do I have to raise 2 to, to get 0.5. The answer is, if you raise 2 to the -1 power, you get 0. 5, i. e.,
$$2^{-1} = 1/2 = 0.5, \text{ hence } \log_2 0. 5 = -1.$$

[xii] The formula for information is easily generalized to N solutions.

INDEX